Augustine and Gender

AUGUSTINE IN CONVERSATION: TRADITION AND INNOVATION

Series Editor: Kim Paffenroth

This series produces edited volumes that explore Augustine's relationship to a particular discipline or field of study. This "relationship" is considered in several different ways: some contributors consider Augustine's practice of the particular discipline in question; some consider his subsequent influence on the field of study; and others consider how Augustine himself has become an object of study by their discipline. Such variety adds breadth and new perspectives—*innovation*—to our ongoing conversation with Augustine on topics of lasting import to him and us, while using Augustine as our conversation partner lends focus and a common thread—*tradition*—to our disparate fields and interests.

Titles in Series

Augustine and Gender
Edited by Maggie Ann Labinski and Kim Paffenroth
Augustine and Ethics
Edited by Kim Paffenroth and Sean Hannan
Augustine and Time
Edited by John Doody, Sean Hannan, and Kim Paffenroth
Augustine and Politics
Edited by John Doody, Kevin L. Hughes, and Kim Paffenroth
Augustine and Literature
Edited by Robert P. Kennedy, Kim Paffenroth, and John Doody
Augustine and History
Edited by Christopher T. Daly, John Doody, and Kim Paffenroth
Augustine and Liberal Education
Edited by Kim Paffenroth and Kevin L. Hughes
Augustine and World Religions
Edited by Brian Brown, John A. Doody, and Kim Paffenroth
Augustine and Philosophy
Edited by Phillip Cary, John Doody, and Kim Paffenroth
Augustine and Apocalyptic
Edited by John Doody, Kari Kloos, and Kim Paffenroth
Augustine and Social Justice
Edited by Teresa Delgado, John Doody, and Kim Paffenroth
Augustine and Kierkegaard
Edited by Kim Paffenroth, John Doody, and Helen Tallon Russell
Augustine and Wittgenstein
Edited by Kim Paffenroth, John Doody, and Alexander Eodice

Augustine and Gender

Edited by Maggie Ann Labinski
and Kim Paffenroth

LEXINGTON BOOKS
Lanham • Boulder • New York • London

Published by Lexington Books
An imprint of The Rowman & Littlefield Publishing Group, Inc.
4501 Forbes Boulevard, Suite 200, Lanham, Maryland 20706
www.rowman.com

86-90 Paul Street, London EC2A 4NE

Copyright © 2024 by The Rowman & Littlefield Publishing Group, Inc.

All rights reserved. No part of this book may be reproduced in any form or by any electronic or mechanical means, including information storage and retrieval systems, without written permission from the publisher, except by a reviewer who may quote passages in a review.

British Library Cataloguing in Publication Information Available

Library of Congress Cataloging-in-Publication Data

Names: Labinski, Maggie Ann, 1981- editor. | Paffenroth, Kim, 1966- editor.
Title: Augustine and gender / edited by Maggie Ann Labinski and Kim Paffenroth.
Description: Lanham : Lexington Books, 2024. | Series: Augustine in conversation: tradition and innovation | Includes bibliographical references and index.
Identifiers: LCCN 2023051313 (print) | LCCN 2023051314 (ebook) | ISBN 9781666954852 (cloth) | ISBN 9781666954869 (epub)
Subjects: LCSH: Augustine, of Hippo, Saint, 354-430. | Gender identity. | Desire (Philosophy) | Marriage--Religious aspects.
Classification: LCC BR65.A9 A827 2024 (print) | LCC BR65.A9 (ebook) | DDC 189/.2--dc23/eng/20240104
LC record available at https://lccn.loc.gov/2023051313
LC ebook record available at https://lccn.loc.gov/2023051314

Contents

Introduction ... vii

PART I: DESIRE AND THE PASSIONS ... 1

Chapter 1: Sex and Love in the World that Was ... 3
Patricia Grosse Brewer

Chapter 2: The Effectivity of Women in Augustine's *Confessions*:
The Erasure of Agency and the Regulation of Desire ... 19
Richard A. Lee, Jr.

Chapter 3: The Intersection of Gender and the Emotions:
Concupiscence and its Discontents ... 39
Eileen C. Sweeney

PART II: SEX AND MARRIAGE ... 57

Chapter 4: Augustine and Anatomical Virginity: The Problem of
Double Integrity ... 59
Julia Kelto Lillis

Chapter 5: Between Exegesis and Naturalization: Gender and
Creation in Augustine ... 79
Willemien Otten

PART III: LANGUAGE, SPEECH, AND EXEGESIS ... 103

Chapter 6: Beyond God the Father: Augustine's Feminine Images
of God and His Concerns for Human Women ... 105
Jennifer Hockenbery

Chapter 7: Women's Talk: Silent Voices and Inarticulate Cries—
Augustine on Conceiving and Giving Birth to the Word   123
Carol Harrison

Chapter 8: Variations on Eve   143
Karmen MacKendrick

PART IV: EDUCATION AND COMMUNITY   161

Chapter 9: Promise and Peril   163
Maggie Ann Labinski

Chapter 10: Augustine's *Confessions* and Monstrous Recognition   181
Daniel Jean Perrier

Chapter 11: Finding an Ally in Augustine   189
Anne-Marie Schultz and Michael R. Whitenton

Bibliography   205

Index   223

About the Contributors   229

Introduction

The volumes in this series have tended to explore the relationship between Augustine's thought and a specific theme or discipline—for example, politics, education, theology, time. In each case, there is little doubt that the topic in question is one to which Augustine made a valuable contribution. While scholars may dispute the particulars of his ideas, very few would argue that Augustine's insights into things like education or theology failed to impact the Western intellectual tradition in significant and meaningful ways. Accordingly, the "problem" that this series has typically addressed is not Augustine *per se*. The problem is that modern readers have forgotten him. With all the pressures that define contemporary life, with all the forces that prioritize hurried production over the slow and steady pursuit of wisdom, it has become easy to overlook the gifts of the past. This series has invited readers to linger—to sit with the writings of a man who became one of the most influential thinkers of the West.

The theme of the current volume requires a different approach. Augustine's impact on the subject of gender is decidedly more complicated. Here, with the question of gender, there is no broad consensus that readers would do well to return to Augustine. Instead, scholars have raised pointed and legitimate concerns about the limits of his thinking. The assumption that Augustine's contribution to gender studies has been inherently positive is all but impossible to maintain. As such, the issue this volume faces is not so much that the full extent of Augustine's significance has been lost in the shuffle. The trouble would appear to be the late bishop of Hippo himself.

Historically, those who have taken on such challenging work have largely fallen into one of three hermeneutic camps. Some scholars have argued that, as is the case with topics like time and politics, Augustine's ideas about gender have (in fact) been profoundly influential. The catch, on this view, is that they are also gravely mistaken. More specifically, Augustine's remarks about women would seem to be deeply misogynistic and partially to blame for the long practice of gender-based oppression in the West. As Elaine Pagels has suggested, Augustine's culpability in this regard exists whether such social, political, and religious marginalization was his explicit goal. Given the power and privilege Augustine held within the early Christian church, he is responsible for both his ideas and their legacy.[1] This has led scholars like Mary Daly to propose that those who wish to analyze gender should avoid Augustine altogether.[2] For, nothing good can come from a poisoned well. To continue focusing on his misguided ideas is to continue to support a tradition of oppression.

A second group of scholars has argued that gender is a modern construct, one developed to support the concrete action of women's liberation movements in the 1900s. So understood, any attempt to "force" Augustine to articulate something about gender would be wildly anachronistic. It is simply unreasonable to expect the good bishop to be able to address the concerns of the twentieth and twenty-first centuries from his decidedly fourth/fifth-century context. By way of example, one might consider the otherwise meticulously detailed encyclopedia, *Augustine Through the Ages*. Amid a near exhaustive list of entries, the line for "gender" is left nearly blank. Instead of offering its characteristically robust synopsis and corresponding bibliography, the text directs readers to see, "Asceticism, Women."[3] As Judith Chelius Stark has maintained, it would be interesting to unpack the apparent equivocation between "gender" and "women" (and the corresponding inference that men are absent of any gender identity).[4] Regardless, the absence of any real content under this entry reflects the general view that it is unfair, if not unscholarly, to insist that Augustine deal with such a theme.

Finally, there are those who have advocated for a more nuanced approach. Other scholars have suggested that, while many of Augustine's conclusions about gender leave much to be desired, there are other textual passages where he appears to push the envelope in provocative ways. So, too, though it is true that Augustine did not have a twenty-first-century understanding of gender, this does not mean that he did not notice the gendered dynamics of his community in his own fourth/fifth-century way. To this end, scholars like Kari Elisabeth Børresen, Elizabeth Clark, Margaret Miles, and Kim Power have highlighted the benefits of encountering Augustine's treatment of gender with a spirit of both trust and suspicion.[5] There are certainly aspects of his conclusions that should give us pause. However, there are also (if not hidden) surprises that offer much needed hope.

The chapters before you follow in this third vein. Each of our authors finds in Augustine a kind of fallible sage: an all-too-human thinker who offers wise words and makes mistakes. By allowing Augustine to occupy this both/and, by giving him permission to be wholly imperfect, these essays bring us closer to the real flesh-and-blood man who stands behind the myth. This volume will ask readers to meditate on the "big ideas" to which Augustine continually returned—themes like love, language, and the truth. It will provide original interpretations of how Augustine read scripture with his God, interacted with his students, and prayed with his church. It will summon new responses to the questions that were near and dear to Augustine's heart—e.g., Who am I? Who is my neighbor? Who is the divine? Moreover, it will do all of this by and through careful readings of Augustine's steps—and missteps—around gender.

Our first section is focused on desire and the passions. Patricia Grosse Brewer's contribution explores the intersection of gender and desire in Eden. The chapter starts with an examination of the role of sex and desire within Augustine's varied interpretations of the early books of Genesis. Grosse Brewer argues that sex is possible in Eden because there is nothing necessarily inordinate about sexual desire. In so doing, she expands upon certain traditional views of *concupiscentia* as mere disordered lust and *caritas* as sterile love. Grosse Brewer concludes that, in the world that is to come, the messiness of *concupiscentia* is not abandoned for the sake of *caritas*. Instead, it is transformed into a newfound eroticism. As point of reference, she draws a comparison between Adam's relationship with Eve and Augustine's personal experiences with his longtime partner. Grosse Brewer's insights will encourage readers to reconsider the real nature of love and how it might help us determine why Adam chose to eat the fruit of the Tree.

For many scholars, the foundational text within Augustine's corpus is his *Confessions*. In our next chapter, Richard A. Lee Jr. offers a compelling interpretation that traces Augustine's representation of women across this seminal work. Lee suggests that there are two interwoven threads that run throughout Augustine's autobiography. First, the *Confessions* can be understood as a meditation on the nature of desire. More specifically, insofar as desire represents an opportunity for human beings to return to God, Augustine seeks to understand what it might mean to live life with properly regulated desire. Second, the *Confessions* can also be read as a piece that erases women. While many of the most significant moments in Augustine's life involve women, few of these individuals are given sustained textual attention. Lee argues that this erasure of women's agency is directly linked to Augustine's understanding of desire. To explain, he investigates Augustine's (if not limited) depictions of his nurses and long-term partner. Lee concludes that the liberation of women in the *Confessions* depends upon the liberation of desire. As such, he invites new analyses of the ways gender continues to shape our ideas about bodies, sex, and love.

The final chapter in Section One investigates the intersection of gender and the passions/emotions. Eileen C. Sweeney begins with an overview of the gendering of the passions in Greek and Roman thought, including sexual passion. Two models of passion as gendered emerge, both of which position women as inferior—i.e., women as passive receiver and as victim of limitless desire. Sweeney argues that Augustine's reception of this tradition is complex. On the one hand, his critique of the Stoics suggests that he embraces the passivity of female desire, at least insofar as it concerns the search for God. On the other hand, in his debates with the Manichees, Augustine would appear to develop a moral psychology that blames the "feminine" for any and all failures in virtue. Sweeney concludes by considering the specific example of sexual passion in Augustine's engagement with Julian. The scope of her analysis raises pointed questions about how gender impacts our sense of the fragility and vulnerability of human emotion today.

Our second section addresses issues surrounding sex and marriage. To begin, Julia Kelto Lillis provides an exploration of Augustine's gendered understanding of virginity. Recent scholars have argued that Augustine recognized virginity as a matter of the will instead of the body. An individual's sexual honor, in other words, depends upon their moral agency (not what might occur to particular body parts). This would seem to suggest that Augustine believed that virgins who experienced sexual violence could still be considered virgins. However, Kelto Lillis argues that texts like *City of God* reveal that Augustine's position is more troubling. She suggests that while Augustine locates chastity in the will, he understands female virginity in terms of will and body. Thus, while his critique of traditional Roman norms about chastity might bear important social and ecclesial implications, those implications are cut short by the gendered nature of his ideas about virginity. This chapter is an important addition to current conversations about the relationship between gender norms and responses to sexual violence.

From here, we have a rich analysis by Willemien Otten on gender and creation. Augustine is often criticized for his views in this area. Scholars have accused him of trying to naturalize a gender hierarchy and of sanctifying this hierarchy through biblical exegesis. In contrast, Otten argues that a more complex and layered interpretation is possible in the tension between naturalization and exegesis. Otten discusses several examples, including Augustine's view of marriage, his seeming suppression of natural desire, and his attitude toward sexual enjoyment in paradise. To shed further light on this original reading, and Augustine's foregrounding of Adam and Eve, the author draws a comparison with Gregory of Nyssa. Otten concludes that, contrary to certain scholarly trends, the paradise vignette of Adam and Eve as married partners serves as a kind of "magna carta" for Christians. By extension, Otten prompts readers to reexamine the scholarly prejudices that often follow Augustine, given his position as the Western Christian thinker par excellence.

Section Three takes on the area of language, speech, and exegesis. In the first piece, Jennifer Hockenbery offers an account of the gendered nature of Augustine's images of God. Augustine's background in rhetoric would have left him well aware of the power of language. This includes the ways in which religious imagery can shape our understanding of both the spiritual and the secular world. Hockenbery argues that, because of this, and despite the failings of most English translations, Augustine's deliberate and intentional use of feminine pronouns and images for God must be taken seriously. To this end, she explores several examples of these images and draws attention to the feminine face of God within Augustine's theology. In so doing, the author raises important questions about whether such imagery ultimately serves as a challenge to patriarchy, including contemporary views of women as teachers, leaders, and lovers. This chapter not only provides a valuable contribution to the field of philology. It also pushes readers to rethink the intersection of theology and politics today.

Next, Carol Harrison investigates gender and voice. She begins by arguing for the importance of situating any such analysis within a theological framework defined by the Eternal voice. Harrison suggests that this is clear in Augustine's account of the the archetypal female voice found in the faithful conception and humble bringing forth of the Word of God by Mary. In the example of the Annunciation and Incarnation, Augustine discovers a voice that communicates through speechlessness and silence. As such, it is a voice that subverts the classical understanding of human speech acts that Augustine, as a former teacher of rhetoric, would have likely preferred. Harrison concludes that, by giving prominence to Mary, Augustine both confirms and subverts traditional gender stereotypes. When it comes to communicating the divine mysteries, "women's talk" is to be preferred to the speech acts of masculine persuasion. As a result, Harrison's chapter serves as a critical response to the widespread social and political silencing of women that occurred in the early centuries of the Christian church.

We then move to a piece by Karmen MacKendrick on Augustine's interpretations of Eve. MacKendrick's premise is that, in both his *Confessions* and *De Doctrina Christiana*, Augustine allows for a generous approach to scriptural exegesis—one that invites, if not encourages, a multiplicity of readings. MacKendrick argues that this methodology is especially useful when it comes to working through Augustine's seemingly contradictory conclusions about Eve. Eve appears in Augustine's texts both analytically and mythically. MacKendrick suggests that when we allow ourselves to read myth and analysis "into" each other, what appears is a more multifaceted account of Eve and of Augustine's understanding of gender. It is one that opens new ways of acknowledging Augustine's unnamed partner—i.e., as a kind of second Eve who appears in Trinitarian and Christ-like manner. MacKendrick's willingness to take seriously Augustine's conviction that any proper speech about the divine is inevitably indirect and "oblique" inspires readers to do the same.

Our last section concentrates on education and community. Maggie Ann Labinski begins with an inquiry into gender and pedagogical desire. Western philosophers have a long tradition of advocating for the educational value of erotic desire. However, recent movements like #MeToo have urged teachers and students to ask whether the erotic is simply too dangerous to allow in the classroom. Drawing from the methods of feminist scholars, Labinski argues that Augustine is well aware of both the perils and the promise of such desires. She suggests that Augustine's interactions with two of his students (i.e., Licentius and Monica) reveal a change in his understanding of the erotics of pedagogy. It is a transformation that recenters the classroom around the longings of his students and encourages readers to reassess the gendered dynamics of the classroom. Labinski concludes that, in this way, Augustine prompts new appreciation of the political possibilities of education today.

Daniel Jean Perrier's chapter returns us to Augustine's *Confessions*. Here, readers will find a persuasive exploration of gender and autobiography. Perrier argues that, in his *Confessions*, Augustine shares the details of his past unabashedly for both himself and for the sake of others. Augustine's position in society gives him the power and privilege necessary to speak with the expectation that others will hear him authentically. In contrast to this, Perrier suggests that transgender persons are often denied such recognition when it comes to their own storytelling. Under the watchful eye of a cisnormative society, transgender folks are pressured to hide themselves for the sake of personal safety and acceptance. By way of example, Perrier draws from recent scholarship on the early autobiographies of transsexual persons. These texts underscore both the dangers of self-narrative for trans folk and their personal and political need. While autobiography can lead to rejection and violence, it can also lead (as Augustine shows) to love. Perrier's chapter calls readers to reexamine the nature of narrative recognition and what it means to find community through embodied personal narrative.

Augustine's significance within the Western intellectual tradition is, in part, due to his lasting practical value. This has been particularly true in the context of the classroom. In our final chapter, Anne-Marie Schultz and Michael R. Whitenton share some of the ways that Augustine's writings can be used in contemporary higher education. They argue that Augustine is an important resource to help navigate the sometimes-pernicious divide between gender inclusivity and traditional Christian understandings of human sexuality and marriage. To this end, the authors discuss how they teach Augustine at their historically conservative Christian university. They propose that Augustine's struggles with his own sexuality, his treatment of Monica, and his view of biblical interpretation are useful for rethinking male/female dichotomies and new issues that arise from sexual diversity in the classroom. They conclude by describing the difficulties an LGBTQ+ student group on their campus faced in trying to get a university charter and some potentially hopeful institutional responses. This chapter raises crucial questions about what it might mean for educational communities to embody the ideals of Christian love and charity with purpose and authenticity.

Nuance is, in some ways, less objectively fun. People tend to like clean lines between their intellectual/spiritual heroes and anti-heroes. However, the contributions in this volume reveal that the space between can be infinitely more satisfying. Furthermore, when at its best, the complexity of Augustine's position calls us to acknowledge our own. Much has happened within the study of gender since Augustine's time. There are good reasons to celebrate how far we have come. Nevertheless, if current events are any indication, we still have a very long way to go. It is, perhaps, thusly that the present volume continues in the spirit of prior books in this series. Augustine, and all he represents, remains a figure whom we would do well not to forget.

NOTES

1. Elaine Pagels, *Adam, Eve, and the Serpent* (New York: Vintage Books, 1988).

2. Mary Daly, *Beyond God the Father: Toward a Philosophy of Women's Liberation* (Boston: Beacon Press, 1973).

3. Allan D. Fitzgerald, ed., *Augustine Through the Ages: An Encyclopedia* (Grand Rapids: William B. Eerdmans, 1999), 376.

4. Judith Chelius Stark, "Introduction," in *Feminist Interpretations of Augustine: Re-Reading the Canon*, ed. Judith Chelius Stark (University Park: The Pennsylvania State University Press, 2007), 39.

5. Kari Elisabeth Børresen, *Subordination and Equivalence: The Nature and Role of Woman in Augustine and Thomas Aquinas*, trans. Charles H. Talbot (Washington, D.C.: University Press of America, 1981); Elizabeth Clark, *Women in the Early Church* (Collegeville: Liturgical Press, 1983); Margaret R. Miles, *Augustine on the Body* (Miissoula: Scholar's Press, 1979); Kim Power, *Veiled Desire: Augustine on Women* (New York: Continuum, 1996).

PART I

Desire and the Passions

Chapter 1

Sex and Love in the World that Was

Patricia Grosse Brewer

The Yahwistic story of Adam and Eve goes as follows: God, upon seeing the loneliness of Adam, makes him a companion from his side.[1] In exchange for a rib, Adam gets a wife. Eve is quickly deceived by a serpent, eats of the forbidden fruit from Tree of the Knowledge of Good and Evil, and, seeing that it is good, gives a bite to Adam. The subsequent expulsion from paradise—and with it the loss of original, prelapsarian bodies and the creation of secondary, postlapsarian bodies—haunts Western thought. In some respects, this story seeks to make sense of many basic things about the human condition: the myth makes a case for why women suffer so much in childbirth, why humans must work and toil throughout their lives, and even why there is a natural enmity between humans and snakes. Augustine takes this story to mean something more.

Throughout his post-conversion writing career, Augustine takes up this original story in order to come to understand what it means to be human. In doing so he outlines a theology (or, perhaps, theologies) of Original Sin[2] as an explanation for much if not all of the evil in the world. Theologian Jessie Couenhoven has argued in "St. Augustine's Doctrine of Original Sin" that "what we call Augustine's doctrine of original sin is actually a handful of doctrines, some more closely related than others, but each capable of independence, and possibly in tension with the others."[3] Augustine's "doctrine" of Original Sin is a theodic reading of myth: it is a story that explains something about why bad things happen to us and by us.

The view of Original Sin as an explanation for evil in the world is seen by some scholars as a direct admission that the "fallen," post-Eve world is bad and evil. For example, Elaine Pagels takes this view in her influential *Adam, Eve, and the Serpent*:

> To the sufferer, Augustine says, in effect, "You *personally* are not to blame for what has come upon you; the blame goes back to our father, Adam, and our mother, Eve." Augustine assures the sufferer that pain is unnatural, death an enemy, alien intruders upon normal human existence, and thus he addresses the deep human longing to be free of pain.[4]

However, Augustine does not come to this theory lightly or clearly. Indeed he is "seeing through a glass, darkly"[5] at a past as distant and as blurry as the future. Augustine picks up the Genesis myth again and again, telling and retelling these myths over and over. Retellings and analyses of the Genesis myth come up in his major works (*Confessions* XI–XIII, *City of God* XII–XIV, *The Literal Meaning of Genesis*) as well as in many non-major works (*On Genesis, Against the Manichees,* the unfinished *On the Literal Interpretation of Genesis,* and various sermons[6] and letters[7]). Each text represents not only his own theological beliefs concerning the original pair but also his social, political, and historical needs at the given moment of his writings.

In this chapter, I will explore Augustine's readings and re-readings of the creation and fall of humankind in order to unpack Augustine's complicated relationship with gender and desire. My reading of Augustine's mythopoesis is benefitted and influenced by the incitement I take from feminist readings and interpretations of reason and emotion as well as insights into human cognition as extended into the world. Indeed, "figuring out" why Adam would eat of the fruit of the Tree of Knowledge of Good and Evil is made more possible by beginning with these insights. I begin by discussing some of the political, social, and personal motivations for Augustine's readings of Genesis. I then discuss ways in which Augustine reads love in the original story: love as *caritas* and *concupiscentia,* love as heavenly and earthly, and love as foolish. Next, I weave together Augustine's relationship with his wife (as outlined in his *Confessions*) and his reading of the Genesis mythology. I conclude this chapter by discussing some of the philosophical ramifications of Augustine's conception of Edenic love. For Augustine, Edenic bodies are not sexless, desireless bodies, they are gendered and generative. This is an important point because it makes a claim about human nature today: sex, reproduction, desire, and love are all part of the "nature" of humans.

LOVING THE SINNER: AUGUSTINE'S MYTHOPOESIS

Augustine's *Confessions* is a prayer to God; it follows Augustine's life from his early days through his conversion to Christianity. Augustine, early in his life, was a member of the cult of Mani, which solved the problem of embodiment like many such cults by claiming that the human body and her world is the evil work of an evil god, and that the goal of life was to get closer to the principle of light, the good god. Both the light and the dark gods in this dyad are material, and thus the problem remains: when he searches just in Manichean matter, Augustine does not find God.

In Book VII of his *Confessions*, we learn that Augustine has left his cult and has read some "books of the Platonists." While he "discovers" an immaterial God in Platonist heavens, he cannot maintain a lasting connection. In his *Confessions*, after he recounts his conversion scene and the death of his mother, Augustine spends three books discussing the Genesis narrative; the creation of the world depicted in the Hebrew Bible. Augustine, thrown about by his own desires and embodiment, turns to the cause of that embodiment to try to make sense of his own alienation.

Augustine was drawn away from Christianity as a youth by the roughness of the stories of the Bible and toward the beauty of the Manichean origin myths. However, he came to despise that beauty and, upon conversion to Christianity, sought to discredit it as a false beauty. It is no surprise that, in his early works on Genesis, Augustine seeks to both disprove and distance himself from the Manicheans, who see even the light, good god as matter. Augustine comes to realize that the Manichean explanation for why there is evil in this world is not enough. The older Augustine interprets the Genesis narrative and does not feel despair at the utter fallenness of the human condition but rejoices in the possibility of redemption hidden within the text.

Augustine goes on to use interpretations of the Genesis narrative as a philosophical, theological weapon in various debates with seemingly heretical[8] groups. In my view, many, if not most, of these discussions have at their core the debate as to whether it is possible to achieve perfection in this life; for example, the Donatist heresy is one he faced early on in his career as priest and bishop and involved the question of whether or not those who committed sins after baptism should be allowed to remain in the community. Augustine's interpretation of the Eden expulsion illustrates why it is not possible to be wholly perfect in this life: humans have an innate incapacity for complete control of their bodies and wills due to their Fallen state. This is not due to a Manichean evil of the flesh but in the twisted nature of the human will that is a result of the first sin of Adam. This twisted will is identified with *concupiscentia*, which I will speak more of below.

One aspect of human nature that Augustine examines in his undertaking of the Genesis myth is human sexuality. *The City of God*, perhaps Augustine's most famous achievement, is bookended with analyses of the moral implications of women's bodies and relies on an exegesis of the Fall of Adam and Eve to do so.[9] In Book I, Augustine spends a significant amount of time analyzing the effects of the rape of women during Alaric's three-day sack of Rome. It is surprising that Augustine blames the sin of the rape on the rapist and not the victim.

In contrast to many thinkers of his time and ours, Augustine claims that women are not tied morally to the "purity" of their bodies. Augustine places women's virtue in their souls, not their flesh. In the last book of *The City of God*, Augustine concludes that resurrected flesh will remain gendered, though women will be spared the pain of childbirth as there will be no need to continue to populate the world that is to come. What happens in between these two conclusions is a long exegesis of the creation of the current world through the sins of the first couple. During this exegesis Augustine makes clear that, though women were punished with painful childbirth after the Fall, the necessity of childbirth itself is not a result of original sin after the Fall. Childbirth itself is not a result of the original sin of the first pair. Sex was possible and permissible in Eden—Adam and Eve would have had full control of their bodies in such circumstances. Augustine describes prelapsarian sex as not only possible but likely—had there been but time.

In his discussion of Edenic relationships in *The Literal Meaning of Genesis*, Augustine reinforces this notion of Edenic sex: "I do not see what could have prohibited them from honorable nuptial union and the bed undefiled (*torus immaculatus*) even in Paradise."[10] The way Augustine describes how this union might take place seems to verge on the comical: "The first couple before they sinned could have given a command to their genital organs for the purpose of procreation as they did to the other members which the soul is accustomed to move to perform various tasks without any trouble and without any craving for pleasure."[11] This strange, seemingly passionless version of Edenic sex is often taken at face value.[12] I am more inclined to see what this reinterpretation of sex might lead to.

In his fascinating article "Feeling Right: Augustine on the Passions and Sexual Desire," John C. Cavadini reads Augustine together with Andrea Dworkin's *Intercourse*, in which she points out the lie that is equality in heterosexual pleasure. Writes Dworkin:

> Because a woman's capacity to feel sexual pleasure is developed within the narrow confines of male sexual dominance, internally there is no separate being.

... There is only the flesh-and-blood reality of being a sensate being whose body experiences sexual intensity, sexual pleasure, and sexual identity in being possessed: in being owned and fucked.[13]

This account of female sexuality under patriarchy as existing only in relation to male sexuality is one that might sound familiar to Augustine. Of course Augustine could not conceive of consensual, nondominant, earthly friendships between men and women under the misogynistic patriarchy of his time!

As I discussed in my article, "Love and the Patriarch: Augustine and (Pregnant) Women," it has been claimed that Augustine could not conceive of an earthly friendship (much less a sexual relationship) between a man and a woman that might be considered equal.[14] Cavadini does an excellent job calling into question modern notions of a "healthy" sexual, psychic, and somatic life. For Cavadini, there is a conflation that occurs in thinking about "passion," "feeling," and "emotion" that causes one to look askance at any call for a rethinking or rebuking of passion. Writes Cavadini: "But if it is accepted that lust is a pathologized desire, trying to imagine sex without lust is not the same thing as trying to imagine sex without feeling, even intense feeling. And yet it almost amounts to the same thing because lust has such a firm grip on the emotional life of the fallen that it is hard to imagine or to speak beyond it."[15] In this way Cavadini speaks to the complex nature of modern discussions of emotion, feeling, and love, and the necessity to consider one's terms carefully. It is important to consider that one always reads an Augustine under the weight of the current manifestation of patriarchal and political oppression. One must embrace that weight, to read Augustine as an outsider, and to think critically of what being an outsider in this context could mean.

Cavadini calls on readers of Augustine to hold off on critiquing his seemingly sex-negative views until they consider *why* Augustine takes such a stance. To fault Augustine in this context for not realizing that "sexual pleasure" can enrich a couple's relationship, or to assess Augustine's views against our own more "positive" view, may be, with all due respect, to beg the question. For Augustine, the question would not be whether sexual pleasure can enrich a couple's relationship, but whether there is any sexual pleasure possible without a taint of violence or complacency ("self-pleasing") in it. The question would be, what are we taking pleasure from?[16] Cavadini entreats readers to not assume that Augustine's views on sex stem from a hatred of women or pleasure. Rather, for Augustine it is important to consider the nature of pleasure and pleasure's effect on the individual. A view toward the political dimension of Augustine's texts on Genesis leads one to see not the absurdity in Adam and Eve performing their sexual duties without unbidden lust, but what such a union might mean about sexual congress today.

What I take to be of particular interest for feminist philosophy is Augustine's insistence that women were created gendered, *as women*. Eve burst forth from Adam's side as a female capable of giving birth. A bursting, Augustine scholar James Wetzel has argued, which causes no damage to Adam:

> The parting of a woman from a man's side recalls the Genesis paradigm of parting (Gen. 2: 21–25): so that Adam may have a partner and not be alone, God sends Adam into a deep sleep, opens his side, and crafts a living being out of one of his ribs—man and woman emerge from the process, unashamedly naked in one another's presence. . . . The original Adam was not wounded by having a woman parted from his side; he was initiated into a fullness that he could enjoy only in relation to his partner.[17]

Gender difference is placed at the beginning of the human species—the *imago dei*, image of God, that humans were created in refers to both genders, as Adam and Eve do not achieve fullness until they are differentiated from each other. The image they are made in is their capacity for Reason.[18] And indeed, if reason is relation, women must possess it in order to exist in the world as something more than just an object for men's domination. Along with Eve's generative potentiality, Augustine makes clear that sex is possible in the Garden because there is nothing *natural* to sex that is illicit or immoral. Concupiscent desire need not necessarily be inordinate—*concupiscentia*, rather than merely being wild desire, is in fact the love of others that are not God. Love of others is natural to what it is to be human, for Augustine.

CONCUPISCENCE, THEN AND NOW

The punishment for their sin was swift. They eat the sweet flesh, look down and across to each other in horror at their nakedness, and hide for fear of their punishment. This opening of their eyes, the eyes of Adam and Eve, has been linked by Augustine and others to the stirring of *concupiscentia* in their flesh—a stirring that originates not in their minds but seemingly in their flesh.

Augustine has a large vocabulary for love, a vocabulary which is not easily pinned down. As previously stated, most Augustine scholars divide up Augustine's reading of love (*amor*) into the stately, steady love of God (*caritas*), and the wild, unbidden, uncontrollable desire (*concupiscentia*). *Concupiscentia* is often translated as something like sexual desire in the particular, but also any kind of ravenous, consuming desire. The reason I linger on sex in this chapter—and indeed the title of this chapter refers to the possibility for sex in Eden—is that, in philosophy and theology, sex is often depicted as a falling away of reason, and sexual desire and love is depicted as something to deny rather than embrace. The contrast readers of Augustine make between *caritas* and *concupiscentia* often reads as a battle between true love and false love. This is a fundamental misreading of Augustine and the nature of human love.

Magazines and Internet lists will tell brokenhearted singles: "You have to be happy with yourself before you are happy with another person," "You can't find your happiness in another person." These modern proverbs imply that love is not something for the lacking; it is something for the whole. And, of course, this is fundamentally untrue. Although one cannot be whole through another, love itself in its very nature requires a lack. *Concupiscentia* and *caritas* both call to that which is different than us: we love what we lack.

In *The Literal Meaning of Genesis*, Augustine firmly states that Eve was created "to be [Adam's] helper in begetting children."[19] If God sought to find Adam someone to help in menial tasks or to be a nice conversationalist and companion, says Augustine, then he would have created another man for Adam:

> Now, if the woman was not made for the man to be his helper in begetting children, in what was she to help him? She was not to till the earth with him, for there was not yet any toil to make help necessary. If there were any such need, a male helper would be better, and the same could be said of the comfort of another's presence if Adam were perhaps weary of solitude. How much more agreeably could two male friends, rather than a man and woman, enjoy companionship and conversation in a life shared together.[20]

It is passages like this that alienate feminist readers from Augustine. It is possible, however, to glean from this a more positive view of women. In his essay "Augustinian Pessimism? A New Look at Augustine's Teaching on Sex, Marriage and Celibacy," David G. Hunter provides a very informative and compelling history of the development of Augustine's views on marriage. Interestingly, according to Hunter within Christian marriage *concupiscentia* must be transferred in this world into *societas*, the social bond:

> Augustine suggests that the companionship or fellowship (*societas*) of marriage operates as a good quite distinct from the good of procreation. The intrinsically unstable character of sexual desire (*libido*) is given a certain limit and order within the context of a relationship of fidelity. *Fides*, then, is a duty, "a sort of mutual servitude," in which each spouse supports the *infirmitas* of the other. Not even the call that one partner might feel toward celibacy can cancel this duty of fidelity. While unrestrained sexual lust is still a fault, a *culpa*, Augustine writes, it is a "forgivable fault" (*venialis culpa*) owing to the good of fidelity. But fidelity itself, like the chaste use of sexual relations for procreation, is one of the glories of marriage.[21]

In this way, according to Hunter, there is something more to marriage than reproduction and reigning in desire. Augustine emphases that sexual desire does not go away through the magical circumstance of having a bishop at one's marriage ceremony.[22] Rather, through the marital bond one might reign in and control the wildness that is desire. In his *Augustine and the Functions of Concupiscence*, Finnish Augustine scholar Timo Nisula compares this taming of concupiscence to the taming of African wild dogs in Augustine's time and today—one does not train a wild dog to live inside with one's children, but to protect one's property.[23] One accepts its limitations.

Augustine's reading of the good of marriage stands in comparison to the marriage "ceremony" itself, which consisted of signing the *tabulae matrimoniales*, which is composed of a mutual agreement between the interested parties and lays out the necessary property transferals related to a dowry: what happens if the man breaks the union, if the woman is unfaithful, if either dies, and what the inheritance rights of potential and existing children are. Augustine supports this pecuniary reading of marriage; and yet he finds it necessary again and again to return to what the function of desire is in the context of marriage.

Love implies lack, or perhaps resonance—one sees in the other something that resonates in oneself, but also something that one does not already have. Desire (as *concupiscentia*) is the form of love that reaches out in longing for that other, not necessarily in hope of incorporating the other into the self, but in hoping for a kind of reciprocity that makes the lack bearable and fruitful. It is perhaps that reciprocal absence that caused Adam to sin along with Eve. Elizabeth Clark argues in "Adam's Only Companion: Augustine and the Early Christian Debate on Marriage" that Augustine reads Adam's first sin as rooted in unwillingness to leave Eve to suffer God's wrath alone.[24] This unwillingness to leave Eve becomes Adam's undoing. This unwillingness is founded in pride.

Eve is seduced by the serpent because he appeals to her intellect. The serpent offers her a ways of thinking differently than she has been accustomed, and in her pride she takes of the fruit to eat. Adam sees that Eve has eaten and then is left with what seems to him to be an impossible choice: God or companion, Creator or Life. In *On the Literal Meaning of Genesis*, Augustine claims that the folly of Adam's thinking has root in his own broken heart:

> After the woman had been seduced and had eaten of the forbidden fruit and had given Adam some to eat with her, he did not wish to make her unhappy, fearing she would waste away without his support, alienated from his affections, and that this dissension would be her death. He was not overcome by the concupiscence of the flesh, which he had not yet experienced in the law of the members at war with the law of the mind, but by the sort of attachment and affection

by which it often happens that we offend God while we try to keep the friendship of men.²⁵

Thus Adam and Eve were friends, on Augustine's view, and *concupiscentia* of the flesh is described as experienced with the body at war with the mind. The attachment between friends is a dangerous one, as was discussed in Chapter 2. In his pride, Adam decides not to leave her. This is not about sexual desire, according to the passage above. However, it could be well said to be his concupiscent will: Adam actively desires a relationship with Eve at all costs, and in his pride—and perhaps his knowledge that he himself wouldn't die upon eating the flesh²⁶—decides to join her in her sin.

In this section, I've sought to lay out the nature and dangers of *concupiscentia*. It may seem contrary to the task of outlining and emphasizing the importance of *concupiscentia* for the human psychosomatic and even religious life. But it is important to consider that *concupiscentia* can be dangerous and overwhelming. Like a sudden flash of light in one's eyes, *concupiscentia* can cause confusion and chaos, and from this confusion comes bad decision-making. However, the denial of wild desire as a function of the human person does no good for those trying to understand what it is to be human, to think like a human, to feel like a human. Not everything about the psyche is nice.

CONFESSIONS OF LOVE: AUGUSTINE'S PERSONAL EVE

Going back to my discussion above of Augustine's flirtation with Platonism and full-blown romance with Manicheanism, I'd like to return to the supposedly ecstatic experience of God Augustine claims to have had after his exposure to some books of the Platonists in Book VII of his *Confessions*. He claims that he found himself "crashing down" back into his *consuetudo carnalis*, which I translate as his "worldly habits." Many translators, such as Henry Chadwick, translate *consuetudo carnalis* as "sexual habit."²⁷ This translation seems to be supported by the fact that Augustine's vision in Book VII is immediately preceded by the loss of his wife in Book VI and the claim that he'd taken a lover in Book XIII. Augustine writes, "*adhuc tenaciter colligabar ex femina,*" concerning what was causing his difficulty to finally convert to Christianity. Chadwick translates this phrase as "But I was still firmly tied by woman."²⁸ James Wetzel has pointed out that this "*ex femina*" in this sentence is wildly misread: "*ex*" is not "*by*," *ex* means "*out of, from*"—*ex femina* means "from woman," meaning his nature as a human, born from a mother, his material nature, was the last thing keeping him from converting to

Christianity. As Wetzel writes, "Fathered by immaterial spirit and mothered by nothing at all, it is little wonder that Augustine has come to think of his closeness to creation *ex femina* as a snare of some sort."[29] Augustine is not caught between sex and God before his conversion; he is paralyzed between the two poles that he sets up for himself: he is struck by the impossibility of thinking materiality and divinity both as knotted and as distinct. Without a mother, how can there be any goodness in body at all? And yet, there cannot be body without soul and no soul without body.

Augustine had a wife but was never married. He describes their relationship in this way:

> She was the only girl for me, and I was faithful to her. With her I learnt by direct experience how wide a difference there is between the partnership of marriage entered into for the sake of having a family and the mutual consent of those whose love (*libidinosi amoris*) is a matter of physical sex, and for whom the birth of a child is contrary to their intention—even though, if offspring arrive, they compel their parents to love them (*diligi*).[30]

Augustine seems to coldly contrast the partnerships of marriage where the goal is children and those "whose *love*" is about sex, not children. Words of love are used twice in this passage and are not directed toward the "partnership of marriage" that Augustine did *not* have. It does one well to remember that Adam and Eve themselves were not married, and it was love for his wife that motivated Adam to choose to betray the command of God (a view that Milton held in common with Augustine).

Augustine did not maintain sexual relationships with women after his conversion. Indeed, before his conversion he and his mother conspired to get him a rich noblewoman to marry, which required the expulsion of his partner of thirteen years, with whom he produced his only child. Readers of Augustine (feminist and otherwise) are often quick to gloss over Augustine's feelings at the rending of his home life—after all, Augustine says clearly that he took another woman to his bed in order to have someone until he could get married to his child-bride. Danuta Shanzer writes:

> Modern scholars have tried to demythologize, deromanticize, and desentimentalize Augustine's (dare one call it?) "relationship". But the language of the passage is a heady and significant mixture of the biblical and the medical. Augustine invites one to read a world of emotional, and indeed theological, significance into the trauma. Maybe one should be slower to mock this "terrible separation" or French scholars who take the dismissal of mistresses seriously.[31]

It is interesting to note that Augustine does not say that he is healed of the festering wound caused by the cutting away of his lover[32]—he is not necessarily "healed of that wound," as he says about his grief at the loss of his mother.

Danuta Shanzer makes a compelling argument that the wound at Augustine's side caused by the loss of his wife is a direct reference to Adam's loss of a rib in the creation of Adam. While Adam loses a rib and gains a help-mate, she writes, "Augustine, instead of gaining a wife, loses a bedmate . . . And instead of emerging miraculously intact from the process, he is left with a bleeding wound that will not heal."[33] Virginia Burrus and Catherine Keller write, concerning Augustine's seemingly careless taking up of another sexual partner, "Bereft of his soul mate and cleaving to alien flesh, Augustine suddenly finds his own sinfulness nakedly revealed."[34]

I agree with Burrus and Shanzer that Augustine is drawing parallels with the creation of Eve. It seems clear also that Augustine is drawing parallels to the first couple's expulsion from Eden: the sin of Augustine and the sin of Adam are the same in this respect: they both thought that they knew what was best for them as far as their relationship with the women in their lives went. Adam thought that the only way to keep Eve was by joining her in her sin: he thought that he understood what God's vengeance would be. Augustine in turn thought that he knew what was best for himself, in this case an official marriage to a person that could promote his career and social status. *As if that is the boundary to his communion with the Divine.* What foolishness to suppose that his relationship with his wife was the boundary to communion with God, his fear of losing sex in his life is a false fear: he thought he understood divine will and the nature of humanity, and thus why sex was precluded from his conversion process. It is not until he is an older man, reflecting on his life and his transition from sinner to saint, and having read the creation myth again and again, that he could come to realize his fundamental misunderstanding of the relationship between love and the divine. This love, desperate as it is, seeks outward and inward in all directions, it is extended and embodied.

In the political and social context of fourth-century North Africa (as well as twenty-first-century North America), Augustine was *not* married, his son was *not* legitimate. What is marriage, then, if what he had with his partner of thirteen years was not that? In this section, I have sought to draw parallels between Adam's situation and Augustine's. It is a fruitful endeavor, I think, to draw the comparison in another way: Augustine, for all that he bleeds inwardly, may be more like Eve, and his wife, faced with an impossible choice, like Adam. Augustine made a decision that broke his union between himself and his partner of thirteen years. His partner too was left with a choice: Does she move on and have another, and thus become a partner to Augustine's adultery and betrayal, or does she move on and keep the pact that she herself had made? For that is what it comes down to—betrayal or loyalty. Augustine's sin here parallels Adam's and Eve's, but his wife's actions are on a plane of their own. Again, as Augustine writes in *The Literal Meaning of Genesis*, Adam "was not overcome by the concupiscence of the flesh . . . but by the sort of attachment and affection by which it often happens that we offend God while we try to keep the friendship of men."[35] Augustine's wife was neither overcome by concupiscence of the flesh (she is said to have returned to Africa vowing celibacy) nor overwhelmed by the concupiscence of the heart: compelled by desire and love, she makes what seems to be the right choice, which Augustine clearly envies: she is a better Adam.

The examination of myth draws out the nature of the human psyche. Of course, as I have shown in my discussion of Augustine's relationship with his wife, this examination can also tell us more about the examiner than the "nature of humanity" as a whole. When his wife leaves at his behest and takes a vow of chastity, Augustine is left with disgust at his own inability to maintain a proper relationship to her. Reading the women in Augustine's *Confessions* as not only set pieces but actual people who influenced Augustine's life leads a much richer reading of Augustine's thoughts on what it is to be human and what it is to love.

ON HUMAN LOVE

In Book XIV, Chapter 11 of *The City of God* Augustine gives a satisfying solution to the question, Why does the "arrogant angel" go after Eve and not Adam? The Devil sought to "worm his way, by seductive craftiness, into the consciousness of man" due to envy at his "unfallen condition."[36] This envy is of a different sort than caused the Devil to fall in the first place, though is likely related to his own pride. He chose the form of a serpent, and through it chose the women to lie to: "No doubt starting with the inferior of the human pair so as to arrive at the whole by stages, supposing that the man would not be so easily gullible, and could not be trapped by a false move on his own part, but only if he yielded to another's mistake."[37] The tempter knew better than to convince Adam to sin, so seduced "inferior" Eve. Augustine, of course, very well believes Eve (and women) to be inferior to Adam (and men), both bodily and mentally.[38] She was certainly younger than Adam, as if that makes a difference. But I think there is something to the fact that the Devil thought it would be better to convince the woman to sin, and then have her convince the man to follow likewise.

Augustine continues:

They were alone together, two human beings, a married pair; and we cannot believe that the man was led astray to transgress God's law because he believed that the woman spoke the truth, but that he fell in with her suggestions because they were so closely bound in partnership . . . Eve accepted the serpent's statement as the truth, while Adam refused to be separated from his only companion, even if it involved sharing her sin.[39]

Adam did not fall through his use of reason in the sense of being tricked (as Eve was tricked). Once Eve bit the fruit he couldn't *not* follow suit. What is companionship such that one would leap into the abyss and disobey God and all that is holy for the sake of it? There must be something profoundly necessary about friendship, partnership, and marriage, something that is in cuts to our very bones, if the original man sinned because he could not imagine life without his wife. Thus the manner of their sins are different: "They were not both deceived by credulity; but both were taken captive by their sin and entangled in the snares of the Devil."[40] The Devil knew he could get to Adam by going through Eve. Eve was not a trap for Adam, however—how could she be? The Devil did not make Eve. God made her to be Adam's companion, from his very bones. What genius is necessary to assume that Adam could not depart willingly from her, just as we might not part willingly from our limbs and sinews?

CONCLUSION

In this chapter, I have sought to emphasize that, for Augustine, the bodies of Adam and Eve are both gendered and generative. Sex, love, reproduction, desire are all aspects of what it is to be human today, to be sure, but are also vital for understanding the place of creation mythology in both the works of Augustine and the Christian West. I have sought to separate as much as possible the Augustine who, as bishop, had to deal with land and property disputes and had to uphold Roman patriarchal, property-driven morays concerning marriage, and the Augustine who had a wife for thirteen years and, upon throwing her from him bedded another without societal repercussions. Augustine's inability to choose rightly is in stark contrast to his wife, who looked at her impossible task and chose another way, one that he follows only later. This failure was not the failure of mind over body, but a failure of cohesion of self. Augustine could not convert because he felt tied *ex femina*—the rational Augustine could not see a way to be both Christian and worldly. The wildness of *concupiscentia* ought to be respected and upheld, as it is a wildness that has existed in humanity since Adam.

NOTES

1. My thanks to James Wetzel, Sally Scholz, Georg Theiner, Sarah Vitale, and Rachel Aumiller for ealy comments on this chapter. This chapter is based on the third chapter of my doctoral dissertation. See "Embodied Love and Extended Desire" (PhD diss., Villanova University, 2017).
2. I have chosen not to capitalize "original sin," as it so often is in English.
3. Jesse Couenhoven, "St. Augustine's Doctrine of Original Sin," *Augustinian Studies* 36, no. 2 (2005): 360.
4. Elaine H. Pagels, *Adam, Eve, and the Serpent* (New York: Random House, 1988), 147.
5. Augustine often makes allusions to 1 Corinthians 13:12: "For now we see through a glass, darkly; but then face to face."
6. Susan Blackburn Griffith argues that, though Genesis is specifically allegorized in few sermons (Sermons 2, 4, 4A, and 5, specifically), "Numerous allusions to the Creation and Fall, however, as well as citations of verses from Genesis, do occur in the sermons in passing." See "The Figure of Adam in the Sermon of Augustine," *Studia Patristica* 49 (2010): 168.
7. Letter CXXXI to Jerome concerning the nature of the creation of souls and Letter CXLIV to Optatus concerning the same issue both have the creation and sin of the first humans as their heart. These letters are inconclusive—Augustine seeks to show through his exegesis on Genesis that he does not actually know the origin of individual souls. See *The Letters of St. Augustine: Annotated Edition Including More Than 1500 Notes*, trans. and ed. John George Cunningham (Augsburg: Jazzybee Verlag, 2015).
8. It is not the place here to discuss at length the problematic term that is "heresy" when referring to schisms of the early Christian community in Augustine's time. It is through the lens of history that such sects are heretical. Augustine sought reconciliation with fractured groups as well as discussion. He did, of course, think his own version of Christianity to be the accurate one.
9. This insight is developed further in Margaret Miles's 2012 text, "From Rape to Resurrection: Sin, Sexual Difference, and Politics." She writes, "From Book I, in which he considered in detail the rape of Christian women that had occurred in the sack of Rome, to his insistence in Book 22 that female bodies will not become male in the resurrection, the topic of female bodies bookends his massive epic. Female bodies became a paradigm of the eperience of the human race, from rape to resurrection, from abjection to perfection." See Margaret Miles, "From Rape to Resurrection: Sin, Sexual Difference, and Politics," in *Augustine's* City of God*: A Critical Guide*, ed. James Wetzel (New York: Cambridge University Press, 2012), 77.
10. Augustine, *The Literal Meaning of Genesis, Vol. 1 and 2*, trans. John Hammond Taylor (New York: Newman Press, 1982), 9.3.6; 73.
11. Augustine, *The Literal Meaning of Genesis*, 9.10.18; 81.
12. See John C. Cavadini, "Feeling Right: Augustine on the Passions and Sexual Desire," *Augustinian Studies* 36, no. 1 (2005): 195–217. It is tempting to consider,

given Augustine's account of the possibilities of sexual union in Eden, that Eve could have been pregnant with Cain upon the expulsion from Eden.

13. Andrea Dworkin, *Intercourse* (New York: The Free Press, 1987), 67.

14. Patricia Grosse, "Love and the Patriarch: Augustine and (Pregnant) Women," *Hypatia: A Journal of Feminist Philosophy*, Special Issue: Feminist Love Studies in the 21st Century 32, no. 1 (2017): 119–34.

15. Cavadini, "Feeling Right: Augustine on the Passions and Sexual Desire," 204.

16. Cavadini, "Feeling Right: Augustine on the Passions and Sexual Desire," 210 (emphasis mine).

17. James Wetzel, "Agony in the Garden: Augustine's Myth of Will," in *Parting Knowledge: Essays after Augustine* (Eugene: Cascade Books, 2013), 16.

18. Though perhaps women do not have as much reasoning capabilities as men, on Augustine's view. See Judith Chelius Stark's illuminating reading of Augustine's account of how women are in the image God, "Augustine on Women: In God's Image, but Less So," in *Feminist Interpretations of Augustine: Re-reading the Canon*, ed. Judith Chelius Stark (University Park: Pennsylvania State University Press, 2007), 215–41.

19. Augustine, *The Literal Meaning of Genesis*, 9.5.9; 75.

20. Augustine, *The Literal Meaning of Genesis*, 9.5.9; 75.

21. David G. Hunter, "Augustinian Pessimism? A New Look At Augustine's Teaching On Sex, Marriage and Celibacy," *Augustinian Studies* 25 (1994): 162.

22. In another informative essay, "Augustine and the Making of Marriage in Roman North Africa," David Hunter writes of the development of Christian marriages. In Augustine's time, "Only the presence of a bishop in the family home would have distinguished a pagan wedding from a Chrstian one. And the bishop's signature on the *tabulae matrimoniales* (perhaps along with blessing over the couple) would have been the only visible sign that the Christian church recognized this marriage to be a Christian one." See "Augustine and the Making of Marriage in Roman North Africa," *Journal of Early Christian Studies* 11, no. 1 (2003): 76.

23. Timo Nisula, *Augustine and the Functions of Concupiscence*, vol. 116; *Supplements to Vigiliae Christianae* (Boston: Brill, 2012).

24. Elizabeth Clark, "'Adam's Only Companion,' Augustine and the Early Christian Debate on Marriage," *Recherches augustiniennes* 22 (1986): 139–62.

25. Augustine, *The Literal Meaning of Genesis*, 11.42.59; 176.

26. Augustine, *The Literal Meaning of Genesis*, 10.30.39; 162.

27. Augustine, *Confessions*, trans. Henry Chadwick (Oxford: Oxford University Press, 1998), VII.xvii.23; 127.

28. Augustine, *Confessions*, VIII.1.2; 134.

29. Wetzel, "Agony in the Garden: Augustine's Myth of Will," 14.

30. Augustine, *Confessions*, IV.ii.2; 53.

31. Danuta Shanzer, "*Avulsa a Latere Meo*: Augustine's Spare Rib: *Confessions* 6.15.25," *Journal of Roman Studies* 92 (2002): 159.

32. Augustine, *Confessions*, VI.xv.25; 109.

33. Shanzer, "*Avulsa a Latere Meo*," 159.

34. Virginia Burrus and Catherine Keller, "Confessing Monica," in *Feminist Interpretations of Augustine*, ed. Judith Chelius Stark (University Park: The Pennsylvania State University Press, 2007), 84.

35. Augustine, *The Literal Meaning of Genesis*, 11.42.59; 176.

36. Augustine, *Concerning the City of God against the Pagans*, trans. Henry Bettenson (London: Penguin Books, 2003), XIV.11; 569.

37. Augustine, *Concerning the City of God against the Pagans*, XIV.11; 570.

38. E. Ann Matter discusses Augustine's view of women at length in "*De cura feminarum:* Augustine the Bishop, North African Women, and the Development of a Theology of Female Nature." She emphasizes the fact that Augustine was not necessarily "weird" about sex and women, rather that he was a man in his own time dealing with the theology of his era. See "*De cura feminarum:* Augustine the Bishop, North African Women, and the Development of a Theology of Female Nature," *Augustinian Studies* 36, no. 1 (2005): 87–98.

39. Augustine, *Concerning the City of God against the Pagans*, XIV.11; 570

40. Augustine, *Concerning the City of God against the Pagans*, XIV.11; 570.

Chapter 2

The Effectivity of Women in Augustine's *Confessions*

The Erasure of Agency and the Regulation of Desire

Richard A. Lee, Jr.

It is perhaps not an exaggeration to say that the entire narrative arc of *Confessions* is contained in a single sentence: "You arouse (*excitas*) us so that praising you may bring us joy, because you have made us and drawn us to yourself, and our heart is restless until it rests in you."[1] Here he indicates three main points that together move the action of the text along. First, there is the arousal or excitation that constitutes, to a large extent, the relation of God and the human. Second, there is a quasi-natural restlessness—that is, a desire that belongs to the human as such, or at least as fallen (and hence the desire is quasi-natural). Finally, Augustine indicates that the restlessness ceases, though the desire continues, when the human desires God. It is this restless desire that opens in infancy, propels the acquisition of language, accounts for many sins (theft, lust, fornication, the love of games, etc.), and moves Augustine's intellectual inquiries, culminating in his conversion to Christianity.

Contained within both this short summary of the narrative motor and the journey that is depicted in *Confessions* is the demand that desire be regulated. More specifically, the restlessness will not cease unless desire is turned toward the unique "object" that is God. Desire as such is not a problem and is certainly not *the* problem as that desire constitutes the appropriate relation of the human to God. Therefore, it is a question of properly ordering that desire, of making desire ordered or ordinated—ordered toward the appropriate end

(God), ordered and not chaotic, ordered from the proper concept of what the human is.

As well documented as this narrative arc is, so too is the erasure of women in the text of *Confessions*. With the exception of Monica, his mother, few, if any, of the other women who play significant roles in Augustine's life are named or even sketched out in any detail. We should be careful not to accuse Augustine of failures that can only be named in our own time. That his treatment, even of Monica, can be accurately termed misogynist is clear. What is less clear, however, is the role in which the erasure of women and of women's agency in particular play in relation to the regulation of desire. There are three pivotal moments in *Confessions* that are occasioned by characters identified as women and yet, as I will argue, their agency is erased so as to make way either for Augustine's own agency or for the action of God. No wonder their names are not given—a name would imply a subject that is capable of acting.

In what follows, I will investigate the role of Augustine's nurses in the regulation of desire toward language and the role of his partner—the mother of his child—in the regulation of desire away from sensuous pleasure. Given the already extensive discussion of the role of Monica in the literature, I will leave a discussion of her aside. That being said, I would argue that she is a haunting presence in the narrative and her agency is often expropriated from her and given over to God. My argument will be that it is Augustine's conception of desire and its relation to pleasure that compels this erasure of feminine agency. A shift in this conception of desire would enable Augustine to see the active contributions these women make on his journey toward a certain kind of self-understanding.

This will entail an investigation into several inter-related concepts that form, I argue, the background to Augustine's understanding of pleasure and desire: the distinction between use and enjoyment, the idea of sensuous reality as deficient, and the identification of woman with sensuous reality, frequently through the identification of women with mother. In the end, I hope to show that the route to the liberation of woman from *Confessions* is through a liberation of pleasure and desire from its regulation.

THE REGULATION OF DESIRE THROUGH ORDER

If desire can be the subject of regulation, that would mean, at a minimum, that there is something desired properly or an object of desire that is appropriate. Already here lies a duplicity. If desire has a proper object, then the appropriateness of that object can be determined either internally or externally to desire. If determined internally, then an analysis of desiring as such would show that it tends to an object or several objects simply because of what desire is. We might say, as Augustine will come close to saying, that desire is for happiness. Then, the proper objects of desire would be only those things that can bring (true) happiness. This internal determination, in turn, requires an analysis of what brings about happiness. Yet this very quickly makes a completely internal determination difficult, if not impossible. One might argue that a good wine, a tasty meal, or other physical pleasures make one happy. Frequently, then, the argument moves to "true" happiness—that is, a determination from outside of happiness itself of what *really* makes us happy. It seems, therefore, that a purely internal determination of the proper object of happiness is impossible.

On the other hand, an external determination of the proper object of desire will turn on a normative claim that arises from a different source. For example, one might argue in this way: If humans are directed toward God through God's creative activity, the only proper object of desire will be God.[2] In this case, however, we need to be on guard as to the source of the "ought." Is there a metaphysical grounding of it? Natural? Social? The difficulty only increases. If the proper object of desire is determined externally, how can we ever be sure that it is not, itself, determined on the basis of a desire that, because determining the proper object of desire, does not itself have a proper object? The experiment with alcohol prohibition in the United States might be an example of this. I desire the "social cleanliness" of a society that does not permit the production of alcohol. I then determine that the desire for alcohol, or even drunkenness is "inappropriate," i.e., the wrong kind of object of desire. Yet the desire for a certain kind of social order is itself without a proper object as it is what determines the proper objects of desire.

One way to avoid these problems is to insist that desire is fundamentally tied to need. No one desires what they do not need. Yet how do I determine need? Do I have a need for beauty? Do I have a need for pleasure? Do I have a need friendship? Frequently, desire as tied to need emerges from a lack, particularly a lack of what is necessary. This understanding of desire as tied to need as lack is another way of determining the proper object of desire.

In all of these ways, desire comes under an order or regulation that is outside itself. In fact, what I mean by the "regulation of desire" is just this insistence on desire being ordered. For Augustine, desire is proper only when ordered, and the order requires both an origin (what desire is, as such) and the assignation of a proper object. The goal or object of desire is determined as appropriate and on this basis the desire is determined to be proper or ordered. I will return to the nature of this ordering in the final section. The relation between desire and order, however, is not immediately obvious.

The Invention of Order

In *De Doctrina Christiana*, Augustine distinguished between what is to be used and what is to be enjoyed:[3]

> There are some things, then, which are to be enjoyed, others which are to be used, others still which are to be enjoyed and used. Those things which are objects of enjoyment make us happy [*beatos nos faciunt*]. Those things which are objects of use assist, and (so to speak) support us in our efforts after happiness [*beatitudo*], so that we can attain the things that make us happy and rest in them.[4]

That Augustine did not mean a dichotomy here is clear for otherwise there could not be things [*res*] that can be *both* used and enjoyed. Yet, as I will show below, there is a decisive distinction here. The root of sin is in enjoying those things that are to be used and, perhaps, in using those things that are to be enjoyed.

That Augustine did not also intend the Kantian distinction between means (use) and ends (enjoyment) is less clear. O'Donovan puts this interpretation immediately aside because "The subordination of the world to God is not primarily a decision of the subject; it is an ontological reality which confronts the subject and demands that he conform his love to it."[5] Even if on the ontological level, without any subjective decision, this is still a distinction between ends and means; for those things that are to be used "assist . . . and support us in our efforts" that are directed toward happiness. To find happiness in those things is *inordinate*, i.e., goes against that very ontological order. However, we can try to find happiness in those things, and so something like will is involved. Even if the distinction is based on an "ontological reality," still, for Augustine, if sin is culpable, the choice for or against that reality is the root of the blame:

> We ourselves, again, who enjoy and use these things, being placed among both kinds of object, if we set ourselves to enjoy those which we ought to use, are hindered in our course, and sometimes even led away from it; so that, getting entangled in the love of lower gratifications, we lag behind in, or even altogether turn back from, the pursuit of the real and proper objects of enjoyment.[6]

The translation here makes a choice that I think is not called for. We are not "placed" among both kinds, but *constituted* between them. That is, if we are "placed" among (note here that English grammar requires "between") that which is to be used and that which is to be enjoyed, we have, precisely, a decision. If we want/will [*voluerimus*] to use that which is to be enjoyed, *then* our course is hindered. What is more, the willing itself is what holds us back (the Latin has the passive *retardemur*) or also calls us back from (again the Latin has the passive *revocemur*) the things which are to be enjoyed. And this is because we are tied down [*praepediti*] by the love [*amore*] of inferiors.

The between what is to be used and what is to be enjoyed is ripe for deconstruction in the proper sense. If a text distinguishes between two concepts or things—and here it is not clear whether "that which is to be used" and "that which is to be enjoyed" are things or concepts—and yet cannot define one term without the other, then we should strive to find out how the one cannot be defined *except in terms of the other*. And if that is the case, then the distinction itself is a construct and the mutual implication of the distinct concepts/things needs to be further investigated.[7] That which is to be enjoyed is, in fact, to be used precisely so as to achieve happiness. Those things are to be enjoyed that can make us happy. A thing that cannot make us happy should be only used. We can only distinguish what is to be used and what is to be enjoyed on the basis of what constitutes our happiness. Yet happiness itself is not determined either on the basis of what *usus* means or on the basis of what *fruitio* means. This distinction is based on a determination of happiness [*beatus*] as if that determination is obvious or self-evident.[8] As I will argue below, Augustine attempts to give an ontological ground to the determination of happiness and yet, that ground itself is neither obvious nor self-evident.

As Augustine continues, the distinction becomes more unstable or, at the very least, is transferred elsewhere, "For to enjoy is to abide in the love of some thing on account of itself. To use, however, is to refer what will come into use for obtaining that which you love, if, nevertheless, that should be loved."[9] Whether by a subjective decision or not, what is to be used is referred—one might even say "transferred"—to that which is to be loved, i.e., enjoyed. A restriction is immediately applied—if that is to be loved, if that ought to be loved, if that should be loved. The problem, as I said, is transferred elsewhere and yet we do not know where. How can one determine what *should* be loved? If it is happiness, what kind? In the end, the useful is useful only in obtaining that which is to be enjoyed. Yet that which is to be enjoyed is itself useful in that, as I quoted above, they make us happy. However, one of Augustine's central concerns here is that we are able to enjoy those things that, properly speaking, should be used. That is, we can be "tied down" to "inferiors" through enjoying that which should only be used. It is not impossible (an ontological condition) that I enjoy what I use. And this is sin (a normative designation). The distinction, therefore, is not between use and enjoyment but between what *should* be used and what *should* be enjoyed. The distinction cannot be ontological, therefore, as long as I can enjoy those things that *should* be used.[10]

That the distinction between what is to be used and what is to be enjoyed is precisely a means/ends distinction is made clear through the analogy Augustine raises—an analogy that shows Augustine's understanding of the human condition as being stretched between use and enjoyment. Imagine you are in a country that is not your home and you wish to return home because you are unhappy where you are living. You start on a journey home and you come to enjoy being on the plane/train/automobile and, in addition, you stop in a country during your journey that you come to find delightful. The problem here is that we have an end, namely to go home, and enjoying the means of transport or a delightful layover "turns us away" [*conversi*: even stronger, "turns us back from"], what we should use into enjoying. The result is that we forget the end toward which we set out and we do not want the journey to end quickly, forgetting that our happiness would only come when we return home. But it is only being at home, so the analogy goes, that would make us happy.

We can, it seems, move from is to ought only if we smuggle in what belongs to the ought as a condition of being. We cannot be happy unless we are "at home" and this home can only be in God, because, it seems, of God's immutability. In this respect, we should only use those things that can bring us "home." Enjoyment should belong only to our being with God. This, I would argue, cannot be understood except on the basis of an ends/means distinction. Given the end (being at home), the means are useful to that end and, as useful to that end, are only to be chosen on the basis of that end. O'Donovan seems to insist that the Kantian distinction can be put out of play because there is in Augustine no subjective decision. Yet if I were to translate "decision" back into Latin, I would choose a verb much like *volere*, and that term is pervasive in these passages. However, he might be on to an insight with his term "subject." It is certainly worth questioning whether there is a "subject" (in the Kantian and post-Kantian sense) in Augustine's thought. My issue is not with the post-Cartesian subject, rather, the problem lies with whether we can understand Augustine's claims here as "ontological" and, so an argument would have it, not normative.

In order to return to *Confessions*, I would point out three features of this distinction between what is to be used and what is to be enjoyed. First, it hinges on a more primary distinction, which is also normative, between what remains and what passes away. Second, and following from the first, it hinges on a distinction between what is only materially pleasing, even if a necessary condition of life as such, and what *should* be enjoyed. Third, while O'Donovan is certainly correct in arguing that Augustine is not insisting that other humans are "mere means," it turns out that the distribution of use and enjoyment in *Confessions* seems to fall on his implication that women are *only* to be used while some men can also be enjoyed.

MATERIAL REALITY

That Augustine is either a Platonist, a neo-Platonist, or a semi-Platonist should, I think, be beyond question at this point.[11] To take the proper name "Plato" out of this equation, I think it is hard to deny that Augustine, even the Manichean Augustine, held the fundamental position that the world that is available to our senses is material, changing, subject to time (and this might just bring together the first two) and therefore not always true. This is, in a certain sense, a tautology. "I weigh 250 pounds is true . . ." today. Tomorrow, I could weigh (hopefully) 220 pounds or (realistically) 260 pounds. On strictly verificationist grounds, the truth of my weight depends on changing circumstances. Yet truth, if it is to be a measure, ought not rest on shifting grounds. If truth is to be a measure, that is, if we can say "this is true" and "this is not true," then what allows for the determination of truth seems to demand a nonshifting ground.[12]

In *On Christian Doctrine* and *Letter 18*, Augustine insists that material reality and bodies are the lowest form of reality. This notion, in fact, drives much of the narrative of *Confessions.* In Book IV, Augustine says "I was miserable, and miserable too is everyone whose mind is chained by friendship (*amicitia*, i.e., love) with mortal things, and is torn apart by their loss, and then becomes aware of the misery that it was in even before it lost them."[13] In *Letter 18*, Augustine posits that:

> There is a nature that is changeable in place and time. And there is a nature that is changeable in no way by place but only in time, as is the soul. And there is a nature that is neither through place nor through time able to be changed. This is God. . . . Since, however, everything that we say "it is," we say insofar as it perdures, and insofar as it is one, furthermore the form of every beautiful [thing] is unity. You see, therefore, in this distribution of natures what would be the highest, what would be the lowest, and what would be the middle, greater than the lowest and less than the highest. The highest would be happiness itself [*ipsa beatitas*], the lowest, which neither is happiness nor misery, and the middle, truly, which lives, when inclined to the lowest, miserably and on the contrary when inclined toward the highest, lives happily.[14]

So much happens in so few sentences. That Augustine makes a distinction between natures is not surprising.[15] That this distinction is based on the ways in which a nature is mutabile or not is also not surprising or suspect. That mutability is a deficient mode of being goes back at least to Plato and is also an aspect of Aristotle's philosophy. This is why Augustine says that we say "it is" only of that which remains, i.e., is unchangeable. Furthermore, that a thing is insofar as it is one has its origins in Plato, is explicitly identified by

Aristotle, and forms the core of the neo-Platonic tradition. Augustine, however, identifies that unity with the form of a beautiful thing. This seems to be an aside, and yet it indicates that we are moving from an ontological description to a normative insistence. The identification of such a nature with God also seems obvious.[16] That this is all obvious is indicated when Augustine asserts, "You see [*vides*] . . . what would be the highest, what would be the lowest, and what would be the middle. . . ."

That permanence is "higher" than change, as I indicated, is as old as Plato, if not older. However, it is not immediately obvious why this should be the case. That which is capable of the most change might seem the highest, from a certain perspective. A superhero, for example, with the capacity to change to meet whatever circumstances require would seem to be a powerful figure. In another context, several animal species have been seen to be capable of switching sexes when the circumstance requires—for example, when only females or males are present in an ecosystem. This mutability ensures the continuity of the species. In fact, evolutionary success depends on maximal mutability.

The denigration of change—and therefore of all material reality—seems to be intimately tied to the recognition that what is capable of change is, therefore, also capable of the greatest change of all, namely from being to non-being. Change is tantamount to death. However, the opposite must also be true: that which is capable of change is able to make the greatest change of all, namely from non-being to being. Change is tantamount to birth. Therefore, the denigration of changeable being is both a denial of death and a denial of birth. As Irigaray points out, the desire for permanence is a rejection of natality. It is, therefore, not that the feminine has an automatic and, therefore, natural connection to materiality. Rather, the denigration of material reality entails a rejection of natality and, consequently, of the feminine.[17]

Irigaray exposes the connection of materiality and natality to permanence in her reading of the analogy of the cave in Plato's *Republic*. On her reading, the story is a story of the masculine being at home in the womb and then emerging into the world. The cave/womb is characterized by lack of truth, the non-reality of images, the material, and nature. The story, however, much like Augustine's, turns the scene of birthing into the activity of the one being born:

> The child . . . will be cut off from any remaining empirical relation with the womb. From everything that might remind him, bring him back toward, turn him in the direction of *his* beginning, an origin that is still inscribed within and also inscribes a *proper* individual history of one's own.[18]

In this way, Irigaray shows the intimate connection between falsity, materiality, and the feminine on the one hand and truth, the Idea, and the masculine on the other. And the dichotomy between these is possible only on the basis of the erasure of the mother.

The division of these three natures turns out to be a ranking is both obvious ("You see what would be the highest . . .") and in need of motivation, if not argumentation. The division has been carried out in terms of *naturae*, natures, and this is thought initially in terms of change. In this sense, it belongs more to natural philosophy than to first philosophy. A translation is possible, however, from physics to metaphysics. Being—"it is"—belongs to that which "perdures," that which remains through a significant or substantial duration. What is holds on and is least affected by the onslaught of change, of coming to be and passing away. If "it is" is said of that which refuses or resists change then change must include some form of "it is not" or non-being. The three natures were first divided according to susceptibility to change and this can now be translated into susceptibility to non-being: what is susceptible to change both in terms of place and time tarries most with non-being; what is susceptible to change neither in terms of place nor in terms of time does not tarry with non-being at all. It is said to be most of all. The division is a ranking and being ("it is") is open to degrees.

There are three further quick steps that complete the thought. The first step is to link "it is" with unity, a step that, as I indicated above, is prepared by Plato and neo-Platonism. To the extent that change is or includes non-being, to that extent it includes distinction or otherness. In fact, it might just be this otherness that opens a changeable thing to change in the first place. The second step is the assertion, which is not argued in the Letter, that unity and beauty are in some sense the same. Then comes the third step and the "quickness" of this is, to repeat, signaled by the appeal to the addressee: "You see. . . ." What is seen is what is highest, lowest, and middle. Or rather, what is seen is just the ordering of highest, lowest, and middle. On the basis of this quick step, the conclusion "follows" that the highest is happiness, the lowest misery, and the middle (i.e., the human) is either happy—when inclined to the highest—or miserable—when inclined to the lowest.

What started as an analysis of natures—a physics—changed into an analysis of being—an ontology—and ended with an analysis of happiness—an ethics. The first analysis borrows from the third as its condition. Why is change the basis of this distinction as opposed, for example, to color, or height, or being knocked over by a cat? There are a number of differentiae according to which natures could be distinguished. As Foucault points out in *The Order of Things*, classifications, on one hand, are arbitrary and, on the other hand, once made, become obvious if not necessary.[19] That change is the principle of ordering picked out by Augustine, therefore, is a normative question and not a physical or metaphysical one. No wonder that the physics of change yielded an ethics according to which happiness is tied only to the permanent.

Augustine dances in reverse. That happiness is linked normatively to the permanent entails that change is linked misery.

Two points follow from this directly. First, everything that belongs to the world in which we find ourselves is indexed to misery rather than happiness. That is, as he already pointed out in *De Doctrina Christiana*, we are stretched along between what is to be used and what is to be enjoyed, between happiness and misery, between the constantly changing and the unchanging. But since happiness is indexed to the permanent, it does not belong to this world and, therefore, not to us as long as we are of this world. There is, in all this, an origin of our being in this world, namely natality. It is an origin into change that cannot be properly understood according to the traditional ontological tools. If birth is the origin into change, then our happiness cannot be indexed to this event. It therefore must be oriented elsewhere. But to where? It must be expropriated from natality and factical existence beyond death to the permanent. This orients the narrative trajectory of *Confessions* and it also entails the occlusion of women in the beginning and the erasure of female effectivity as a result.

In what follows, I want to analyze two moments in *Confessions* where women play a significant structural and also narrative role. The first moment comes at the opening of *Confessions*, namely the role of Augustine's mother and unnamed nurses. The second moment will be an analysis of the role of the mother of Augustine's child, also unnamed.[20]

DESIRE, SIN, AND WOMEN IN *CONFESSIONS*

Already at the outset of Augustine's life and the outset of his narrative, desire is present. And so too is God. "Allow me to speak, though I am but dust and ashes, allow me to speak in your merciful presence, for it is to your mercy that I address myself, not to some person who would mock me."[21] In an odd way, however, Augustine the author of *Confessions* is not there:

> But this I know, that I was welcomed by the tender care your mercy provided for me, for so I have been told by the parents who gave me life according to the flesh, those parents through whose begetting and bearing you formed me within time, *although I do not remember myself*.[22]

Although Augustine the author is not present, he is the center of the narrative, indeed of the world, as he tells the story.[23] If Augustine has no memory, then it is not present for him, it is not knowledge for him. And yet he tells the story. Perhaps he can tell the story without knowledge because it is the story of women. More specifically, without memory and, therefore, without presence, he can tell the story of the women who themselves, in his narrative, also are not present.

The story of his infancy is strange and not just because he ought not be able to tell it. It starts with feeding and ends with the first stages of language acquisition and is propelled by the women who play a central role from behind a constructed curtain. The curtain is put up in front of the women at the very beginning. "The comforts of human milk were waiting for me, but my mother and my nurses did not fill their own breasts; rather you gave me an infant's nourishment through them in accordance with your plan . . ."[24] The indirect object here, "for me" turns the thought away from the subject, the comforts [*consolationes*], and even further from the agents, the women who were providng the milk. The comforts of milk are not the doing of anyone, except, perhaps, God. The comforts were there to be taken by Augustine. And Augustine takes the comforts. But there are two Augustines here, the one taking the comfort and the one telling the story. Of course every infant experiences the world as there exclusively for them. The adult Augustine ought to know better. And so he seems to. Except he turns the actual state of affairs backward.

The providing of nourishment is removed from the agency of the women and handed over directly to God. "You gave me an infant's nourishment through them . . ." This turns the women into nothing more than means, i.e., that which is to be used. Since they women are to be used, two consequences follow. First, there should be no love attached to them. To love what is only to be used would take Augustine away from what he ought to be. He ought not have *amor* nor any of its cognates, including *amiticia*, friendship. Behind the curtain, though with milk available, the contribute nothing, they do nothing. And, as we shall see, they are silenced.

Before those issues can be reslovled, the narrative turns the need/desire for nourishment into a tool for the acquisition of language:

> Little by little I began to notice where I was, and I would try to make my wishes [*voluntates*] known to those who might satisfy them; but I was frustrated in this because my wishes were inside [me] while other people were outside and could by no sense of theirs be able to enter into my soul.[25]

There are desires [*voluntates*], presumably for food primarily and comfort secondarily, that cannot be satisfied because the infant Augustine has no way to externalize them. The infant has some "signs" by which to make their desires known—tossing, crying, screaming, etc.—but such signs are insufficient to express Augustine's desires. The adults, however, are unable, they lack the power, to penetrate the interiority of Augustine's soul. As signs, the flailing limbs and the screams are similar to Augustine's desires but they were not similar to the truth.[26] Still, the lack is hung, most of all, on those around him who failed to enter into his soul.

The paucity of signs for expressing desires is the motor that drives Augustine to the acquisition of language. Augustine has signs. The problem is that the signs are not similar enough to his true desires. And so while he screams and flails, his desires go unmet. The women, apparently, are silent. Being behind the curtain that the narrative has constructed, the women are now robbed of a second moment of effectivity. While in the case of nourishment, the women had at least the effectivity of being a means to an end, in the acquisition of language they play no role whatsoever. Augustine himself is the agent of his own language acquisition: ". . . [I]n the end of my infancy, I began to search for signs by which I could make my ideas [*sensa*] known to others."[27] That the infant Augustine could be the sole agent of his own development requires that the women be silenced—but not the "womenfolk" [*mulierculae*]. *Even* their authority is to be trusted on this matter. Yet their authority would never indicate that the child develops language without being spoken to. Augustine here refers to the "womenfolk" to attest to what we can come to know about infancy. Would they say of Augustine that he was the one who began to look for language? Would they acknowledge that, while they remained silent, a child began to speak in language? Would they admit that the very language they were speaking to the child was not the language into which the child emerged as speaking?

Yet Augustine develops language on his own. Apparently he learned to speak Latin without ever having heard it from those around him. He does not indicate that his language had a mimetic stage that would entail that his nurses spoke.[28] His nurses are behind a curtain and silent. No, rather, they are silenced. It is impossible to think that Augustine was raised in a household that did not include speech, particularly the speech of women. From behind the curtain, we are led to understand, Augustine's care takers do nothing and say nothing.

Augustine, on his own account, develops language from his own infant agency. Here, apparently, the sin of infancy is not operative. It is a redoubled desire that propels his language development: first, the desires he has and wants to satisfy and, second, the desire to express those desires. The first desires are what we might call natural or material and are desires we share with all animals (and maybe even plants). The second desire is the beginning of Augustine's crucial distinction between the inner human and the outer human, crucial in that it sustains the threefold division of natures that I analyzed above. The external/outer is inextricably tied to matter and to sensuousness. It is his interior that *deserves* expression. The difference between the interior and the exterior produces a distinction that is another site of desire. It is the failure of signs like flailing and screaming that produces an internality and externality. In infancy, Augustine must find a way to express his interior desires to the external world. This, it turns out, is the moment of original sin:

> Who is there to remind me of the sin of my infancy (for sin there was: no one is free from sin in your sight, not even an infant whose span of earthly life is but a single day). . . . What then was my sin at that age? Was it perhaps that I cried so greedily for those breasts? Certainly if I behaved like that now, greedy not for breasts, but for food suitable for my age, I should provoke derision and be very properly rebuked. My behavior then was equally deserving of rebuke, but since I would not have been able to understand anyone who scolded me, neither custom nor common sense allowed any rebuke be given.[29]

The crying for food was initially a sign for a desire. That desire is now cast as sin [*peccatum*] because, it seems, it is disordered. Augustine says, more literally, "Was it because my mouth was agape [*inhiabam*] crying for the breasts?" His mouth opens, it seems, for two reasons: to accept the nourishment his nurses are providing and to scream for that very nourishment. Clearly if the adolescent or adult Augustine were to behave in this way, it would be disordered. And that order is retroactively applied to the infant and therefore the infant sins. But there is a second, or perhaps originary, sin, namely the direction outward of an interior desire. But where, exactly, is the sin? Is the sin in language itself, i.e., in the expression of the desire? It must be, for the desire itself is not disordered—a child needs to eat, after all. The expression of the desire, therefore, must be the sin. Not the expression as such but the excess of the expression over the (ordered) need. Now the interiority of the desire is judged on the exteriority of its expression. But it is the same gaping mouth that opens to the breast that also expresses too much.

Here, then, is the final occlusion of the women involved in his early care. They are now present only as breasts [*uberes*]. While Augustine here acknowledges, for the first time, the language of others in the form of their rebukes and scoldings, that language is as unintelligible to the infant Augustine as his signs are to them. If the women who cared for him as a baby spoke, their language would have been gibberish to the infant Augustine. And he could only speak his own gibberish back to them. Silenced and behind a curtain, only their breasts appear. And they appear not as love, care, concern, or even duty, but only as the occasion of Augustine infant sin: "The only innocent feature in infants is the weakness of their limbs; not the soul of infants."[30]

It is telling that the next episode in which a woman "plays" a role occurs in Book IV, a book that is so rich in content and significant episodes that it merits study in its own right. Interestingly, toward the beginning, Augustine recasts the scene of nursing in a fully positive light: "Or what am I when things are well with me but sucking your milk or eating from you food that does not corrupt?"[31] Sucking the milk of women is the site of sin, sucking the milk of God is the origin of the good. This leads Augustine to ask what is a human that is only human. The answer: Not a human at all. Nursing is a site of sin when related to the milk of a woman. The actual nourishment that Augustine's nurses provided is now turned into a deficient copy of the food that God provides, a food that does not corrupt. Yet how is it that his nurses corrupted him by providing food? It could only be that their nourishment was the occasion of Augustine's sin because it was material, subject to change, and, most importantly, an opportunity for Augustine's happiness.

"ILLEGITIMATE ONE"

Book IV deals with Augustine's life from ages nineteen to twenty-eight. He was teaching rhetoric, the art of using, in his words, "tricky language." Referring, whether intentionally or not, to the "crime" of which Socrates was accused, Augustine insists that he did not teach how to make it that the innocent are guilty or that the guilty are innocent. He was still enjoying theater and enjoying his friends who shared similar interests. In all of this, language continues to be an occasion for sin. The origin of language in the sinful desire of the infant Augustine continues to taint language throughout Augustine's life.

In the midst of what appears like a recap and introduction to the next plot point, Augustine slips in this bit of information:

> At this time I had somone [*unam*] not known by that union that would be called legal [*legitimum*], but who wandering desire lacking prudence sought out, but nevertheless the only one I had, and I was sexually faithful to her, in whom I would have learned by my own example what a distance there is between the kind of suitable marriage that is founded for generating a family and an agreement of libidinous love, where children may be born even against the wishes of the parents, though once born one is driven to love them.[32]

The very next sentence begins, "I also remember," and goes on to speak of a poetry contests and the offer of a sorcerer to help him win. That is, although Augustine was faithful to this women who he does not name, it is listed among a series of events at the time.[33]

While Augustine's nurses are presented behind a curtain, his partner is introduced as offstage.[34] It is clear that, in the time about which Augustine is writing, his son, Adeodatus, is already born.[35] Yet here Augustine does not speak of the love he had for her and certainly not of the love she had for him. He does not speak of her role in his life again until she is "torn from his side." As an agent, her effectivity is erased. This erasure happens by casting the desire he had for her against the appropriate order of sexual desire. The desire he has for her is libidinal, the true ordering of that desire should be to generating a family.[36] The pleasure of sex must be regulated. That is, there is nothing inherently sinful in sexual pleasure. The sin emerges when that pleasure is not regulated toward its proper order, namely a "suitable marriage" the purpose of which is to generate a family. "Family," therefore, is not mere generation of offspring but must be something more, i.e., something legitimate or legitimated by its proper order.

The pleasure of sex is, therefore, not to be enjoyed but only to be used: "Loving and being loved were sweet to me, the more so if I could also enjoy a lover's body; so I polluted the stream[37] of friendship [*amicitiae*] by the filth of desire [*concupiscentiae*] and clouded its purity with the hell of lust . . ."[38] There is a love that is not polluted and Augustine names this love *amicitiae*, friendship. What polluted friendship was not that Augustine enjoyed [*fruerer*] the body of the beloved, at least not that alone. Rather, it was the kind of desire—concupiscence—that stains the purity of love/friendship. Augustine's desire brings him to enjoy what should be merely used. And in this case, what is properly used is the body of another. But what does love look like when the body of the beloved is used and not enjoyed? It is a love whose pleasure is expropriated from the body and even from the relationship and appropriated by the proper end toward which love, including carnal love, ought to be directed. And that is where happiness will be found, not in the body of the beloved.

Love, therefore, can be enjoyed, but only when it is properly ordered, properly regulated. Lust [*libido*] is a disordered desire aimed, it seems, only at pleasure. Augustine reports that the state of his soul was "not well," covered with wounds [*ulcerosa*] and longed to be scratched/titillated [*scalpi*] by the touch of sensible things. The disorder of the desire leads to a disease of the soul that Augustine can only describe by a corporeal analogy, as if the lust is the cause of a venereal disease of the soul. And the sores burn and itch. Augustine's partner in all this provides a means for scratching that itch of his soul. She was, however, part of the disease, in his telling, not part of the cure. Indeed, she is present here only as the occasion for Augustine's disordered desire.

Book III does provide sufficient indications that the only proper, i.e., properly ordered way to soothe his wounds would be either to find a relationship that is the foundation of a family or, perhaps better, to understand that the itch can only be scratched by God. In either case, Augustine is clear in Book III that his desire is only properly satisfied when it moves away from the sensible and the sensuous. In all of this, his partner, offstage the entire time, is stripped of her effectivity in the name of the proper regulation of desire. As the site of his disorder, as the cause of his psychic venereal disease, she must be removed. In this, she is also reduced to mere materiality/sensuousness. That is, she is the "thing" against which Augustine scratches his sores or titillates his desire that is itself material and sensuous.

As with his caregivers in infancy, here again the erasure of the effectivity and agency of women is carried out by means of two gestures that are presented as ontological and existential: that natures are not just different but hierarchized (God being the highest, matter being the lowest) and that only those things are to be enjoyed that are not only a means to enjoying something else. That these two gestures seemed "neutral" in their presentation cannot be sustained any longer. They are normative in an expansive sense and they together work to erase the effectivity of women. And that erasure is "natural" or ontological only on the basis of these two normative gestures.

CONCLUSION:
THE RETURN OF AGENCY

The story of Augustine's partner and the mother of Adeodatus comes to an end in Book VI:

> Meanwhile, my sins were multiplying, for she, with whom I was used to sleeping, was torn from my side as an impediment to marriage, where [my] heart cleaved [*adhaerebat*], was for me cut and wounded and drew blood. And she returned to Africa, vowing to you to be unknown to another [lover] and the son that was my natural son she left to me. But I, unhappy, was not able to imitate this woman.[39]

One could use this as an occasion to, once again, mark the erasure of the effectivity of Monica. However, Augustine notes, for the first time, the agency, if not effectivity, of his spouse/partner. It should be noted that this is one of the occasions in which Augustine goes out of his way to not use a name. The simple perfect passive (with an understood *est*) *avulsa* suffices because it requires an unstated feminine subject—"she." Still not named, she is given a designation: "the one with whom I usually/was accustomed to sleep" [*cum qua cubare solitus eram*]. All of this is still off stage. And then she acts. She vows, she returns to Africa, and she leaves behind their son. The vow she makes looks both backward and forward. She would not know—clearly in a sexual sense—another. This is a proclamation of a faith. She has faith in her own agency and that faith is expressed precisely in relation to her capacity to desire. It is not that she vows to properly order her desire and thus control it. Rather, she vows to Augustine that she will remain faithful to the desire they shared together. She has faith in her effectivity. But it is also a faith in Augustine (who, on his own acknowledgement, is not worthy of this faith), and a faith that Adeodatus's future would be better in Augustine's hands than in hers, as the former common law spouse of Augustine. She vows and, as a result, leaves their child in his hands.

Given that their son would have belonged to her family had she not acted in this way, she acts toward a faith in another, perhaps, future for their son. There is a thorny problem, however, with her vow. All vows are addressed. "I vow to you," "I vow to the republic," "I vow to humanity." Augustine says that she vowed "to you" [*tibi*]. To whom is this vow, put in her mouth, addressed? The very next paragraph begins "tibi laus," "praise to you." Augustine, in fact, frequently addresses God with forms of the same pronoun. Already in Book I Augustine asked "But who will grant me to rest in you? Who will grant me that you will come into my heart and inebriate it, that I would forget my evils and that I would embrace you, my one good."[40] Augustine takes his partner to be making her vow to this same "one." In his telling, she vows to God to order her desire and pleasure toward the only proper good. But in this proclamation of faith of Augustine's spouse, even as Augustine is writing it, the "to you" could just as well mean "to you, Augustine." In this sense, she vows to Augustine that she will not have another relationship and, vowing this, she demands that Augustine provide for their child. She vows and does not "leave behind," but expects a vow from her other, from Augustine: "I won't have another lover, here's our son, take care of him." With that being said, she leaves the narrative. She moves again offstage, this time with the proclamation of faith in her own agency and the effectiveness of that agency.

Yet her exit leaves (as did her entrance) a gaping wound. Augustine was torn apart and left bleeding from her loss. And yet he says, unhappily, he could not follow a "woman's example." But he understands her "example" in the only way Augustine can understand what a woman vows. He takes her "example" as giving up on pleasure. Even on his telling, she vowed no such thing. She vowed "to you" only to not know a man as she knew Augustine. It is Augustine who takes her proclamation of faith as also a regulation of pleasure. It is not her vow. Her vow is appropriated by another vow, by Augustine's vow. And it is a vow that he cannot and does not keep. While acknowledging her, he turns it toward his himself and his own desires. Her desire is multiple. It is for the happiness of Adeodatus, and probably of Augustine, but it is also toward the love they had together. "I will never know someone as I know you" is probably the proclamation of faith that founds any relationship that is worthy of the name "love." In this, she, the one, Augustine's spouse has the final agency that he cannot recuperate: We loved, now vow! And Augustine failed.

NOTES

1. Augustine, *Confessions*, trans. and intro. Maria Boulding, O.S.B., vol. I/1 *The Works of Saint Augustine: A Translation for the 21st Century*, ed. John E. Rotelle O.S.A. (Hyde Park: New City Press, 1997), 1.1. I cite *Confessions* using the convention of Book and paragraph number to allow ease of consultation to both the Latin and other translations. I have altered this translation slightly. The translation inserts the phrase "and drawn us" where the Latin simply state "*fecisti nos ad te*," that is, "you have made us toward/for you." While the difference is not great, Augustine pauses frequently in the text to ask, "Where were you (God)?," in order to show that God is always that toward which we tend. There is no need for a further action of drawing us toward that end.

2. This, for example, is an argument Thomas Aquinas makes in *Summa Theologiae*, Part I, Question 1, article 1.

3. It is generally though that *De Doctrina Christiana* is written around the same period as *Confessions*.

4. The translation is from Augustine, "On Christian Doctrine," in *St. Augustine's City of God and Christian Doctrine*, trans. J. F. Shaw, series 1, vol. 2 *Nicene and Post-Nicene Fathers*, ed. Philip Schaff (Buffalo: Christian Literature Company, 1887), 523b. As with all texts from Augustine, I will refer to book and chapter to allow easy reference to all editions in all languages. I will refer to this text as *De Doct. Chr.*, followed by book and chapter.

5. Oliver O'Donovan, "*Usus* and *Fruito* in Augustine, *De Doctrina Christiana I*," *Journal of Theological Studies*, New Series 33 (1982): 362.

6. Augustine, *De Doct. Chr.*, I.3.

7. I take this basic idea of deconstruction from both Derrida and Michael Naas. In several lectures and personal conversations, Michael Naas has referred to "Deconstruction 101," and this is what I think he means. For Derrida, the perhaps original version of this is in Jacques Derrida, *Speech and Phenomena: And Other Essays on Husserl's Theory of Signs* (Evanston: Northwestern University Press, 1973).

8. To this point, I have not commented on the translation of various forms of *beo*, including nominal and participial forms, as "happiness." I think that this translation is entirely warranted. That Augustine does not use *felicitas*, with its relation to luck or happenstance, is telling in ways I cannot engage for the purposes of this paper. *Felix* is certainly different from *beatus*. *Beatus* seems to imply a wholeness, if not completion. And here we see again why the "means/ends" distinction might prove relevant: *beatus* is an end in itself.

9. Augustine, *De Doct. Chr.*, I.4 (translation mine). The Latin reads: "*Frui enim est amore alcui rei inhaerere propter seipsam. Uti autem, quod in usum venerit ad id quod amas obstinendem referre, si tamen amandum est.*"

10. That the distinction is normative is indicated, in part, grammatically by Augustine's use of the jussive. However, it is also indicated by the fact that what ought to be used *can* be enjoyed by us but it should not be. The ground of the ought/should seems to be happiness (*beatus*). O'Donovan's argument is aided, however, by Augustine's insistence that when we enjoy that which is to be used, we are "impeded in our

course," that is, we are (perhaps by our nature) set within an order and we are made disordered (turned aside or even called away from where or course is going) by enjoying what is to be used.

11. For an overview of these influences, see Roland Teske, "Ultimate Reality According to Augustine of Hippo," *Ultimate Reality and Meaning* 18, no. 1 (March 1995): 20–33.

12. Augustine, to my mind, is not a Platonist nor a neo-Platonist precisely because he is attentive to human experience. However, I will argue that when it comes to pleasure and also truth, Augustine turns away from him experiential concerns and that is where he turns normative.

13. Augustine, *Confessions*, 4.6.11.

14. Augustine, *Letters (1–82), Vol. 1*, trans. Sister Wilfrid Parsons, S.N.D., vol. 12 *The Fathers of the Church,* ed. Ludwig Schopp et al. (Washington, D.C.: Catholic University of America Press, 1951); *Letters*, in *Opera Omnia: Patrologiae Latinae Elenchus*, edited by J.P. Migne (Paris, 1865), 33:85.

15. In his last published work, *Des Hégémonies Brisées,* Reiner Schürmann argues that *natura* is the "hegemonic phantasm," i.e., the posit around which a way of thinking turns, of the age of philosophy that is inaugurated by Cicero, given a ground by Augustine, and holds sway until (self-)consciousness emerges with its first sparks in Descartes. On this tripartite division of "nature," Schürmann says, "In this dialectic [of the 'I' as singular and the 'I' subsumed under law], nature is encountered in three sites, though it is not the same in each. Only in the second site is nature common and commonly imposed, that is to say, normative. The vicissitudes at one pole can only be shown—these are conspicuous objects. At the other pole, the concluding point is what has to be created—it will come into being through subjection. Only the mediating term can be demonstrated; it is the object of reflection." Reiner Schürmann, *Broken Hegemonies*, trans. Reginald Lilly (Bloomington: Indiana University Press, 2003), 213; Reiner Schürmann, *Des hégémonies brisées* (Mauvezin France: Trans-Europ-Repress, 1996), 278.

16. However, below we will look to Luce Irigaray's reading of Plato's cave as a womb and see that this identification of what is with what is permanent is a feature of what she identifies as part of the patriarchal exclusion of the feminine.

17. I do not insist, in saying this, on a strict (or any) binary between either biological contributions to reproduction or genders. On the contrary, it is Augustine's insistence on an ordering that is possible only on the basis of a preference for permanence that demands a binary at all.

18. Luce Irigaray, *Speculum de l'autre Femme* (Paris: Le Éditions de Minuit, n.d.), 365–66; Luce Irigaray, *Speculum of the Other Woman*, trans. Gillian Gill (Ithaca: Cornell University Press, 1985), 293.

19. Michel Foucault, *The Order of Things: An Archaelogy of the Human Sciences* (New York: Vintage Books, 1973), xv.

20. A third character could, obviously, be Monica, Augustine's mother. I will not treat that here simply because there is a wealth of scholarship on the role of Monica.

21. Augustine, *Confessions*, I.6.7.

22. Augustine, *Confessions*, I.7 (emphasis mine).

23. As Teske points out, memory is, for Augustine, "the mind itself." Teske points out that memory is crucial in both Book X and XI of *Confessions*, the first leading to a knowledge of God and the second leading to an understanding of time. See Roland Teske, "Augustine's Philosophy of Memory," in *The Cambridge Companion to Augustine*, ed. Eleonore Stump and Norman Kretzmann (Cambridge: Cambridge University Press, 2005), 148–58.

24. Augustine, *Confessions*, I.7.

25. Augustine, *Confessions*, I.8 (translation modified).

26. The Latin reads: "*Itaque jactabam membra et voces, signa similia voluntatibus meis, pauca quae poteram, qualia poteram: non enim erant veri similia.*"

27. Augustine, *Confessions*, I.10.

28. There is some evidence that Monica, Augustine's mother, may have spoken a Berber/Amazigh language.

29. Augustine, *Confessions*, I.11.

30. Augustine, *Confessions*, I.11.

31. Augustine, *Confessions*, IV.1.

32. Augustine, *Confessions*, IV.2.

33. On Augustine's partner, see Margaret A. Miles, "Not Nameless but Unnamed: The Woman Torn from Augustine's Side," in *Feminist Interpretations of Augustine*: *Re-Reading the Canon* (University Park: Pennsylvania State University Press, 2007), 167–88.

34. I do not mean to indicate that she is "offstage" because Augustine does not name her. As Kim Power has pointed out, Augustine frequently avoids using proper names. Kim Power, "*Sed Unam Tamen*: Augustine and His Concubine," *Augustinian Studies* 23 (1992): 51. One case to which she refers, that of the death of his friend that had a profound impact on Augustine, seems relevant. That he does not name his partner should not be taken as an indication of his lack of love for her. Rather, she is offstage because Augustine is presenting his relationship with her, including the birth of their son, as something that is not happening *in* the narrative but on the side of it. It is worth noting that the death of Augustine's father also happens offstage.

35. As Boulding points out in her translation, Augustine seems to indicate in Book 9 that Adeodatus was born in 371/2. See Augustine, *Confessions*, 93, n. 5. Therefore, when Augustine was nineteen, Adeodatus would have been between one and two years old.

36. As Power and others point out, "concubinage" was not an uncommon practice in Augustine's milieu. However, any offspring of such a relationship would not belong to the father's family but to the mother's. In this case, even though his relationship produced a son, it did not produce a family for Augustine.

37. *Vena*, coming from the root meaning "to carry" is most frequently used for a blood vessel. However, it came to mean the course water takes (hence "stream") but in addition can also mean the inside of something and hence its nature or what is innate to it.

38. Augustine, *Confessions*, III.1.

39. Augustine, *Confessions*, VI.25.

40. Augustine, *Confessions*, I.5.

Chapter 3

The Intersection of Gender and the Emotions

Concupiscence and its Discontents

Eileen C. Sweeney

This paper explores the intersection between gender and the passions/emotions in Augustine. I consider, first, whether, and to what degree, Augustine engages in the gendering of the passions/emotions as female weakness and passivity as opposed to male control, domination of the self or others. Because it is illustrative of, but also different from, the other emotions/passions, secondly, I examine Augustine's account of the particular passion of sexual desire and his view of its place and role in marriage. As we shall see, Augustine's position on the gendering of the passions is complex, we might even say ambivalent. On the one hand, he criticizes the Stoic position on the passions and virtue, strongly endorsing emotions, both positive and negative, as part of a fully human good life, modelled importantly in the life of Jesus Christ himself. On the other hand, he also characterizes the life of virtue as successful struggle against the passions, gendering the point of failure in sin as the female lower reason, having contact with and transmitting desire/lust to the higher reason in his opposition to the Manichees. On sexual desire, Augustine completely rejects any except the most tangential and accidental positive role for sexual desire and activity, allowing us to see his deeper concerns and anxieties about the feminine aspects of passion/emotion in general, especially in his opposition to Julian's views on sexuality.

GREEK AND ROMAN GENDERING OF
EMOTION AND SEXUAL DESIRE

In order to make the connection between passion and gender, I must begin in the complex and controversial account of the gendering of the passions in Greek and Roman thought. The most well-known and now questioned account of the gendering of sexual desire (and by extension all the passions) is that of Kenneth Dover. His monograph, *Greek Homosexuality* (1978), argued essentially that the right way to understand sexuality in ancient Greece is by distinguishing between hetero- and homosexuality but rather between active and passive roles in sex.[1] What is criticized in ancient Greece Dover argues is not attraction between men or sexual activity between men, but men or young boys who consent to play the passive role in sex. That passive position is the position of the female and a male who plays that role does something shameful, essentially giving up or betraying his gender. This account of Greek sexuality among men has been to be seen as the example proving the rule that sexuality cannot be understood in terms of fixed essential categories (e.g., homo vs. heterosexuality or male vs. female) but is structured, even determined, but cultural and social expectations and practices.

John Rist's *Augustine Deformed: Love, Sin, and Freedom in The Western Moral Tradition* describes something like this view as part of the "canon of Greek love," according to which there is a strong distinction between the role of lover and beloved. The lover is "aroused and heated" while the beloved/object of love is "receptive . . . cool and complacent."[2] He cites Xenophon's *Symposium*, which describes the older lover of the beautiful younger man, loving merely his body, as engaging in intercourse driven by passion, while the (proper) young man should merely receive these attentions. Xenophon contrasts the young man's lack of engagement and activity to that of the wife who "shares with her husband in their nuptial joys."[3] This is not quite what is going on in Dover's account of homosexual relations in ancient Greece. But Xenophon, following Socrates, is describing the distinct roles of lover and beloved to critique the view (not unlike Dover's) which approves and praises the virility/activity of the older lover. Rather Xenophon makes the old man look a bit foolish and the young man nonplussed. As in Plato's own *Symposium*, Xenophon wants to persuade the reader/listener that the proper direction of sexual desire is not toward the beautiful bodies of young men but away from the body to the soul. Xenophon preserves the opposition of lover and beloved, active and passive, but reverses who is seen as passive and active. The young beloved is impassive, receiving but not desiring the attentions of the lover; he is right not to return the love of the lover, while the lover is the one "drunken with the wine of passion," and therefore passive subject to his own desires.

There are, however, reasons to question Dover's view as *the* account of Greek sexuality as centered around approbation for the active and shame for the passive partner. Davidson's revisiting of the sources shows that on closer examination, criticism of young men for engaging in sex with older men was not for their passivity, their allowing themselves to be penetrated, but rather more often for "whorishness, revealed by acceptance of payment, excessive eagerness or random promiscuity that was to be avoided."[4] To be sure, gender is part of this sexual morality, one in which the female role is also maligned but for different reasons. As Davidson explains, "Female sexuality was not constructed along Victorian lines as an inert frigid receptivity, but, on the contrary, in terms of an inability to master sexual desire. Whereas men ejaculated, so finding a release and an end for desire, women's desire for sex was never-ending."[5] He continues, "the focus is on avoiding the terrifying abyss of limitlessness, conjured up in images of the wicked in Hades: Tantalus; Sisyphus; filling leaky jars with leaky sieves, eschatology and images of desire, linked the '*kinaidoi.*'"[6] "*Kinaidoi*" are the "catamites" Callicles so objects to being compared to in Plato's *Gorgias*.[7] As Davidson also points out, this construction of sexual morality—that what is bad is being a leaky jar of endless desire—fits well with the more general notion of morality based on the value of "self-mastery (*enkrateia*)." This is exactly what Socrates makes a case for against Callicles, that Callicles' moral model of having more and greater desires and satisfying them amounts to the "life of the catamite." It is also analogized in the dialogue to the life of the "leaky jar" in which the problem is being so taken over by a desire, one must constantly, almost in the mode of the addict, work to satisfy.[8] Passivity/activity is still lurking in this picture; the catamite/addict becomes in effect the passive subject of the addiction, reduced to being or seeking the object that satisfies the desire.

Davidson admits that the distinction between active/passive parties in sexual intercourse does have some more validity (though, he asserts, less so than in our present day) in the Roman as opposed to the Greek world.[9] Jonathan Walters explores the notion that in Roman culture men are "impenetrable penetrators," and that this is part of "a wider conceptual pattern that characterized those of high social status as being able to defend the boundaries of their body from invasive assaults of all kinds."[10] Seneca refers to woman as having been made by nature to be sexually passive; what amount to a perverse acting against that nature is the female attempt to become penetrators rather than penetrated.[11] "*Vir*" ("man") is a term not accorded to all males; young men, adult slaves and ex-slaves are referred to as "*homines*" or "*pueri*." The logic, Walters argues, is that "*viri*" are the ones with the status and power to protect their own bodies from penetration and able instead to perpetrate rather than suffer such humiliation. The situation of women of status then becomes somewhat complex. They are not impenetrable but only to be penetrated by their lawful husband and protected from sexual assault by anyone else.[12] Similarly a slave, unlike a free man, can be beaten. Walters concludes,

> The inability to defend one's body is a slavelike mark of powerlessness. It is within this wider pattern, which sees the body as potentially subject to invasion from a more powerful external force, and social superiority as, symbolically at any rate, consisting in the ability to protect one's body and even invade the body of others, that the Romans' obsession with seeing sexual activity in terms of an active/passive polarity, and their linking of this polarity with a conception of manhood, should be placed.[13]

Though I shall have more to say about this below discussing Augustine's critique of Stoic and Roman virtue, it is worth noting here that Greek notions of morality and virtue, from Socrates, to Aristotle to the Stoics, to some degree at least, set the standard for virtue as self-mastery and control. Whether or not Plato is actually endorsing the virtue as "self-mastery/control" view in Book IV of the *Republic* or in his argument against Callicles in the *Gorgias*, he certainly traffics in this model, using it in a context where he takes it to be appealing and persuasive; Aristotle's notion of moderation in some ways softens (!) this picture, admitting that the "suffering" of the passions is fully human and not to feel is to miss the mean of virtue; still, at least when he gets to the picture of the magnanimous man, Aristotle idealizes a kind of self-sufficiency and invulnerability in the highest virtue. Having this kind of virtue is equated with rationality, a quality, of course, only imperfectly present in women (as well as in children, slaves, etc.).

There are two models of passion (especially sexual passion) as gendered here: women as passive receiver or, alternately, as the victim of limitless desire; both associate the morally (and in every other way) inferior position with the female, and both, though defining it in different ways, describe the superior position as mastery/ control. We could say that what we have are two strategies in response to male sexual desire: satisfy it or control it. Women are denied having the ability to do either. To be able to do neither is to be in the weaker, more subordinate position. To be the one who desires, without the power to put an end to it, is to be avoided by one means or another. And this is true whether the means of escape from this position of vulnerability and weakness is to seize the object to satisfy desire or to seize control of the desire itself, quieting its overwhelming need.

AUGUSTINE ON THE ETHICS OF LOVE AGAINST THE STOICS

Augustine makes the most important basic claims about the centrality of love in the good life, transforming Stoic principles by placing them into an ethics of love, one in which the affections are both primary and outwardly directed. Of the passions, Augustine writes, "[They] are all bad, then, when the love is bad, and they are all good when the love is good."[14] Augustine adds loving in the right way also orients the emotions, "because their love is right, they have all these emotions in the right way."[15] In these contexts, there is no mention of restraint or control of emotion or passion. Rist argues that in his early work, *The Catholic Way of Life and the Manichean Way of Life*, that Augustine is "correcting a presumably Stoic account of the nature of virtue whereby the virtues are modes of right reason," in contrast, "Augustine claims that they are modes of love."[16] Augustine goes so far as to define the particular virtues in terms of love: "Temperance is love offering itself in its integrity to the beloved. Fortitude is love easily tolerating all things on account of the beloved. Justice is love serving the beloved alone and as a result ruling righteously. And prudence is love that wisely separates those things by which it is helped from those by which it is impeded."[17]

In these passages, the language of love has in effect superseded the language of virtue. Augustine's rejection of this picture becomes especially clear in his powerful critique of pagan virtue in the *City of God*. Their vaunted cardinal virtues are unable to do much more than forcibly restrain evil, he argues, in their very acts witnessing to their own defeat: temperance is nothing more than "internal warfare," fortitude "bears the most witness to human evils, because it is precisely these evils that it is compelled to endure with patience," while prudence teaches about evil but fails to remove it from life, and justice labors continually but does not achieve its end of giving each their due.[18] Moreover, they do not just fail but become vices when not directed toward service of God but for oneself.[19] Augustine describes the Roman empire as fueled by the desire for glory and honor, and criticizes Cicero for praising glory as a motive for virtue.[20] He connects that pride directly to the supposed virtue of self-control or mastery:

> If this city has any citizens who appear to control and in some way to temper these emotions, they are so proud and puffed up in their impiety that, for this very reason, the tumors of their pride expand as the pangs of their pain shrink. And, if some of these, with a vanity as monstrous as it is rare, are so enamored of their own self-restraint that they are not stirred or excited or swayed or influenced by any emotion at all, the truth is that they are losing all humanity rather than gaining real tranquility. For the fact that something is difficult does not

make it right, nor does the fact that something has no feeling mean that it is in good health.[21]

The desire for glory is the sin of pride, and it easily degrades to one for domination, since it rejects the notion of human beings as equal before God.[22] As Rist puts it, for Augustine, "wishing to be one's own master is inseparable from wishing to have power over others, and not only over their bodies."[23] Augustine understands the pagan virtues as pretensions to self-mastery, to invulnerability, and to be both unsuccessful in their aspiration and sinful when they succeed.

Importantly, Augustine praises emotion or passion, and he defends this connection of feeling not just with humanity but with the model of Christ, citing with approval Jesus's real emotion, angry at the hardhearted, shedding tears for Lazarus, and grieving before his own suffering and death.[24] In his *Tractate on the Gospel of John*, Augustine repeats his praise of Jesus's emotions and explicitly calls out the Stoics on their account of fear, sorrow, love and gladness as the four perturbations of the soul. The mind of the Christian should *fear* lest others be lost to Christ, *sorrow* over such a loss, *desire* to be and *rejoice* in the *hope* of being with Christ. In this they "dissent from the error of the Stoic philosophers" who "just as they esteem truth to be vanity, regard also insensibility as soundness; not knowing that a man's mind, like the limbs of his body, is only the more hopelessly diseased when it has lost even the feeling of pain."[25]

Even more completely re-writing Stoic moral psychology, Augustine counsels *feeling* and not just *doing* for those who suffer: "So when you perform a work of mercy, if you're offering bread, feel sorry for the hungry; if you're offering drink, feel sorry for the thirsty; if you're handing out clothes, feel sorry for the naked; if you're offering hospitality, feel sorry for the stranger and traveler; if you're visiting the sick, feel sorry for the people who are ill; if you're burying the dead, feel sorry for the deceased; if you're patching up a quarrel, feel sorry for the quarrelers."[26] Augustine repeats the list of works of mercy from Matthew 25, adding to each the exhortation to feel sorry for those who suffer as one offers solace. Seneca, considering whether one should feel as well as act for those who suffer, argues vehemently that feeling adds nothing and even interferes with the moral act. Commenting on the story of a Stoic sage, who succumbed to what looks like fear as the boat on which he was traveling was buffeted by a strong storm, Augustine points out something most commentators have missed, that after analyzing whether this was merely a disturbance the Stoic managed to resist consenting to, Augustine adds, "how much more honorable it would have been if the Stoic in Aulus Gellius's story had been disturbed by compassion for a person in need of being saved rather than by fear of being shipwrecked himself."[27]

What is significant about this critique is its account of glory as a pretense to self-sufficiency and self-mastery, a manifestation of the sin of pride; they are, fundamentally, a rejection of vulnerability. Augustine embraces the opposite picture of our actual and aspirational affective state. He councils an openness to emotion instead of their mastery or control; he bids us aim not for self-sufficiency but compassion for ourselves and others. The object of desire, God primarily and others secondarily, is not conquered by our action, but one that one waits in longing for, a desire we are unable to satisfy ourselves or control or extirpate. Thus, Augustine embraces rather than flees both modes of Greek/Roman characterization of female desire, both receiving/passivity and limitless, unsatisfiable desire. As Rist notes, contrasting Augustine on love to the Platonic ascent in the *Symposium*, since Origen, "all souls are female with reference to God (or Christ)" which would imply—doubtless to Augustine's satisfaction—that receptivity/humility (*Fiat mihi* . . .) would be a necessary part of all theistic, as distinct from Platonic Impersonal–seeking, ascent.[28]

PASSION AS SIN, VIRTUE AS STRUGGLE AGAINST SIN

However, even *The City of God*, in the context of defending the passions of Jesus and criticizing the Stoics, Augustine slides easily from a positive into a negative view of the passions. From emotions as kinds of responses to pain or pleasure, he moves to anger and sexual lust/desire as the sources of vice, and then to the ways in which sexual desire is worse, because it is so completely beyond the control of the will. This slide is because Augustine turns from the emotions in the "city of God" to those in the human city, but more significantly to the emotions/passions as transformed by the fall. First he takes care to note that the "pains of the flesh" are actually pains of the soul "experienced in the flesh and from the flesh," responses of the soul—versions, lusts, or sorrows at what is happening to the flesh.[29] Though there are many kinds of lust—for revenge (anger), money (avarice), for winning (obstinacy), glory (self-promotion), and domination (without its own name) but "lust" by itself is sexual desire ("lust in the lewd parts of the body"). This way of being subject to the passions is as a result of the fall. Since we did not serve God, Augustine notes, our flesh does not serve us.[30]

Though lamenting all the versions of lust, Augustine goes on to sharply distinguish the psychology of sexual desire from other sorts of desires.[31] First he notes the overwhelming character of sexual desire and its satisfaction; "[sexual desire] not only takes over the whole body externally but also seizes the person inwardly. When it moves the whole man by combining and intermingling the emotion of the mind with the craving of the flesh, there follows a pleasure greater than any other bodily pleasure; and, at the moment this pleasure reaches its climax, almost all mental alertness and cognitive vigilance, so to speak, are obliterated."[32] Next he explains how the role of the will is different for sexual desire vs. the other lusts. For the other passions, the will "sets them in motion, when it gives its consent." In the throes of the other passions, the will retains "complete control" over its other members. In anger, when one speaks in anger or even strikes out in anger, the tongue and the hand are "set in motion by the will's command." The situation is different with sexual desire: "In the case of the sexual organs, however, lust has somehow taken such complete control of them that they are incapable of being moved if lust is absent, and they do not move at all unless it arises either on its own or in response to stimulation. It is this that causes shame; it is this that, in embarrassment, shuns the eyes of onlookers."[33] Augustine makes the same point in *On Marriage and Desire*, singling out sexual desire as the only passion, "which arouses, as if by its own command, the members which cannot be aroused by the will. In that way it shows that it is not the servant of a will that is in command, but the punishment of a will that is disobedient; it shows that it is a servant which has to be moved, not by free choice, but by some seductive stimulus and is, therefore, something to be ashamed of."[34]

Continence is the companion to concupiscence as diseased desire, cast as the restraining of desire. Continence is the "control of sensuality," something it "certainly would not toil to restrain our desires, if we had no inclination toward anything improper, if there were no resistance to our good intentions from evil desires."[35] Augustine goes out of his way in interpreting Paul's comment in 1 Corinthians (3:3): "Are you not carnal persons, who are walking in a human way?" to equate "walking in a human way" to "walking according to the flesh," identifying human nature with this fallen carnality (even though later in the same text Augustine says that spirit and flesh, and the human being made of both are good).[36]

Augustine, however, has not abandoned his critique of pagan self-mastery, distinguishing between true and false continence. Just as true patience is not putting up with torture to resist confessing to crime, so not all self-control is a virtue. Self-control can be in the service of injustice, "as, for example, when a spouse refuses to have sexual union with the other spouse, because he or she can now control that bodily urge. Some practice self-control too because they are deceived by false beliefs and with futile hope are striving for vanities."[37] It seems a necessary distinction, for what is eviler than a highly disciplined person who marshals that self-control for nefarious ends? Yet, it also means that the moral task involves *both* the turning of one's loves and the restraint of one's desires.

AUGUSTINE'S MORAL PSYCHOLOGY: THE ALLEGORY OF WOMAN AND OPPOSITION TO THE MANICHEES

There is a similar feel to the multiplication of moral tasks and an even greater narrowing of the way to go "right" and multiplying of the ways (and responsibility) for going wrong in the particular moral psychology Augustine develops in opposition to the Manichees, the Stoics, as well as Pelagius and Julian. We have already seen Augustine's opposition to Stoic *apatheia*. Even though Augustine rejects the Stoic model of self-mastery and *apatheia*, Augustine takes over and the Stoic distinction between the sudden involuntary movements or perturbations, sometimes called pre-passions, as well as the notion that it is not vice (or sin) until one (or one's reason) consents to the feeling and does its bidding.[38] According to Nisula, Augustine's first opponent on the passions is the Manichees, in opposition to which he sides with the Stoics that the passions are "inordinate movements only in the sense that they do not always obey rational control, but not in the sense that they would be a compulsive essence, alien to the human soul."[39] Augustine rejects the Manichean view that passion is somehow "not-me" but some other will, a bad will, that takes over my good will; the Manichean view, for Augustine, leans fully into the passions as *passive*, something that simply happens to us involuntarily. On the quasi-Stoic view Augustine constructs, the perturbations or 'pre-passions' come over us suddenly as a basically physical involuntary response neither consented to nor rejected by reason and/or the will, but "passion" strictly speaking requires consent and thus becomes both voluntary and active. Thus, one cannot escape responsibility for having acted under the influence of passion; there is no 'the devil made me do it' defense. Once one consents, which is active not passive, one is responsible.[40]

In *On Genesis, Against the Manichees*, Augustine turns the story of the fall of Adam and Eve into an account of this moral psychology—and a critique of the Manichean account. Here is where gender explicitly enters the picture. It is worth citing Augustine's way of mapping on the story of the fall to the story of giving in to or resisting the (wrongful) urges of the passions at length:

> Even now, when any of us slide down into sin, nothing else takes place but what then occurred with those three, the serpent, the woman and the man. First of all, you see, comes the suggestion, either in the thoughts, or through the body's senses, by seeing or touching or hearing or tasting or smelling something. If, when the suggestion has taken shape, our desire or greed is not roused to sin, the serpent's cunning will be blocked; if it is roused, though, *it's as if the woman has already been persuaded*. But sometimes the reason valiantly puts the brake on greed even when it has been roused, and brings it to a halt. When this happens,

we don't slide into sin, but win the prize with a certain amount of struggle. If however the reason does consent and decide that what lust or greed is urging on it should be done, then the man is expelled from the entire life of bliss, as from paradise. Sin is already put down to his account, you see, even if the actual deed doesn't follow, since the conscience incurs guilt just by consent.[41]

It is worth noting that the serpent isn't just the physical bodily desires but both bodily desires (symbolized by its belly) and pride (symbolized by its bosom); he uses both to bring desires to consciousness.[42] Moreover, Augustine also makes the serpent the heretic who tempts the church, in this case clearly the Manichees. For the serpent both urges Eve to taste the delicious fruit (fleshly desire) *and* tells her it will make her like the gods, with knowledge of good and evil (pride). The serpent, like the Manichees, appeals to two (or actually three) things (pride, lust, and curiosity):

> [E]ither the proud, who arrogate to themselves a status that is not theirs, and readily come to believe that God most high and the human soul share one and the same nature, or else those tangled up in the desires of the flesh, who are only too happy to hear that whatever they do as they kick over the traces is not being done by themselves but by the race of darkness, or else finally the curious and inquisitive, who are worldly wise and enjoy the taste of earthly things, and go looking for the spiritual with a fleshly eye.[43]

The Manichees claim, on the one hand, a kind of divine state, the pure soul that would never go astray, and, on the other hand, a "race of darkness" that can take over and fully overwhelm the pure soul.

Augustine's criticizes the Manichees for splitting off our physical selves and desires in order to claim a specious purity, and in opposition to their view, he might have chosen to fully reintegrate these aspects of the self. But Augustine instead offers a different kind of "split" *within* the self as one part struggles against its own desires. That split within the self is symbolized by the woman, Eve, in the story of the fall, over against the roles of the serpent, the bodily desires, and Adam. Augustine says explicitly that the relationship between Adam and Eve illustrates the interior structure of the self. In a kind of reverse of the *Republic* where Socrates says we can see more easily the polity by looking at the structure of the individual soul (reason, spirit, and appetite), Augustine says Adam and Eve together show the interior structure of the self:

> In this way what can be seen more clearly in two human beings, that is, in male and female, may be considered in a single person; that the interior mind, like the manly reason, should have as its subject the soul's appetite or desire, through which we put the limbs and parts of the body to work, and by a just law should

keep its help within bounds—just as a man ought to govern his wife, and not let her lord it over her husband, because where this happens the result is a topsy turvy and miserable household indeed.[44]

The reason God creates enmity between the *woman* and the serpent and not the *man* and the serpent is "to show clearly that the only way we can be tempted by the devil is through that animal part which the author has shown to exist in every single human being, represented by the likeness or model of a woman. . . ."[45] First there is the suggestion (what the serpent provides); in response, one can withhold consent to those pre-passions and resist, but if desire or greed are roused, he notes, "it is as if the woman has already been persuaded."[46]

On this psychological scheme, Eve is the hinge that can either turn toward good or toward evil. Augustine makes this clear in explaining the significance of the pain of childbirth that is a consequence of the fall. That pain is from "restraining the will from any desire of the flesh," but when the flesh has been reformed (through painful resistance) into better habits, that is a kind of giving birth. The next phrase, "and your turning round shall be toward your man, and he will lord it over you" (Gen. 3:16), Augustine reads as describing the inner struggle against sin:

> [W]hen that part of the soul, which is taken up with the joys of the flesh, wishes to overcome some bad habit, it experiences difficulty and pain, and in this way brings forth a good habit; and that this now makes it all the more careful and eager to submit to the reason as to its husband; and that now, as though taught a lesson by the pains themselves, it turns around to the reason, and willingly follows its instructions, to avoid again trickling away into some destructive habit.[47]

"Most women," he notes, do not "turn around" to their husbands after delivery but in fact become proud, lording it over their husbands rather than the contrary.[48] Hence, the husband ruling over the woman is, when read spiritually, Augustine argues, not a curse but a commandment.[49] Why, then, does Adam, after the curses are pronounced, name the woman "Life" "because she is the mother of all the living" (Gen 3:20), when she seems more aptly named 'death' than life, having brough mortality down on herself and all her children? She is "life" in her turning back to her husband after giving birth in pain, Augustine answers. What this corresponds to in the individual is when one submits to reason "as to a husband," going through the "labor" of self-restraint to resist an evil habit, "giving birth" to the good habit of acting rightly, thus becoming the "mother of the living," i.e., of "rightly performed acts."[50]

Augustine describes the moment of her turn back to her husband as the moment of re-integration, in contrast to the Manichean split self, where we can know that "that there is not one part of us belonging to God as its author, and another belonging to the race of darkness, as these people say, but rather that both that in us which has the right to govern (*regendi*) and that lower element which has to be governed (*regendum est*) come from God."[51] Augustine follows this with the passage from Corinthians about women veiling their heads, but not men. (1 Cor 11:7–12). But, of course, this is an integration achieved through both pain and submission. And it is an integration in which the split is only partially healed over, knit together by scar tissue that is both sore and inflexible. "Woman" as an allegory for the lower or practical reason, having heeded the serpent, is at fault. Though not split off as "not me," as the bad will is for the Manichees, woman/lower reason cannot be in control and must be ruled by the male/higher reason.

SEXUAL DESIRE AND MARRIAGE: AUGUSTINE VS. JULIAN

When we look at how Augustine thinks of the role of sex within marriage we get an even stronger sense of the way in which there is no real healing of the wound, both that internal to the self and that between man and woman. Augustine's response to the special problem of sexual desire is a mix of taboo and resignation. Sexual desire is a "disease" we make progress against only by resisting and waiting for its lessening in old age.[52] Within marriage, he sometimes speaks the language of restraint and control of sexual desire but with a resigned sense that it can never by extirpated:

> Concupiscence itself, after all, is not now a sin in those who have been reborn, provided they do not consent to it for acts that are forbidden and the mind, remaining sovereign, does not hand over the members to it to carry out those acts. Thus, even if we do not fulfill the words of scripture, *You shall not desire* (Ex 20:17), we at least fulfill what we read in another passage, *Do not go after your desires* (Sir 18:30).[53]

Resignation also comes in the form of the two pieces of advice: first, to subordinate this bad desire to the good of children, and second, to serve the desire of the other partner in order to at least keep their sexual activity within the marriage. Augustine also repeats in the context of marital concupiscence and continence that married parties should not refuse to consent to the other partner's desire for sex nor take any pride in any kind of ability to resist their own desire.[54] Augustine is very careful *never* to assert a good or natural end for sexual desire. Even the welcoming of children is a good end achieved by evil means; sex itself is not transformed into good. And the obligation to have sex with a partner rests only on the obligation to keep them from great sin in pursuing an outlet for their desire outside of marriage. That the will cannot directly arouse the sexual organs, Augustine argues, "shows that it is a servant which has to be moved, not by free choice, but by some seductive stimulus and is, therefore, something to be ashamed of." In Augustine's careful parsing, "[T]his concupiscence of the flesh *is no longer counted as a sin* in those who have been reborn, but it *comes to our nature only from sin*."[55]

Julian's attempt to understand and defend sexual desire as a good meets with stinging criticism from Augustine. For Julian, *concupiscentia*, like the other emotions/passions, is natural, and not a fleeting thing like the pre-passions; like any created thing, it is good and has a good use, designed by God to enrich the human experience. While Augustine does in effect have this view of the other passions (e.g., the good sorrow modelled by Jesus), he refuses to budge on his view that that sexual desire is "an affection of evil quality."[56] There is what Augustine calls "disordered disobedience," the multiple ways will and desire are out of sync with each other, at the heart of sexuality: "it is aroused even when it is not needed, and when it is needed, it sometimes heeds their command too quickly and at other times too slowly, manifesting its own independent movements."[57]

The conclusion to *On Marriage and Desire* is an extended diatribe against Julian, outlining the inhumane outcomes of Julian's view of sexual desire as a natural good. Julian's view, Augustine, argues, amounts either to the view that the will commands the desire and so the desire is always correct, or the desire precedes the will, but such that the will would immediately follow. "On this account," Augustine asserts, "the wife ought always to be at hand, and whether about to conceive or already pregnant, she would be brought to him. And so, either a child would be conceived, or natural and praiseworthy pleasure would result with the loss of the human seed, so that the desire of a good conscience would not be frustrated."[58] If beyond this "unnatural intercourse" attracted them, if the passion itself is praiseworthy, they should follow it, or, if they resist, Julian's claim of "the peace of such great felicity" is shattered.[59] On Julian's view, this desire would never need to be repressed and the consent of the will would never be denied. "Heaven forbid," Augustine exclaims sarcastically, "after all, that in such beatitude one could either not have what one wants or could feel in body or in mind what one does not want."[60]

Augustine only imagines an escape from sexual desire and the humiliation of our lack of control over it in Eden and at the resurrection. Augustine claims that in Eden, the sexual organs respond to the command of the will, like the legs to the command to walk, and Adam would deposit his "seed" just as a farmer plants his field.⁶¹ Julian, according to Cavadini, found Augustine's comparison of Eve to a field (in Eden), as dehumanizing as Augustine finds the consequences of Julian's view.⁶² At the resurrection, Augustine maintains, women will not become men (a view with some currency) but their sexual organs will be transformed such that they do not arouse male desire.⁶³ Of course, what Julian and Augustine might have missed, is that Augustine's view of how sexuality would work in Eden or at the resurrection simply asserts the perfect coincidence—no gaps, temporal or otherwise—between desire, consent, and act that Julian asserts can happen in this life and that Augustine finds so impossible and dehumanizing.

CONCLUDING THOUGHTS

There is an important sense in which Augustine maintains the fragility and vulnerability of our humanity, both in emotions and in sexual desire. At least for me, the most compelling criticism he makes against Julian's naturalized version of sexual desire is of it as an attempt to deny vulnerability, to relieve us of the difficulties of wanting what we cannot have or not wanting to want what our passions long for. Here Augustine is willing to dwell (and exhorts all to dwell) in what he takes to be the authentically human and uncomfortable situation, the gap between wanting and not having, and between not wanting and having. Augustine, unlike Julian, leans into the *wound* of sexuality—Julian wants to heal it by making it unproblematic, without discomfort, frustration, or embarrassment. In an important sense, Augustine affirms the human position as the "feminine" one—receptive rather than active, with a desire whose object is beyond one's ability to control or acquire, rejecting male assertions of control and self-sufficiency, able to either achieve or successfully extirpate desires that disturb one's peace. What Augustine reacts most strongly against are attempts to deny or speciously heal that wound—Stoic assertions of self-sufficiency, Manichean attempts to achieve integration by splitting off the woundedness as an alien force, and, lastly, Julian's attempt to decree a state of healthy integration at odds with what Augustine takes to be the conflict and mismatch between desire and its object he argues is universal human experience.

Augustine's allegorical readings of "male" and "female" are not, at least in principle, directly transferrable to an account of actual gender relations in Augustine's thought. Nevertheless, what Augustine finds illuminates the psychological struggles within the self—the story of Adam and Eve and the serpent—illuminates something about Augustine's own struggles and fears, his way of describing and accounting for what he sees as human woundedness. In all these different engagements—with the Stoics, the Manichees, and Julian, Augustine's account of emotion/desire is marred by his inability to actually live with the fragmentation and vulnerability he is so good at pointing out. He rejects Stoic notions of control (which make for invulnerability), yet still returns to the model of struggle from which one can emerge victorious, successfully ruling over the lower (female) part; he rejects the Manichean attempt to achieve integrity by splitting off the "bad" will, yet he tells a story which splits the male from the female part of the soul and only achieves their integration by subordinating one to the other in a relationship of ruling and domination; he rejects Julian's picture of unproblematic sexual life in which we get what we want and always approve of what we want, yet still idealizes in Eden and heaven the perfect harmony of desire with will and action, making of the woman only the passive fertile field on which Adam sows. Thus, Augustine rejects male self-sufficiency but cannot escape from his discomfort with feminine passion, reverting to its need to be mastered by the male reason.

NOTES

1. Kenneth Dover, *Greek Homosexuality* (Cambridge: Harvard University Press, 1978).

2. John Rist, *Augustine Deformed: Love, Sin, And Freedom in The Western Moral Tradition* (Cambridge: Cambridge University Press, 2014), 69.

3. Xenophon, *Symposium*, 8, 19–22, in *Memorabilia Oeconomicus; Symposium; Apology*, trans. Jeffrey Henderson, E. C. Marchant, and O. J. Todd, in *Loeb Classical Library* 168 (Cambridge: Harvard University Press, 2014).

4. James Davidson, "Dover, Foucault and Greek Homosexuality: Penetration and the Truth of Sex," *Past & Present* 170 (Feb. 2001): 27.

5. Davidson, "Dover, Foucault and Greek Homosexuality," 25.

6. Davidson, "Dover, Foucault and Greek Homosexuality," 26.

7. Plato, *Gorgias*, in *Plato: The Collected Dialogues*, ed. Edith Hamilton and Huntington Cairns (Princeton: Princeton University Press, 1961), 494e.

8. Plato, *Gorgias*, 493a–494b.

9. Davidson, "Dover, Foucault and Greek Homosexuality," 28.

10. Jonathan Walters, "Invading the Roman Body: Manliness and Impenetrability in Roman Thought," in *Roman Sexualities*, ed. Judith P. Hallett and Marilyn B. Skinner (Princeton: Princeton University Press, 1997), 30.

11. Seneca, *Ep.* 95.21: "These women are as bad as men in their sexual appetites, and, though nature made them sexually passive, they think up a new form of perversity and even . . . penetrate men." Cited in Walters, "Invading the Roman Body," 31, n. 9.

12. Walters, "Invading the Roman Body," 34.

13. Walters, "Invading the Roman Body," 37.

14. Augustine, *The City of God*, trans. and intro. William Babcock, vol. I/6–7 *The Works of Saint Augustine: A Translation for the 21st Century*, ed. Boniface Ramsey (Hyde Park: New City Press, 2012–13), 14.7.

15. Augustine, *The City of God*, 14.9.

16. John Rist, *Augustine Deformed: Love, Sin, and Freedom in The Western Moral Tradition* (Cambridge: Cambridge University Press, 2014), 74.

17. Augustine, *The Catholic Way of Life and the Manichean Way of Life*, in *The Manichean Debate,* trans. and notes Roland Teske, S.J., vol. I/19 *The Works of Saint Augustine: A Translation for the 21st Century*, ed. Boniface Ramsey (Hyde Park: New City Press, 2006), I.15.25.

18. Augustine, *City of God*, 19.4.

19. Augustine, *City of God*, 19.25.

20. Augustine, *City of God*, 5.12–13.

21. Augustine, *City of God*, 14.9.

22. Augustine, *City of God*, 19.12. And so pride is a perverse imitation of God. For it hates a society of equals under God and instead wishes to impose its own domination on its fellows in place of God's rule.

23. Rist, *Augustine Deformed*, 82. Cf. Augustine, *On Music*, in *The Immortality of the Soul; The Magnitude of the Soul; On Music; The Advantage of Believing; On Faith in Things Unseen*, trans. Robert Catesby Taliaferro, vol. 4 *The Fathers of the Church* (Washington D.C.: Catholic University of America Press, 2002), 6.13.41, https://ebookcentral.proquest.com/lib/bostoncollege/ebooks/detail.action?docID=3134830.

24. Augustine, *City of God*, 14.9.

25. Augustine, *Tractates on the Gospel of John*, trans. John Gibb, series 1, vol. 7, *Nicene and Post-Nicene Fathers,* ed. Philip Schaff (Buffalo: Christian Literature Publishing Co., 1888), 60.3.

26. Augustine, *Sermons (1–400)*, trans. Edmund Hill, O.P., vol. III/1–10 *The Works of Saint Augustine: A Translation for the 21st Century*, ed. John E. Rotelle, O.S.A. (Hyde Park: New City Press, 1990–95), 358A. This sermon is found in the *Patrologia Latina* edition of Augustine's sermons but is not included in the *Corpus Augustinianum Gissense*. Susan Wessel cites some concern that it is a modern insertion. See her *Passion and Compassion in Early Christianity* (Cambridge, Cambridge University Press, 2016), 231, n. 121.

27. Augustine, *City of God*, 9.5.

28. Rist, *Augustine Deformed*, 72, n. 5.

29. Augustine, *City of God*, 14.15.

30. Augustine, *City of God*, 14.15.

31. While it is true that Augustine lists the many types of lust before differentiating between the mechanisms of sexual lust vs. the others, surely Hunter distorts the issue to note only their common ground, not the crucial differences. Hunter writes, "that the 'lust of the flesh' associated with sexual desire takes its place as merely one of many *libidines* that scourge the human heart as a result of Adam's sin: anger, greed, obstinacy, vanity, and many others, above all, the lust for domination. See David Hunter, "Augustinian Pessimism? A New Look at Augustine's Teaching on Sex, Marriage and Celibacy," *Augustinian Studies* 25 (1994): 170.

32. Augustine, *City of God*, 14.16.

33. Augustine, *City of God*, 14.19.

34. Augustine, *On Marriage and Desire*, in *Answer to the Pelagians II*, trans., intro., and notes Roland J. Teske, S.J., vol. I/24, *The Works of Saint Augustine: A Translation for the 21st Century*, ed. John E. Rotelle, O.S.A. (Hyde Park: New City Press, 1998), I.24.27.

35. Augustine, *On Continence*, in *Marriage and Virginity*, trans. Ray Kearney, vol. I/9, *The Works of Saint Augustine: A Translation for the 21st Century*, ed. John E. Rotelle, O.S.A. (Hyde Park: New City Press, 1999/2005), 3.6.

36. Augustine, *On Continence*, 4.11; cf. 7.18.

37. Augustine, *On Continence*, 12.26.

38. There is some difference of opinion about whether he misunderstands or in fact adds to this account. See Sarah C. Byers, "Augustine and the Cognitive Cause of Stoic Preliminary Passions (Propatheiai)," *Journal of the History of Philosophy* 41, no. 4 (Oct. 2003): 433–448m, and Johannes Brachtendorf, "Cicero and Augustine on the Passions," *Revue des Études Augustiniennes* 43 (1997), 289–308.

39. Timo Nisula, *Augustine and the Functions of Concupiscence,* vol. 116 *Supplements to Vigiliae Christianae* (Boston: Brill, 2012), 208.

40. Nisula, *Augustine and the Functions of Concupiscence*, 216.

41. Augustine, *On Genesis: A Refutation of the Manichees*, in *On Genesis*, trans. Edmund Hill, O.P., vol. I/13 *The Works of Saint Augustine: A Translation for the 21st Century*, ed. John E. Rotelle, O.S.A. (Hyde Park: New City Press, 2002.), 2.14.21 (emphasis mine).

42. Augustine, *On Genesis: A Refutation of the Manichees*, 2.17.26.

43. Augustine, *On Genesis: A Refutation of the Manichees*, 2.25.40.

44. Augustine, *On Genesis: A Refutation of the Manichees*, 2.11.15.

45. Augustine, *On Genesis: A Refutation of the Manichees*, 2.18.28.

46. Augustine, *On Genesis: A Refutation of the Manichees*, 2.14.21.

47. Augustine, *On Genesis: A Refutation of the Manichees*, 2.19.29.

48. Augustine, *On Genesis: A Refutation of the Manichees*, 2.19.29. Oddly Augustine also remarks with apparent disapproval that most women do not give birth with their husbands present.

49. Augustine, *On Genesis: A Refutation of the Manichees*, 2.19.29.

50. Augustine, *On Genesis: A Refutation of the Manichees*, 2.21.31.

51. Augustine, *On Genesis: A Refutation of the Manichees*, 2.26.40.

52. Augustine, *On Marriage and Desire*, 1.24.28.

53. Augustine, *On Marriage and Desire*, 1.23.25.

54. Augustine, *Sermons (1–400)*, trans. and notes Edmund Hill, O.P., vol. III/1–10 *The Works of Saint Augustine: A Translation for the 21st Century*, ed. John E. Rotelle, O.S.A. (New Rochelle: New City Press, 1992), 153.VI.8-VII.9 (PL 38, 829–30) and 155.III.3 (842). Cited in Michael R. Rackett, "Anti-Pelagian Polemic in Augustine's *De Continentia*," *Augustinian Studies* 26 (1995): 37.

55. Augustine, *On Marriage and Desire*, 1.24.27.

56. Augustine, *On Marriage and Desire*, 1.28.

57. Augustine, *On Marriage and Desire*, 2.35.59.

58. Augustine, *On Marriage and Desire*, 2.35.59.
59. Augustine, *On Marriage and Desire*, 2.35.59.
60. Augustine, *On Marriage and Desire*, 2.35.59.
61. Augustine, *On the Literal Meaning of Genesis*, in *On Genesis*, trans. Edmund Hill, O.P., vol. I/13 *The Works of Saint Augustine: A Translation for the 21st Century*, ed. John E. Rotelle, O.S.A. (Hyde Park: New City Press, 2002), IX.3.6; IX.4.8. Cf. Augustine, *On Marriage and Desire*, 2.14.29.
62. John C. Cavadini, "Feeling Right: Augustine on the Passions and Sexual Desire," *Augustinian Studies* 36 (2005): 195.
63. Augustine, *City of God,* 22.17. Cited in Kari Elisabeth Børresen, "Patristic 'Feminism': The Case of Augustine," *Augustinian Studies* 25 (1994): 146.

PART II

Sex and Marriage

PART II

Chapter 4

Augustine and Anatomical Virginity

The Problem of Double Integrity

Julia Kelto Lillis

In his opening book of *The City of God*, Augustine of Hippo makes a famous intervention in Roman thought about chastity. He argues that Christian holiness and sexual honor are dictated not by what happens to a woman's (or any person's) body parts, but by her own moral agency. His intervention, however, was not as complete as many readers think. Numerous recent publications claim that Augustine located virginity squarely in the will instead of the body, thus making it possible for Christians to count virgins who experienced sexual violence as virgins. In fact, both in this and in other writings, Augustine locates *chastity* in the will but understands female *virginity* as a combination of moral chastity and bodily integrity. He challenged a conventional belief about chastity that adversely affected victims of sexual violence, yet the definition of virginity he endorsed makes it difficult to consider chaste but violated women truly virginal. By promoting the belief that girls and women possess a distinctive, anatomical form of virginity, Augustine impeded the promising trajectory of his own reasoning about chastity.

This essay lays out the tension in Augustine's thought about virginity and chastity in *City of God* 1.16–29 with reference to his terminology and claims in other works.[1] The first section of the essay situates Augustine within a larger history of virginity discourse. The second briefly situates his comments in *The City of God* as a response to historical events and a continuation of earlier Roman deliberation about the resilience of chastity. The third and fourth sections examine his ways of describing virginal integrity, resilient chastity, and threatened virginity in various texts. The final two sections discuss his position in *The City of God* on chastity and virginity in the wake of sexual violence and the unsettling implications of his position.

THE BROADER HISTORY OF ANCIENT VIRGINITY DISCOURSE

In Mediterranean antiquity, "virginity" was never a single or static concept with a predictable meaning. On the broadest level, what made a "virgin" different from a "woman" could be her age, marital status, sexual status, or reproductive status: the term "virgin" might refer variously to a teenager or to a woman who is not married, has not experienced penile-vaginal penetration, or has not yet had children. Among Christian thinkers—even those who assumed that a lifelong vow of virginity entailed eschewing marriage, sex, and childbearing altogether—one finds a stunning variety of conceptual configurations, including diverse understandings of "bodily" virginity.[2] Discourse on women's virginity had surprising moments of convergence and contrast as its Christian significance grew.

In late antiquity, a new "common sense" about virginity arose. Beginning in sources of the very late fourth and early fifth century, writers from numerous regions and differing religious and intellectual traditions rather suddenly show a shared investment in the idea that female virgins have perceptibly virginal sex organs—features of either genital anatomy or genital physiology[3] that make virginal or nonvirginal status evident. Some authors subscribe to the physiological idea that bleeding during penetration provides proof of prior sexual virginity to a sex partner or observer, while other sources equate virginity with a narrow, tight, or dry vagina. Several writers appeal to the emerging notion of a hymenal membrane that occludes the vagina.[4] These beliefs were not timeless and universal, nor a foregone conclusion. Medical science and social valuation of women's sexual purity had proceeded for centuries without them, with isolated instances of physiological notions before and during the Common Era and sporadic reference to anatomical notions like hymens beginning in the Common Era.[5]

The longer view of virginity discourse reveals that Augustine's ideas about female virgins' bodies were not the only options but—despite their relative novelty—had already gained a firm hold in his region. Anatomical conceptualizations of virginity likely arose in Rome and Roman North Africa sooner than in other locales.[6] Writings by Tertullian and Cyprian show that the notion of virginally "closed" sex organs and the idea that midwives can assess virginity by genital inspection surfaced in Carthage in the early third century, long before they appeared in other Christian sources.[7] When later ancient authors began to utilize anatomical configurations for their own purposes, they merged models that could not fully cohere, for Christians not only drew from multiple available social meanings for virginity but developed their own theological and moral discourse that emphasized virgins' personal holiness, purity of mind, and undivided devotion to God. Writers were hard-pressed to explain how these higher, spiritual aspects of virginity fit together with new notions about the concrete tangibility of virginity that served certain agendas well. Embracing anatomical notions therefore created tensions in reasoning as well as pastoral problems in when and how to apply competing configurations. Augustine's comments and silences on attacked virgins is a prime example of these problems, and his location in North Africa and stance in intra-Christian debates may help explain his inability to think differently about virginity or follow his reasoning about chastity to its logical conclusion.

THE SACK OF ROME AND EARLIER ROMAN REFLECTION ON THREATENED CHASTITY

Augustine's *City of God* 1 responded to difficult questions prompted by the Visigoths' sack of Rome in 410. Many virgins and wives suffered sexual assault during the events, and in Roman culture, suicide was, or was seen as, a common response to such attacks.[8] Augustine discusses the relationship between chastity, purity, holiness, and bodily integrity in order to address the matter of how readers should view survivors who did not kill themselves after being raped.[9] He endeavors to delegitimize self-killing and defend the possibility that assaulted women are undeserving of shame or punishment while also rationalizing why God permitted such attacks in the first place.

Augustine's discussion is part of a longer lineage of deliberation over how to view women's chastity when states of the body and mind do not align. What happens when a chaste woman's body is sexually "corrupted" against her will? Is chastity destroyed by unwanted sexual penetration, or does it ultimately depend on the mind? Augustine shows familiarity with lines of argument found in earlier Latin texts. Works of the imperial period offer multiple views and sometimes voice divergent verdicts within a single work.[10] On the one hand, physical chastity was traditionally seen as a state of purity from the pollution of sexual corruption, which occurs in mechanistic fashion: illicit penetration was thought to pollute the body of a virgin girl, freeborn boy, married woman, or adult man, regardless of a victim's willingness or unwillingness to be penetrated. According to this purity/pollution model (which operated long before the spread of beliefs that sex changes virgins' genital anatomy), being chaste requires staying pure; chastity can be destroyed against one's will. On the other hand, personal character and moral intent mattered, too; one finds in these earlier texts the position that guilt or innocence matters more than corruption.

Augustine takes up the latter position and argues at length in *The City of God* 1 that it is the state of one's own mind, not acts perpetrated upon one's body by others, that determines whether a person is chaste and holy. His broad, inclusive terms, chastity and holiness, speak to the distressing circumstances and potential imputed shame shared by wives, widows, virgins, and consecrated virgins who were attacked.[11] While his arguments against a mechanistic view of pollution and in favor of women's agency constitute an important intervention in the intellectual, social, and pastoral frameworks of his time, his position not only can create other problems for survivors of sexual violence[12] but would have held limited applicability in his own day among those who shared his beliefs about the nature of female virginity. By failing to explain how one can reconcile the anatomical prerequisites of virginity with a moral configuration of chastity, he leaves assaulted virgins' social and ecclesial status precarious.

VIRGINITY AS INTEGRITY IN AUGUSTINE'S OTHER WORKS AND IN *THE CITY OF GOD*

Augustine routinely equates virginity with integrity (*integritas*) in his writings. While both chastity (*pudicitia, castitas*) and virginity (*virginitas*) entail integrity of the soul, it becomes apparent upon examination of his works that he considers integrity of the body necessary for virginity as well. Furthermore, the kind of integrity he associates with female virgins' bodies is not simply a quality of being untouched or pure (as is the case in many earlier Roman sources) but includes a form of genital intactness—undamaged hymen tissue—that he thinks virgins innately possess. No discernible variations or chronological changes on these matters appear in his corpus, despite developments on other aspects of embodiment and sexuality.[13]

The anatomical nature of virginal integrity is particularly clear when Augustine writes about Mary. He depicts Mary's womb remaining closed in childbirth, comparing it with the locked doors Jesus was able to enter after the resurrection (John 20:19, 26);[14] he calls this closed genital state "integrity" and "the integrity of virginity" (*virginitatis integritas*).[15] Several sermons that celebrate Mary's virginal motherhood use the term *integritas*, either interchangeably with "virginity" or to denote its essential bodily characteristic(s). As a virgin even in giving birth, she "gave forth with fertile organs and intact genitals (*genitalibus integris*)," gaining fecundity without losing integrity.[16] Christ "did not take away [his mother's] virginity in any way" during childbirth because he was able to give her both a good thing from marriage and a better thing belonging to virgins: "fecundity in marriage is indeed a good thing, but integrity in consecration is a better one."[17] Augustine is capable of privileging the mind over the body in portrayals of Mary,[18] but he repeatedly refers to her genitally intact state as an essential feature of her virginity.

Though Mary's virginal physical childbearing is exceptional, Augustine makes her physical integrity exemplary for virgins of his day.[19] In Christmas sermons, he urges vowed virgins to rejoice that they can imitate Mary's example of spiritual marriage and (spiritual rather than physical) fertility without loss of bodily integrity;[20] the "integrity of flesh" retained in those who are virgins "by body" augments their minds' fertile production of virtues.[21] The treatise *Holy Virginity* likewise treats her as a model of bodily integrity for consecrated women.[22] Augustine explains that even physical virginity is spiritual as well, for one cannot maintain integrity of flesh without a chaste soul; the virgin's combination of bodily and spiritual virginity is superior to the chastity of married motherhood.[23] Virginity also has heavenly benefits, since "virginal integrity . . . in corruptible flesh is a preparatory practice of perpetual incorruptibility."[24] Integrity is central to Christian virgins' virginity, not only Mary's.

Like many authors, Augustine can speak of a collective, figural, and spiritual sort of virginity that applies to all Christians while maintaining classifications by which the individually and officially virginal belong in a distinct group.[25] "Few (women) have virginity in body; all ought to have (virginity) in heart."[26] Passages that configure virginity as integrity of the mind rather than the body foreground this inclusive capacity without negating the distinction between virginal and non-virginal Christians.[27] Integrity of faith or of the mind and heart can be seen as a kind of virginity shared by the corporate Church, whose virginity is embodied in a fleshly way by some members and not others.[28] Virgins do not have a monopoly on pleasing God but do have a lifestyle superior to other chaste lifestyles.[29]

The same correlation between virginity and integrity, including female genital integrity, is evident in *The City of God*. Besides the prominent instance from book 1 that will appear below, a list of chaste lifestyles for women in 1.27 juxtaposes "virginal integrity" with "widowly continence" and marital fidelity.[30] Other passages link virginity with undamaged genitals and virginity loss with forceful penetration that alters genitals. In 6.9, where Augustine refers to Roman traditions concerning consummation of a marriage, virginity and its loss depend entirely on a husband's use of force against a timid bride. Defloration[31] seems to be an act of inevitable theft and injury: the weak and fearful young woman's virginity must be taken away (from the verb *aufero*), and "a woman does not cease to be a virgin without force (*vis*)."[32] Augustine means to mock non-Christians' association of various deities with this act, but one is left wondering whether he envisions alternative approaches to marital defloration in a fallen world. Things would have been different, however, if sin had not intervened in Eden. According to 14.26, in a world without sin human reproduction would have proceeded in tranquil fashion—without lust usurping the control over body parts that should belong to the soul, and without violence between bridegroom and bride. Augustine writes that a husband, by sheer willpower, could have inseminated his wife without lustful excitement and "with no corruption of the body's integrity," sending semen into her uterus "with the integrity of the female genital (organ) preserved," just as menses flow from a virgin without destroying integrity.[33] As he sees it, a virgin's integrity includes genital intactness that could have persisted in prelapsarian sex but is now destined for destruction in the forceful encounter of the marriage bed. New wives' virginity involves a physical integrity that is taken away by husbands' exertion of physical power.

Within and beyond *City of God*, then, virginity is integrity. It is clear from his comments on Mary and in *City of God* 6.9 and 14.26 that Augustine pictures something like hymen tissue barring virgins' closed, intact vaginas. Even though the sources we turn to next show that the chaste state of the body rests with the mind, virginity entails more than chastity; it is a state that combines spiritual and physical integrity. The equivalence of virginity and bodily integrity in Augustine's works implies that loss of bodily integrity is a loss of virginity as well.

PRESERVED CHASTITY AND THREATENED VIRGINITY IN AUGUSTINE'S OTHER WORKS

Two works besides *City of God* deal with the issue of whether chastity, or sexual honor and virtue (*pudicitia*), can be taken by force.[34] In both works, Augustine prioritizes integrity of the soul over that of the body: the body might be damaged, but it should not be seen as polluted when the victim has been made an object of sin without being a willing participant in sinning. The pertinent passages are instructive for seeing continuities in Augustine's thought on this matter, yet they do not clarify his views on whether a sexually assaulted virgin is still a virgin. A passage from *Holy Virginity*, on the other hand, suggests that virginity can indeed be destroyed against one's will.

The treatise *Lying*, which dates to about 395, posits men as potential victims of bodily violation who are concerned to preserve their *pudicitia*.[35] Several chapters discuss whether it is ethical to tell a lie if lying would prevent the great evil of having one's body violated. Augustine argues that lying defiles the soul, the integrity of which matters far more than that of the body. Bodily goods are temporary, while the soul's integrity and the truth embraced by the chaste mind last forever. Unlike bodily *integritas*, however, the body's *pudicitia* should not be thought of as merely a temporal good, since it depends upon the soul's integrity and cannot be removed against one's will.[36] When an enemy lustfully attacks a chaste person's body, he can accomplish violence but not corruption—"or if every ordeal (like this) *is* corruption, (then) not all corruption is dishonorable, but (is so) to the extent that lust has procured or agreed to it."[37] This means that *pudicitia* remains undamaged: the chaste victim is still chaste, has lost nothing of his virtue, and should not be thought to have lost any honor, since God has judged him innocent. "No one violates the body's *pudicitia* when the soul does not agree to and allow (it)."[38] According to Augustine, the polluting consequences of sexual violence do not take effect when the soul keeps its chastity (*castitas*);[39] the mind dictates the un/chaste state of both mind and body through its culpability or its innocence and integrity. Here we gain insight into Augustine's reasoning on sexual violence and the preservation of *pudicitia*, but not into the question of whether bodily integrity is essential for virgins.

In *Letter* 111, addressed to a priest named Victorianus and probably written in 409, Augustine gives an initial response to the problem of women's sexual vulnerability as war captives during "barbarian" invasions. In this work he describes the capture of chaste women as lamentable, but he remains somewhat optimistic about their fate, relaying a story about the abduction of a consecrated virgin who was restored safely to her family after God struck her captors with illness and healed them by the girl's prayers.[40] Even so, he considers the possibility that not all will be so fortunate. God, he declares, will either protect captive women's chaste bodily members from their enemies' lust or assign culpability only to the perpetrator, not the victim. If the soul and mind remain pure by not consenting to the act, the event is an act of violence that injures members of the body but cannot harm the body's *pudicitia*.[41] Through the chaste integrity of her mind, the violated woman will remain free from sin and in possession of her chastity. Here, Augustine correlates pollution and purity with sin and innocence rather than with the bodily states by which Roman culture traditionally measured sexual honor, but he provides no verdict on a violated virgin's virginity.

Lying and *Letter* 111 anticipate Augustine's reasoning in *City of God*, declaring that *pudicitia* is determined by the soul and not by the body's members. *Virginitas*, on the other hand, is apparently so firmly anchored in the body that violence poses a threat to it. In *Holy Virginity* 4, Augustine claims that Mary vowed herself to lifelong virginity prior to the annunciation. Since Israelite custom demanded marriage, she was espoused to a righteous man who "would not take away by violence what she had already vowed (to God), but could protect it from violent men."[42] This rationalization implies that Mary's virginity would be destroyed by force if a husband or another man raped her, no matter how chaste she might be. Chastity survives assault, but virginity is a bodily possession that can be stolen.

CITY OF GOD 1.16–29: RESILIENT CHASTITY, VANISHED VIRGINITY

In *City of God* 1.16–29, Augustine again makes the case that chastity cannot be destroyed against one's will. Would he attribute the same resilience to virginity? Many readers assume that remaining chaste means staying virginal. Scholars are divided in their conclusions, and though most who discuss sexual violence and chastity do not address this question directly, growing numbers equate retained chastity with retained virginity in Augustine's thought.[43] The author never assures us that a virgin can remain virginal after losing the genital integrity that is part and parcel of female virginity. He declares that the goods of chastity, holiness, and continence cannot be taken by force, but if virginity requires not only a chaste mind and resolute will but bodily integrity as well, then chaste assaulted virgins have lost their virginity after all.

Augustine opens his discussion of sexual assault and chastity with a series of affirmations that place chastity under the control of the will. "Virtue, by which life is lived uprightly, commands the parts of the body from its seat in the mind, and the body is made holy by the exercise of a holy will"; so long as this holy will is unshaken, "whatever another person may have done concerning the body or upon the body that one would not be able to avoid without one's own sinning is irrelevant in terms of guilt for the one undergoing (it)."[44] The subsequent chapters discuss the situation of victims of sexual violence, sometimes turning to famous women of the past who faced the threat or reality of assault and chose whether or not to kill themselves.[45] Augustine argues against the valorization of suicide, portraying self-killing as murder and defending recent rape survivors' decision not to kill themselves.[46] He meanwhile complicates the task of assessing moral innocence and experiences of shame by raising the possibilities of involuntary pleasure and inward voluntary assent.[47] Throughout these chapters, he focuses on the determination of sin and innocence. Virtue and holiness are a matter of the mind and are determined by the state of the will.

City of God 1.18 contains an extended argument for the prioritization of the mind in assessing moral status. First, Augustine turns to an objection that would naturally arise from common Roman notions of purity and pollution: "it is feared that another person's lust pollutes (the rape victim)."[48] On the contrary, he says, "it will not pollute if it is another person's; if it does pollute, it will not be another person's," but the victim's, as well."[49] A victim incurs pollution only by sharing in the sin of the rapist through consent. Augustine calls chastity a "virtue of the mind"[50] and explains that a person exercises control over the mind's approval but not over the events that affect the flesh. If chastity could be destroyed (from *perdo*) by someone else's lustful and forceful use of one's body, it would not belong among the goods that guide moral life but would merely "be counted among goods of the body, of the sort that strength, beauty, sound health, and other things of this kind are."[51] As a good of the mind, chastity cannot be removed by force, and "when the good of holy continence (*continentia*) does not cede to the uncleanness of fleshly concupiscence, the body itself is also sanctified."[52]

Having established that bodily holiness is not affected by external forms of pollution, Augustine next uses several illustrations to argue that it remains unaffected by injuries to bodily integrity; a person's holiness (*sanctitas*) of mind and body depends on the state of the mind.[53] He mentions wounds and surgeries as cases of injury that should not be thought to affect bodily holiness, then employs the similar example of a virginity inspection gone wrong (quoted below). This is followed by a discussion of an inverse situation in which a woman pledges herself to continence but later decides to have sex, thereby losing the holiness of her body even before the sexual act. All these examples support the argument that the holiness of the body as well as of the mind depends on the mind, such that for those who intend continence, "the violence of another person's lust does not take away (*aufero*) the holiness of the body."[54] In the case of that virginity inspection, bodily integrity is lost, but the body's holiness remains:

> It is not by this that the body is holy, (by the fact) that its parts are intact . . . For example, a midwife, when investigating a certain virgin's integrity by hand, destroyed (it), whether by spite or lack of skill or accidentally. I don't imagine anyone to think so foolishly that they would consider anything to have been lost (from) her (sanctity), even from the sanctity of that very body, even though the integrity of that body part has been lost.[55]

His wording specifies that this midwife has destroyed (*perdo*) the virgin's *integritas* and that genital *integritas* has been lost (*pereo*), while no one—in more wooden translation—should picture "anything to have been lost for her from the sanctity even of her body." Her *sanctitas* cannot be destroyed against her will, but her bodily integrity is gone. The virgin victim of rape would likewise retain her holiness while losing the defining bodily feature of virginity.

In *City of God* 1.28, Augustine offers possible rationales for why God has recently allowed the sexual assault of Christians to occur. Noting that attacked women lose some of their former status and their grounds for impressing fellow Christians, he theorizes that women who had become too proud of their chastity or would have become too proud in the future have been forcibly robbed of their reason for pride and redirected to a focus on their inner standing before God. He claims that witnessing one's own inner innocence after an experience of violation can teach women that continence (*continentia*), chastity (*castitas*), and holiness (*sanctitas*) are resilient goods they still possess rather than goods of the body that are susceptible to theft.[56] He seems to assume, though, that such women have indeed lost something that affects their standing in others' eyes.

Augustine's terms in *City of God* 1 form a recurring list of interrelated goods that are salvaged or unassailable in the face of rape: *pudicitia, sanctitas, castitas, continentia*. These goods rely on the will and the state of the mind, not the body. *Virginitas* is not named as one of these higher goods. Since bodily integrity is central to Augustine's understanding of virginity across multiple works, it stands to reason that virginity entails the bodily good of *integritas* as well as the virtue *pudicitia*.

This conclusion about the dual goods that comprise virginity fits well with the verbs and logic we have already seen across *City of God*. Eternal goods like chastity[57] and holiness cannot be destroyed (*perdo*) or taken away (*aufero*) by unwilled acts against the body, but virginity is taken away (*aufero*) from a reluctant bride on her wedding night (6.9), and a virgin's integrity is destroyed (*perdo*) if a midwife ruptures her hymen (1.18). Augustine notably treats rape as an act of violence by an offender and an injury for a victim rather than a primarily sexual act;[58] we might say in today's language that he treats rape as sexual violence rather than a violent form of sex. According to 6.9 and 14.26, however, ordinary defloration in a fallen world is also an instance of violence and injury. While rape is an act of violence against virginal and non-virginal women alike, for virgins, it includes damage to the body that licit sex would also cause. The damage of "opening a womb" has implications for sexual status that other types of injuries do not. Regardless of a virgin's moral innocence and Augustine's categorization of rape as predominantly violent rather than predominantly sexual, in his eyes, the loss of genital integrity appears to signify loss of virginity. Augustine never directly confirms or denies holding this belief, but the tight link between bodily integrity and virginal status in *City of God* and other works suggests that female virginity requires intact genitals and is destroyed by sexual violence as well as by the quotidian violence of marital consummation. A raped virgin's damaged body can remain pure, chaste, and holy, but it seems that for Augustine, it has lost its virginity.

CONCLUSIONS AND IMPLICATIONS

Augustine thought assaulted virgins with chaste minds remained chaste and holy in both mind and body, but he apparently did not think they were still virgins. In the end, he exchanged one mechanistic model for another. Sexual violence does not automatically pollute virgins, but it does automatically alter their bodies. An attacker cannot affect their moral standing against their will but may still affect their status as a virgin. Whether Augustine noticed it or not, his dual trajectories regarding chastity and virginity left an area in his thought in conflict and left injured virgins vulnerable to changes in their social and ecclesial status.

His discourse leaves several questions unanswered and mixes promising resources for practical application with troubling messages about embodied experience and sexual difference. On the one hand, his focus on the will could provide warrant for humane responses to devastating events like wartime rape and potential justification for maintaining a consecrated woman's special status in the church after assault. Against common perspectives held by both Christian and non-Christian Romans, Augustine insists that virtue, holiness, and sexual honor cannot be involuntarily lost from women's bodies and that raped women need not undergo punishment or perform any expiation to rid themselves of attackers' pollution. Disturbing rationalizations about pride notwithstanding, he lays partial groundwork for pastorally sensitive responses to sexual violence. On the other hand, he seems unable to say that raped virgins are still virgins, and he says in multiple works that the loss of virginity is irrevocable.[59] According to *The Good of Marriage*, even the newfound purity of Christian baptism does not cancel the effects of sexual corruption for women who might otherwise have become consecrated virgins.[60]

Moreover, his morality-centered reasoning dismisses the importance of bodies in a situation where bodily trauma might not be dismissed easily by the women themselves. Much as Augustine rewrites Roman history and revises the story of salvation history in *City of God*, he revises the history of what has happened to particular women who suffered assault; in doing so, he "nearly (but not quite) writes the human body out of history" for these women.[61] He deems bodily integrity inconsequential for virgins' and other women's moral state and for the purposes of discerning God's favor toward and protection of Christians in times of crisis. Yet closed wombs and intact flesh are consistently invested with enormous importance when Augustine discusses Mary or the life of consecrated virginity. In stating in *Homily* 191.3–4 that integrity of flesh serves to augment one's production of virtue, he exhibits a conviction that the state of the body can have a positive impact on the state of the soul. In his discussions of assaulted women in *City of*

God, he rejects the body's power to shape the soul. If he indeed believes that virginity can be lost involuntarily, this is one way—and not a very reassuring one—in which the body continues to matter in the first book of *City of God*, and the viewpoint falls startlingly close to those of authors who celebrated "martyrdoms" of female saints who killed themselves to preserve virginity. Neither *City of God* nor another work explains how or if he resolved the disjunction between his moral view of chastity and his moral and anatomical view of virginity.

A chief claim of the discussions in *City of God* 1.16–29 and *Lying* is that others' lust, through damage to the body, affects only earthly and transitory goods and has no effect on eternal ones. Virtue is what matters. Yet consecrated virgins' integrity has eternal implications in *Holy Virginity*. It anticipates the future incorruptibility of the body, and those who possess it reap a greater reward in the afterlife, receiving greater glory than those who have lost it.[62] If hymen tissue is among the parts of the body that will be restored to a state of wholeness and beauty in the resurrection (see *City of God* 22.18–21), its earthly intactness or rupture nevertheless has consequences for eternity.[63] As with many accounts of gender, Augustine's views on permanent female and male sexual difference contain affirmations feminist readers may see as positive while harboring problematic asymmetries and contradictory elements.[64]

We may wonder what so compelled Augustine about the notion of anatomical integrity that he could not sacrifice it for the sake of the trajectory of his reasoning in *City of God*, which aims toward making all forms of chastity a moral matter. Various factors present themselves. His location in North Africa, where the notion of a hymen was naturalized relatively early, would have shaped his assumptions about virgins' bodies. Theologically, genital integrity had lately featured in intra-Christian debates, with figures like Ambrose of Milan arguing that Mary's womb was permanently, perceptibly shut even when she gave birth and that God thus showed the clear superiority of celibacy over marriage; Augustine took part in such debates and shared many of his mentor's views.[65] On another theological front, Augustine gave increasing value to the physical body and its capacity to represent spiritual realities.[66] It is possible he also sensed the need to temper his message about the invincibility of chastity with acknowledgment of the very real harm suffered by invaded bodies in an invaded city.[67]

Overall, Augustine's investment in genital intactness impeded the trajectory of his reasoning about chastity. His logic about the moral nature of chastity sits uneasily beside a genital prerequisite for virginity that is frequently implied, occasionally articulated, and never relinquished in his works. Though he challenged the use of a purity/pollution model for conceptualizing the status of sexually assaulted women, his alternative focus on moral innocence or guilt does not supplant his investment in an equally mechanistic model that defines virgins as chaste women with intact hymens. His attempt to hold together spiritualizing and anatomizing views of virginity left the virginal status of those with misaligned will and body uncertain and generated problems for the coherence of his reasoning. In his schematization, female virginity cannot belong among purely spiritual goods; it is a composite rather than an integral unity befitting its symbolic power, partly a matter of the soul and partly a matter of the body, in whose sphere it remains vulnerable to unwanted or accidental injury. Instead of following his own logic on chastity to the conclusion about retained virginity that many recent readers attribute to him, Augustine produced discourse that leaves violated virgins pure in mind but changed in body, paving the way for other possibilities without being able to realize them himself.

NOTES

1. Sections of this essay also appear in my forthcoming book, *Virgin Territory: Configuring Female Virginity in Early Christianity* (Oakland: University of California Press, 2022).

2. Extended discussion of this variety is available in Lillis, *Virgin Territory*.

3. Anatomy concerns the structures or parts of the body (what the body has), while physiology concerns the functioning and fluids of the body (what the body does).

4. This "perceptibility turn" is discussed extensively in Lillis, *Virgin Territory*. On late ancient Christians' promotion of the idea that virgins' sex organs are enclosed by hymen tissue, see also Julia Kelto Lillis, "Who Opens the Womb? Fertility and Virginity in Patristic Texts," *Studia Patristica* 81 (2017): 187–201.

5. Contra many scholars' assumptions, early texts acknowledging that some virgins bleed when they first have sex do not constitute evidence for belief in hymens or belief that an expert could verify women's sexual status through genital examination. Medical writers offered other explanations for the physiological phenomenon of virginal bleeding during first intercourse, and clear evidence for anatomical conceptualizations and inspections by midwives does not appear until the second and third centuries C.E. References to knowledgeable women assessing virginity are found as early as the Dead Sea Scrolls, but it is unclear whether this entails bodily examination or another kind of investigation. Most ancient sources envision ordeals, not genital inspection, as means of verifying virginity. Hymen tissue's biomedical status today as a functionless and highly variable byproduct of growing a vagina makes it easy to understand why ancient societies might not conceptualize hymen tissue as a discrete body part.

6. The first recorded reference to the idea of a vaginal hymen for virgins occurs in an argument against its existence, written by the medical author Soranus of Ephesus sometime in the early second century. See Soranus of Ephesus, *Gynecology*, in

Soranos d'Ephèse: Maladies des femmes, ed. Paul Burguière, Danielle Gourevitch, and Yves Malinas, 4 vols. (Paris: Les Belles Lettres, 1988–2000), 1.17. Soranus worked in Rome and does not explain whose views he is rejecting.

7. On the frequently misinterpreted scenes in *Protevangelium of James* 19–20, see Julia Kelto Lillis, "Paradox *in Partu:* Verifying Virginity in the *Protevangelium of James*," *Journal of Early Christian Studies* 24, no. 1 (2016): 1–28. It is possible the early rise of institutionally recognized vows of virginity in Carthage sparked an eagerness to distinguish between virginal and non-virginal women and a readiness to apply newly available anatomical notions circulating in Rome to do so.

8. This is evident from both pre-Christian Latin literature and early Christians' praise of women who killed themselves to avoid assault. On the importance of chastity, see Rebecca Langlands, *Sexual Morality in Ancient Rome* (Cambridge: Cambridge University Press, 2006); on motives for self-killing, Timothy D. Hill, *Ambitiosa Mors: Suicide and Self in Roman Thought and Literature* (New York and London: Routledge, 2004).

9. Augustine also downplays the severity of the events for the sake of his apologetic aims. Recent studies that discuss sexual violence in late ancient military contexts and Augustine's or others' responses to it include Melanie Gibson Webb, "Rape and Its Aftermath in Augustine's *City of God*" (PhD diss., Princeton Theological Seminary, 2016); Jennifer Collins-Elliott, "'Bespattered with the Mud of Another's Lust': Rape and Physical Embodiment in Christian Literature of the 4th-6th Centuries C.E." (PhD diss, Florida State University, Forthcoming); Kathy L. Gaca, "Martial Rape, Pulsating Fear, and the Sexual Maltreatment of Girls (παῖδες), Virgins (παρθένοι), and Women (γυναῖκες) in Antiquity," *American Journal of Philology* 135, no. 3 (2014): 303–57; Helen Morales, "Rape, Violence, Complicity: Colluthus's Abduction of Helen," *Arethusa* 49, no. 1 (2016): 61–92. On the difficulties of choosing fitting terminology for non-consensual sex in antiquity, see Jennifer Barry, "So Easy to Forget: Augustine's Treatment of the Sexually Violated in the City of God," *Journal of the American Academy of Religion* 88, no. 1 (2020): 237 n. 6.

10. Especially pertinent are Livy's version of the story of Lucretia in *History of Rome* 1.57–59 and Seneca the Elder, *Declamations* 1.2. On the array of previous views on self-killing, honor, and shame with which Augustine could engage, see J. Warren Smith, *Ambrose, Augustine, and the Pursuit of Greatness* (Cambridge and New York: Cambridge University Press, 2020), 237–68.

11. See Augustine, *City of God (books 1–10)*, Series Latina 47 *Corpus Christianorum*, ed. Bernhard Dombart and Alfons Kalb (Turnhout: Brepols, 1955), 1.16 and 1.28.

12. Critiques of Augustine's moral construal of chastity and its application in present-day legal proceedings appear in Jennifer J. Thompson, "'Accept This Twofold Consolation, You Faint-Hearted Creatures': St. Augustine and Contemporary Definitions of Rape," *Simile* 4, no. 3 (2004): 1–17. Other scholars add nuance that can ameliorate the problem of involuntary pleasure in this moral framework—see Webb, "Rape and Its Aftermath," 77–78 and Smith, *Ambrose, Augustine*, 242–47—but Thompson raises further points regarding the pitfalls of using a conscience-focused framework in today's legal proceedings.

13. See, for example, the developments summarized in David G. Hunter, "Evil, Suffering, and Embodiment in Augustine," in *Suffering and Evil in Early Christian Thought*, ed. Nonna Verna Harrison and David G. Hunter (Grand Rapids: Baker Academic, 2016), 143–60. The sources most frequently cited in the analysis below include homilies that cannot be assigned secure dates and treatises from the very early 400s. On the difficulty of dating Augustine's sermons, see Hubertus R. Drobner, "The Chronology of St. Augustine's *Sermones ad populum*," *Augustinian Studies* 31, no. 2 (2000): 211–18; on dates for *Holy Virginity* (traditionally 401, but perhaps 403–4 or in stages during later years yet) and *The Good of Marriage* (which closely preceded it), see Pierre-Marie Hombert, *Nouvelles Recherches de Chronologie Augustinienne* (Paris: Institut d'études augustiniennes, 2000), 105–36.

14. Augustine, *Homilies (184–229)*, vol. 32/1 *Nuova Biblioteca Agostiniana* (Discorsi 4/1), ed. and trans. P. Bellini, F. Cruciani, and V. Tarulli (Rome: Città Nuova Editrice, 1984), 191.2; *Letters*, vol. 31B *Corpus Scriptorum Ecclesiasticorum Latinorum*, ed. K. D. Daur (Turnhout: Brepols, 2009), 137.2; *City of God (books 11–22)*, Series Latina 48 *Corpus Christianorum*, ed. Bernhard Dombart and Alfons Kalb (Turnhout: Brepols, 1955), 22.8.

15. Augustine, *Homilies (184–229)*, 191.2 (NBA 32/1.46) and 192.1 (NBA 32/1.50). Apart from quoted phrases of more than one word, I will give lexical rather than inflected forms for Latin terms.

16. Augustine, *Homilies (184–229)*, 186.1 (NBA 32/1.12). Similarly, *Homily* 193.1 says that she remained *integra* after giving birth (NBA 32/1.56), and *Homily* 215.3 says that her child kept her organs *integra* (NBA 32/1.238). Mary's miraculous fecundity and preserved integrity also feature in *Homilies* 184.1, 189.2, 190.3, and 195.1–2.

17. Augustine, *Homilies (184–229)*, 188.4 (NBA 32/1.28).

18. For instance, see *Homily* 72A.7 in *Homilies (51–85)*, vol. 30/1 *Nuova Biblioteca Agostiniana* (Discorsi 2/1), ed. and trans. Luigi Carrozzi (Rome: Città Nuova Editrice, 1982).

19. On Mary as a model for consecrated virgins and other Christians, see Geoffrey D. Dunn, "The Functions of Mary in the Christmas Homilies of Augustine of Hippo," *Studia Patristica* 44 (2010): 433–46.

20. See, for example, Augustine, *Homilies (184–229)*, 184.1–2 and 192.1–2.

21. Augustine, *Homilies (184–229)*, 191.3–4 (NBA 32/1.46–48).

22. Augustine, *Holy Virginity*, vol. 41 *Corpus Scriptorum Ecclesiasticorum Latinorum*, ed. Joseph Zycha (Vienna: Tempsky, 1900), especially sections 2, 4, and 11. For an example of the juxtaposition of "virginal integrity" with marital fecundity and the interchangeability of "virginity" and "integrity" frequently found in this work, see section 7 (CSEL 41.240–41).

23. Augustine, *Holy Virginity*, 8; cf. 11. Augustine aims to strike a balance in this treatise that refutes both Jovinian's equalizing of marriage and celibacy and Manichean rejection of marriage.

24. Augustine, *Holy Virginity*, 12/13 (CSEL 41.245; some treatise sections have rival numbering systems). Augustine emphatically teaches that virgins will receive a greater reward in the afterlife than those who have followed lesser paths; see, for

example, *Holy Virginity*, 21–29, and *Good of Marriage,* vol. 41 *Corpus Scriptorum Ecclesiasticorum Latinorum*, ed. Joseph Zycha (Vienna: Tempsky, 1900), 26/35.

25. See especially Augustine, *Homilies (86–116)*, vol. 30/2 *Nuova Biblioteca Agostiniana* (Discorsi 2/2), ed. and trans. Luigi Carrozzi (Rome: Città Nuova Editrice, 1983), 93.

26. Augustine, *Homilies (86–116)*, 93.3–4 (NBA 30/2.140); cf. the concluding sentences of *Homilies* 188.4 and 195.2.

27. For example, Augustine, *Homilies (51–85)*, 72A.7–8; *Homilies (184–229)*, 192.2; *Holy Virginity*, 5–6; and *Good of Widowhood*, vol. 41 *Corpus Scriptorum Ecclesiasticorum Latinorum*, ed. Joseph Zycha (Vienna: Tempsky, 1900), 10/13.

28. Augustine, *Holy Virginity*, 2, 6, 11/12; *Homilies (184–229)*, 191.3 and 213.8. Faithful and chaste Christians do not all qualify as virgins; Christian women live out chastity in various ways, as wives, widows, or virgins (see *Homilies (184–229)*, 196.2, and juxtapositions of virginal integrity with celibate widowhood and marital fecundity in *Good of Marriage,* 8; *Holy Virginity*, 7; *Good of Widowhood*, 17/21 and 19/24).

29. Augustine, *Holy Virginity*, 29–56/57; cf. *Good of Marriage*, 23/28.

30. Augustine, *City of God (books 1–10)*, 1.27 (CCSL 47.28).

31. Antiquated terms like "deflower" are problematic today but aptly render some late ancient views of initial sexual intercourse as an act that changes a virgin's genitals and diminishes her value and appeal on the marriage market.

32. Augustine, *City of God (books 1–10)*, 6.9 (CCSL 47.179). The notion of force is ambiguous here; while the key sense may simply be of action or powerful motion (here, the effort and effect of penetration), Augustine's appeal to the classic image of a reluctant bride touches on the sense of compulsion that the term can also convey in English.

33. Augustine, *City of God (books 11–22)*, 14.26 (CCSL 48.449).

34. Divjak Letters 14* and 15* discuss the assault of a consecrated virgin around the year 419. The letters make it clear that Augustine considers violation of a virgin a grave offense, but neither clarifies whether he understands this criminal act as a destruction of virginity. See *Divjak Letters*, vol. 88 *Corpus Scriptorum Ecclesiasticorum Latinorum*, ed. Johannes Divjak (Vienna: Tempsky, 1981/88).

35. Augustine probably intends for his ethical reasoning to apply to both men and women, but he uses masculine examples here; defilement of the body includes no terms specific to women but includes being made to "suffer womanish things," i.e., as a penetrated sex partner. See Augustine, *Lying,* vol. 41 *Corpus Scriptorum Ecclesiasticorum Latinorum*, ed. Joseph Zycha (Vienna: Tempsky, 1900), 9 and 10 (CSEL 41.434, 436).

36. Augustine, *Lying*, 7 (CSEL 41.427–429). On the complex assignation of temporal or eternal import to these modes of integrity and chastity, see especially the sentence that bridges 427–28 and a later statement on 428: while the body's *pudicitia* "should not be counted among temporal things," *integritas* of body and soul are contrasted by saying that "integrity of soul, which can be preserved into eternity, should be put before integrity of body."

37. Augustine, *Lying*, 7 (CSEL 41.428).

38. Augustine, *Lying*, 19 (CSEL 41.460).

39. While the body's chastity is called *pudicitia*, the soul's is called *castitas* in these passages of *Lying*: see, for example, the repeated parallels in chapter 20 (CSEL 41.462–63).

40. Augustine, *Letters*, 111.7.

41. Augustine, *Letters*, 111.9 (CCSL 31B.102).

42. Augustine, *Holy Virginity*, 4 (CSEL 41.238).

43. Numerous recent studies claim or imply that Augustine sees virginity as a matter of the mind or will, not the body, and sees assaulted virgins as still virginal. Examples include Virginia Burrus, "An Immoderate Feast: Augustine Reads John's Apocalypse," in *History, Apocalypse, and the Secular Imagination*, ed. Mark Vessey, Karla Pollmann, and Allan D. Fitzgerald (Bowling Green: Philosophy Documentation Center, Bowling Green State University, 1999), 183–194; Michael Rosenberg, *Signs of Virginity: Testing Virgins and Making Men in Late Antiquity* (New York: Oxford University Press, 2018), 182–207; Abbe Lind Walker, *Bride of Hades to Bride of Christ: The Virgin and the Otherworldly Bridegroom in Ancient Greece and Early Christian Rome* (London and New York: Routledge, 2020), 80–92; Webb, "Rape and Its Aftermath in Augustine's *City of God*"; Collins-Elliott, "'Bespattered with the Mud of Another's Lust.'" Broad studies with the same claim include Françoise Meltzer, *For Fear of the Fire: Joan of Arc and the Limits of Subjectivity* (Chicago: University of Chicago Press, 2001), 82; Maud Burnett McInerney, *Eloquent Virgins from Thecla to Joan of Arc* (New York: Palgrave Press, 2003), 78–81 (though McInerney thinks Augustine makes it nearly impossible for any virgin to have undamaged chastity); and (for general audiences) Hanne Blank, *Virgin: The Untouched History* (New York: Bloomsbury, 2007) and Anke Bernau's *Virgins: A Cultural History* (London: Granta, 2007). The contrasting position can be discerned in P. G. Walsh's translation of *City of God* 1.18.5 and 1.19.15 in *Augustine: De Civitate Dei (books I & II)*, ed. P.G. Walsh (Oxford: Oxbow Books, 2005). Sissel Undheim's discussion in *Borderline Virginities: Sacred and Secular Virgins in Late Antiquity* (London: Routledge, 2017) posits that Augustine attempts (but struggles) to redefine virginity as a matter of the mind and will (163–64).

44. Augustine, *City of God*, 1.16 (CCSL 47.18).

45. Augustine, *City of God*, 1.19 and 1.26.

46. Augustine, *City of God*, 1.26: He is willing to reserve judgment on some saints of the past who (he suggests) may have been following direct commands from God.

47. Augustine, *City of God*, 1.16, 1.19, 1.25, 1.27. See n. 12.

48. Augustine, *City of God*, 1.18 (CCSL 47.18).

49. Augustine, *City of God*, 1.18 (CCSL 47.18).

50. Augustine, *City of God*, 1.18 (CCSL 47.18).

51. Augustine, *City of God*, 1.18 (CCSL 47.19).

52. Augustine, *City of God*, 1.18 (CCSL 47.19).

53. These are listed within *City of God*, 1.18 (CCSL 47.19).

54. Augustine, *City of God*, 1.18 (CCSL 47.19).

55. Augustine, *City of God*, 1.18 (CCSL 47.19): "*Neque enim eo corpus sanctum est, quod eius membra sunt integra . . . Obstetrix virginis cuiusdam integritatem manu*

velut explorans sive malevolentia sive inscitia sive casu, dum inspicit, perdidit. Non opinor quemquam tam stulte sapere, ut huic perisse aliquid existimet etiam de ipsius corporis sanctitate, quamvis membri illius integritate iam perdita."

56. Augustine, *City of God*, 1.28 (CCSL 47.29–30).

57. Webb makes the interesting point that *pudicitia*, or at least its tie to shame (*pudor*), falls out of view when Augustine turns to depicting the heavenly city in *City of God* ("Rape and Its Aftermath," 79–80)—but he also hesitates to count it as a temporal good, at least at the time of writing *Lying* 7. It seems to belong among the qualities and virtues that lead toward eternal life and last forever.

58. This is compellingly argued in Webb, "Rape and Its Aftermath," 58–99.

59. For example, according to *Holy Virginity* 29, other gifts of holiness are attainable by those who have lost virginity, but virginity loss cannot be reversed.

60. Augustine, *Good of Marriage*, 18/21. In this brief discussion of restrictions for clerical ordination to men who have been married no more than once, Augustine points out that restrictions on male clerical ordination and female consecrated virginity are not a matter of sin but of the unique potential of once-married men and virginal women to signify aspects of humanity's relationship to God.

61. Borrowing a turn of phrase that Virginia Burrus applies to Augustine's broader historical project in this work: Virginia Burrus, *Saving Shame: Martyrs, Saints, and Other Abject Subjects* (Philadelphia: University of Pennsylvania Press, 2008), 129. See Margaret Ruth Miles, "From Rape to Resurrection: Sin, Sexual Difference, and Politics," in *Augustine's City of God: A Critical Guide*, ed. James Wetzel (New York: Cambridge University Press, 2012), 75–92, and Barry, "So Easy to Forget." Barry considers the tension between Augustine's seemingly pastoral claim to exonerate violated women from blame and the dismissive effects of his rhetoric as he proceeds.

62. Augustine, *Holy Virginity*, 12/13–14 and 21–29; cf. 45/46–46/47.

63. On Augustine's varied statements about bodily continuity in the resurrection, see Caroline Walker Bynum, *The Resurrection of the Body in Western Christianity, 200–1336* (New York: Columbia University Press, 1995), 94–104.

64. I count myself among feminist readers interested in the potential as well as the problems of early Christian texts. On the importance of Augustine affirming that femaleness need not be erased in the resurrection and that bodies are integral to human identity, see Kari Elizabeth Børresen, "God's Image, Man's Image? Patristic Interpretation of Gen. 1,27 and I Cor. 11,7," in *The Image of God: Gender Models in Judaeo-Christian Tradition*, ed. Kari Elizabeth Børresen (Minneapolis: Fortress Press, 1995), 187–209, and Beth Felker Jones, *Marks of His Wounds: Gender Politics and Bodily Resurrection* (Oxford and New York: Oxford University Press, 2007). On Augustine's failure to develop fully his own promising lines of reasoning about humans as God's image, see Judith Chelius Stark, "Augustine on Women: In God's Image, but Less So," in *Feminist Interpretations of Augustine: Re-Reading the Canon*, ed. Judith Chelius Stark (University Park: Pennsylvania State University Press, 2007), 215–41.

65. See Lillis, *Virgin Territory*, ch. 5; for fuller background on the debates, see David G. Hunter, *Marriage, Celibacy, and Heresy in Ancient Christianity: The*

Jovinianist Controversy (Oxford and New York: Oxford University Press, 2007). On North African contention over marriage and celibacy that Augustine may have needed to address in a fresh way several years after Jovinian's work circulated, see David G. Hunter, "Augustine, Sermon 354A: Its Place in His Thought on Marriage and Sexuality," *Augustinian Studies* 33, no.1 (2002): 39–60.

66. On the notion of *sacramentum* and the spiritual significance of the body, see Hunter, "Evil, Suffering, and Embodiment in Augustine"; Brian Stock, *The Integrated Self: Augustine, the Bible, and Ancient Thought* (Philadelphia: University of Pennsylvania Press, 2017), 127–43; Joseph T. Lienhard, "*Sacramentum* and the Eucharist in St. Augustine," *The Thomist* 77, no. 2 (2013): 173–92. The bodies of virginal women and once-married men have a powerful symbolic role in *Good of Marriage* 18/21. In *City of God*, virginity also becomes useful for Augustine's reflections on the original and final integrity of human beings as a whole.

67. As Miles observes, Augustine's ideas in *City of God* about the significance of bodily suffering are "hopelessly conflicted," sometimes affirming and sometimes disavowing the importance of the body. See "From Rape to Resurrection," 82.

Chapter 5

Between Exegesis and Naturalization

Gender and Creation in Augustine

Willemien Otten

Augustine of Hippo shares the questionable honor of being the single premodern Christian author whose readership stretches beyond the confines of Christianity. While Origen of Alexandria (ca. 184–253) or Thomas Aquinas (1225–1274) are in many ways equally impressive Christian intellectuals, they are not considered representative of Christianity in the same, near-universal way. This unique status may explain why Augustine is also the one most blamed, and sometimes it seems exclusively blamed, for what are considered Christianity's ostensible flaws, if not outright errors. In recent decades these errors have often involved his views of gender and sexuality,[1] but these are in turn almost always connected, as I will try to show, with his conceptions of nature and creation. At times the criticisms of Augustine can be so powerful that one wonders whether the honor of a wide readership for Augustine stems not more from the critique that has come his way than from the evaluation of his thought.

This article's first goal is to evaluate in survey manner various criticisms that Augustine's positions on *gender*, in stricter or looser connection with his views of creation, have received. Ranging from his relative nontreatment or neglect of gender difference to his lack of documented social interaction with women, these criticisms have yielded an unfavorable comparison with contemporaries like Jerome, who seemed to take women more seriously as correspondents.[2] That Augustine's stance on gender is problematic also holds up in the comparison with Thomas Aquinas. Insofar as the comparison with Aquinas allows us to cover a broader historical spectrum than that of late antiquity,³ it suggests that premodern Christianity has a structural problem on its hands,⁴ exemplified in but not limited to the denial of the priesthood to women in the Catholic tradition.

From there, I review how other Augustine critics, notably Bernadette Brooten and Andrea Nightingale,⁵ see Augustine's failure poignantly in terms of his conception of *nature or creation*. If their analysis is correct, does Augustine's view of creation need correction pursuant to his negative view of gender and sexuality? This is no small question to ask in an age of environmental crisis, even though that issue must remain outside my purview.⁶ Starting from Nightingale, who holds Augustine responsible for downplaying if not disallowing the enjoyment of natural life, including sexuality, in Western culture, I home in on Augustine's thought on the topic of creation or nature. His thought on nature manifests itself not only in his actual treatment of nature but also—in what I have come to see as a kind of Augustinian partiality for thinking in naturalistic terms—in his analysis of heaven and paradise in the *City of God*, even if it means that he pushes these key terms beyond the limits of what they can responsibly bear. After all, ideas about paradise or heaven cannot but be speculative. Instead of seeing such speculation as an anthropological figment of the imagination, might we do better to see it as indicative of what I have elsewhere called a kind of Augustinian surplus?⁷ This surplus allows Augustine to fully accept human life as rooted in day-to-day earthly life but, in a sort of double vision, uphold at the same time that its final significance lies beyond the constraints of the here and now. With paradise and heaven as bookends to our natural, temporal lives Augustine can pull back the curtains on the meaning of created life itself. Here it is good to be mindful of Augustine's undisputed reputation as master of time and temporality.⁸ It is precisely on the point of how best to recalibrate the relationship of *creation* and *procreation* in the face of an ever-present, looming divine eternity that Augustine's rhetoric of temporality tilts and reshapes the language, and the values, of early Christian eschatology.

To clarify what I mean by Augustine's focus on life in the here and now and the end of eschatology as a kind of affirmation of creation and embrace of historical time, I contrast him with a roughly contemporary thinker from the patristic past, namely Gregory of Nyssa (ca. 335–395), whose eschatological outlook makes him more idealistic and perhaps more straightforwardly Platonic. The comparison with Gregory of Nyssa gives a unique view into how both thinkers developed a rather different perspective on sexuality based on their perception of humanity's place in the world and its role in the return of creation. As Peter Brown sees it, Gregory's exegesis of Genesis at the basis of his theology of virginity is aimed at driving out the fear of mortality, which is inherent in procreative marriage as a mark of the fall.⁹ A comparison between Gregory and Augustine on the status of paradisaical creation in

Genesis reveals Augustine to anchor human nature directly in God's material and physical creation, even though humans are the "image of God," whereby it remains a poignant question whether for Augustine this applies only to the soul in distinction of the body.[10] Augustine clearly views paradise not merely as an idealized state but as a grounded, earthly reality. While all of us could have lived in it, it is not the reality we find ourselves in today. Also, human nature is for Augustine ensconced in a view of nature that is broadly construed according to the six days of creation, which makes it even more puzzling that he never wrote a cosmological tract.[11] Whether Augustine's non-anthropocentric view of creation mitigates against any persistent androcentrism remains to be seen.

Finally, we have to address the question of whether to see Augustine, who rejected both the gnostic/Manichaean and the Donatist position, as a theologian of empire. Elaine Pagels sees in his inflexible gender hierarchy more the imposition of Roman imperial order than the expression of intrinsically Christian values.[12] If we couple Pagels's criticism of empire with that of Augustinian nature leveled by Brooten, it seems Augustine failed to employ his religious convictions to counter the Roman ethos on gender with a more capacious (biblically based for Brooten; open to more tolerant, gnostic views for Pagels) Christian position, one that would no doubt meet with a more favorable reception today. Thinking along similar lines, Andrea Nightingale regards Augustine's take on physical existence (including his take on sexuality) as especially pernicious,[13] encapsulated as it is in his attempt to bridle and suppress all natural desires.

At the end of my analysis of creation and gender I aim to formulate a summary statement that is sufficiently representative of the complexity of Augustine's views as situated between exegesis and naturalization. Along the way I hope to demythologize some of the prejudices that have been thrown his way largely, if not exclusively, because he is indeed the Western Christian thinker par excellence.

FROM GENDER TO CREATION

A key gender criticism leveled against Augustine is his reproductive view of marriage, with its implied reduction of the role of women to that of childbearers. The seminal case for this criticism driving much of the discussion that ensued was made by Elizabeth Clark in her 1986 article "Adam's Only Companion: Augustine and the Early Christian Debate on Marriage."[14] Clark points out that Augustine initially had what she called a companionate view of marriage, traces of which we find in his early work *De bono conjugali* (*On the Good of Marriage*), written around 401CE. He later sacrificed this companionate view in favor of what she labels his reproductive view of marriage. Pivotal text for the later view is *The Literal Meaning Genesis* 9.5.9,[15] where Augustine states that if God had wanted to create a friend for Adam, he would have created another man.

Clark relates Augustine's view of reproductive marriage directly to his view of biblical creation, in which the woman is assigned the status of a helpmate. This gives the anchoring of woman's subservient role in nature the final, negative word. While Clark's analysis is relevant for contemporary feminist debate, it also shows her to be influenced by it, as she sees Augustine caving in before the demands of institutional marriage with its goal of procreation. The move to Christianize marriage meant upholding its validity by *naturalizing* it, that is, embedding it in the *exegesis* of paradise and all that transpired there.

As expounded by many Augustine scholars,[16] the discussion of marriage and virginity—what in broader terms can be seen as a discussion about the limits of eschatology for a Christianized Roman Empire—reached fever pitch when Jerome and Jovinian came out around 400 CE with opposing viewpoints about the desirability of the ascetic lifestyle. While for Jovinian the sacrament of baptism sufficed to define Christian identity, keen as he was on avoiding a hardened separation between an ascetic elite and many married Christians, Jerome's polemical *Against Jovinian* exaggerated the contrast by staking out a position that considered marriage to be in effect bad and virginity good. Inserting himself in the debate between Jovinian and Jerome through the writing of his *On the Good of Marriage*, whose title signals support for the institution, Augustine appears to want to take responsibility for an episcopal flock that consisted of both married and ascetic Christians,[17] making his work the equivalent of what Robert Markus has called a kind of *Against Jerome*.[18]

In short, Augustine came up with a relative hierarchy in which marriage was considered good but virginity still better. Around this same time, he also wrote two treatises dealing with asceticism and the monastic life, as monastic communities were likewise entrusted to his episcopal care, namely *On Holy Virginity* (*De sancta virginitate*, 401 CE) and *On the Work of Monks* (*De opere monachorum*, 400 CE).[19] It is therefore hard to think about marriage in Augustine without taking his positions on virginity and on monasticism into account, making for a more complete civic and ecclesial picture. In *On the Good of Marriage* 24.32, Augustine formulates what would later come to be considered the traditional goods of marriage in the Catholic tradition, namely faithfulness (*fides*), sacrament (*sacramentum*), and offspring (*proles*).[20] More important than these goods, however, is what Clark labels his companionate view in the treatise, including the role of friendship, as she deplores that Augustine did not uphold this view over the full span of his career.

Following Clark's positive assessment of this treatise, one cannot but wonder about the meaning of friendship: is it something between the partners alone or does it serve a larger purpose by representing the disposition of peaceful coexistence between all humans? Mining the rich resource that is *Confessions*, one is tempted to think that Augustine's faithful relationship with a concubine who bore him a son could have shown him the importance of friendship as a noninstitutional but binding bond.[21] Yet his episcopal experience and the pastoral duties involved likely also played a role, as Augustine uses friendship to uphold the validity of marriage in case of childless partners or for partners beyond the childbearing age.[22] While I agree with Clark that *On the Good of Marriage* shows Augustine to have a balanced view, I differ with her reading of Augustine's remarkable statement that sexuality can be used in the service of friendship as referring only to the friendship at large among people in society.[23] Since the intra-marital, social and the extra-marital, societal dimension of friendship are intimately connected in Augustine's view of paradise as shown below, they are nearly impossible to distinguish. Hence, I see no reason to exclude sexuality as also informing and cementing the partners' personal bond of friendship, be they concubines or spouses.[24]

While Clark was after the essence of marriage in Augustine, it seems more useful to talk about its function and utility,[25] given that institutional marriage was not inherently Christian but inherited from both Mosaic law, tightened by Jesus in the gospels to exclude divorce, and Roman law. It was always linked to offspring.[26] As an inherited social institution its position was unstable for the first Christians, however, the more so the more they had an eschatological focus. Two centuries before Augustine, Tertullian of Carthage counseled his wife not to remarry after his death, projecting a vision in which not even death could dissolve their marital bond, even as he deemed marriage at the same time a good that was as dispensable as the society he wanted to leave behind.[27] Paul's ambivalent statement that "it is better to marry than to burn" (1 Cor. 7:9) no doubt further impacted the rise of asceticism in early Christianity, that is, the widespread interest in virginity for men and women, and in permanent widowhood for women.

Given Tertullian's strong eschatological outlook as underlying his tepid embrace of marriage, it is instructive to see that a later Christian thinker like Augustine, inhabiting the same North African region but living in Constantinian times, goes back to Adam and Eve in paradise. He sees the couple planted there by God linked in intimate union, since God made Eve from Adam's rib. We are no longer dealing now only with a personal relationship as in Tertullian, but with a blueprint for society filtered through the prism of paradise. For Augustine, Adam and Eve are the ancestral couple and the progenitors of all human beings: Jews and Gentiles, Romans and Christians.

He considers their bond of kinship and human intimacy not just a social but a societal one. In his opening of *On the Good of Marriage*, Augustine stops short of anointing their paradisaical bond formally as one of marriage just yet, but he clearly considers the relationship of the partners natural, that is, divinely ordained, social, societal, and unbreakable.[28] That he presents the natural/divine and social/societal bond as intertwined is important because it explains why the concepts of gender and creation are so hard to disentangle, as Augustine rarely analyzes the one without engaging the other. At the same time, the paradisaical prism adds the dimension of a vision of *longue durée* absent in the more practical, outright eschatological Tertullian. We could say that Augustine sets Christianity in a new key: the key of paradise as humanity's collective socio-historical past rather than a place of mythical origin. Yet even in changed times Augustine can still surprise us with a half-eschatological comment such that it would be better not to marry, hastening the end time.[29]

For Clark, Augustine's adoption of a reproductive view implied the abrogation of marital friendship, the more apodictically so since it was decreed in paradise. Yet questions about the fate of marital companionship remain. Augustine puts indeed a rather crude end to the centrality of friendship by bluntly stating that if God had wanted to create a friend for Adam, he would have created a second man:

> Or if it was not for help in producing children that a wife was made for the man, then what other help was she made for? . . . (For example, a man would have been a better help for tilling the earth. . . .) The same can be said about companionship, should he grow tired of solitude. How much more agreeably, after all, for conviviality and conversation would two male friends live together on equal terms than man and wife?[30]

Clearly, in his formal exegesis of paradise in Genesis, Augustine gives *biblical* sanction to the relationship of Adam and Eve as a union that *naturally* prioritizes procreation.

Clark's appreciation of companionate marriage may have been bolstered by her study of the correspondence that Jerome and Chrysostom had with female ascetics, which presupposes a form of friendship based on mutual respect.[31] While Augustine's view of friendship at the root of a companionate marriage seemed a viable alternative for a time, his comment on the creation of Eve all but eliminated that option. And yet, the companionate model may have left a more lasting imprint than Clark thought. For while Tertullian heaps the blame for humanity's transgression in paradise on Eve alone,[32] in *City of God* 14.11, Augustine upbraids both Adam and Eve:[33] Eve for her transgression and Adam for the fact that his loyalty to Eve was greater than his obedience to God's commandment. By companionate standards, Adam seems to have been the perfect paradisaical spouse.

FROM CREATION TO GENDER

If we now make the opposite journey, namely from creation to gender, we encounter a similar reaction of disappointment in Augustine in Bernadette Brooten's view that Augustine is aligned with ancient Mediterranean views of immovable nature. In her carefully laid-out article "Nature, Law, and Custom in Augustine's *On the Good of Marriage*," she compares Augustine's classification of sexual acts to the classical scheme laid out by the second century author Artemidoros, whose *The Classification of Dreams* tallies sexual dreams according to the categories of nature, law, and custom (*Oneirokritika* 1.78–80).[34] Brooten is dismayed by the similar pattern of gender subordination found in both authors, as she clearly expected better of Augustine. Her comparative, cross-cultural analysis of *On the Good of Marriage* yields a more negative judgment than Clark, exemplified in the contrast between Augustine's tolerance of polygyny in the patriarchs and his rejection of polyandry.[35] Taking the focus off sexual acts, however, we do well not to overlook Peter Brown's comment about the value of marriage in ancient patronage society. Since free spouses stood like philosophers on one side of political life, they could through their use of *parrhesia* also be one's best and perhaps only "unmotivated friend."[36] The dynamic of valuable trust, though far from creating equal partnership, made for a more lasting and powerful relationship inside marriage than in other, less regulated sexual relationships, as Plutarch makes clear in his *Praecepta conjugalia*.[37]

When comparing the permissibility of certain sex acts in Artimidoros and Augustine Brooten appears to make ancient nature rather than Jewish or Christian creation the determinative criterion. As I have argued elsewhere,[38] in doing so she seems to discount the importance of history for Augustine. Augustine condoned the polygyny of the patriarchs because he deemed the offspring which such polygyny could yield in accelerated fashion important not merely as the fulfillment of the commandment in Gen. 1:28 "Be fruitful and multiply," but because of the need for the Savior to be born. Once the incarnation had occurred, the unfolding of history pivoted. Bearing out this incision, Augustine identifies Christ's birth as the beginning of the sixth "day" of history. In this world-week, Christ's birth marks the starting-point of the last thousand years after which the eternal Sabbath sets in.[39]

Aside from marking a temporal incision the birth of the Savior seems to have had dispositional consequences for Augustine's view of sexuality and procreative marriage, insofar as he is more measured about the need for offspring after Christ's birth. Patriarchal polygyny is no longer needed, or tolerated, though Brooten is correct that there remains a double standard about what is sexually allowed for women vis-à-vis what is permissible conduct for men. Still, while the classification of sexual acts links Artimidoros and Augustine, there is also a noticeable dispositional difference, for example, between Plutarch's "Advice to Bride and Groom" and Augustine's *On the Good of Marriage*, with the latter generally more pastoral in tone.[40] The difference may be due in part to the fact that Augustine, unlike Plutarch and other more prescriptive early Christian texts by Tertullian or Cyprian of Carthage, proceeds through exegetical and moral-theological (self-)reflection. As he situates marriage on a wider spectrum of Christian conduct and comportment, Augustine's tone may well reflect his episcopal experience alongside his personal one.

While Augustine's tone in *On the Good of Marriage* is remarkably companionate and even compassionate, structural shifts in his thought about marriage occur over time, making his sexual views increasingly restrictive. Clark attributes this increased restrictiveness to the impact of the Pelagian controversy.[41] In his recent introduction to Augustine's treatises on marriage and virginity, David Hunter has adopted her approach.[42] Although situating Augustine's thought vis-à-vis the theological controversy in which he was embroiled seems straightforward enough, it potentially occludes important continuities by privileging Augustine's opponents in determining the upshot of his development. Adam's choice to side with the sinful Eve shows that there is no good reason why the focus on procreation in the context of God's creation of woman excludes companionship.

Continuing the discussion in his Genesis commentary that God could have created a second man if he wanted Adam to have a friend, Augustine grapples with the question if and how in that case the equal, male partner could still be a helpmate:

> While if it was expedient that one should be in charge and the other should comply, to avoid a clash of wills disturbing the peace of the household, such an arrangement would have been ensured by one having been made first, the other later, especially if the latter were created from the former, as the female was in fact created. Or would anyone say that God was only able to make a female from the man's rib, and not also a male if he so wished? For these reasons I cannot work out what help a wife could have been made to provide the man with, if you take away the purpose of childbearing.[43]

If two male friends and supposedly equal partners could be in a hierarchical relationship, could not also the reverse be true? That is to say, could there not be a friendship between man and woman despite the hierarchical relationship between them? But friendship is not Augustine's point here. Only a female partner can give Adam offspring, and a male cannot, which is why Augustine embraces procreative marriage. While this seems to justify Clark's label of reproductive marriage, her language draws Augustine uncomfortably into contemporary juridical and political debates on reproductive rights and, via the stress on partner inequality, also on misogyny. Add to this an oft-found miscasting of Pelagius as a tolerant liberal, although in point of fact he was rather the opposite,[44] and we see how Augustine's views can become easily misconstrued as those of a proto-American neoconservative evangelical.

The ripple effect of seeing Augustine's view as one about reproductive rather than procreative marriage is not to be underestimated. In his recent book *Sex and the Constitution*, constitutional law scholar Geoffrey Stone only needs a few brief pages to indict Augustine for turning Western culture against sexual enjoyment. Setting Augustine up as someone "who gave himself up as a young man to lust, an experience that profoundly shaped his later theology," Stone continues by saying that "having dedicated himself to continence, Augustine turned his pen against the temptations of sex."[45] Stone's reading culminates in his view that the sin of Adam and Eve was sexual. Augustine is known to see their sin as pride and not sex, but for Stone "Adam's transgression, he [Augustine] reasoned, had not been one of disobedience, as the ancient Hebrews believed, but one of sex."[46] This leads him to draw the following conclusion:

> Augustine's triumph was unprecedented in the history of man's attitudes about sex. Before Augustine, most Western societies had condemned adultery (at least by wives); some had denounced same-sex sex; and a few had censured fornication. But no Western culture had ever before condemned *all* human sexuality except marital intercourse for the sole purpose of procreation. Every prior Western culture has regarded most forms of sex as natural and properly pleasurable facets of human existence. By early in the fifth century, however, the dominant strand of Christianity left no doubt of its stance: Sexual desire and its fulfillment, in every manifestation, was sinful and must be suppressed.[47]

What Stone fails to grasp is that Augustine seizes on sexuality to portray the human condition as a collectively (rather than individually or personally) sinful one by inscribing it in humanity's origin story of paradise and the fall.[48] It is true that Augustine does not give us a narrative of liberation, which is what Stone seems to have wanted him to do, as liberation is the key in which much postmodern scholarship on gender and sexuality is set. That he does not even do so when he retroactively describes pre-fallen sexuality is because for Augustine paradise is the beginning of a collective journey. We find Augustine even go so far as to say that in terms of their hope for the future, Adam and Eve were not fully happy in paradise, since they were uncertain of their destiny.[49]

In another ripple effect of a skewed reading, we find literary scholar Andrea Nightingale depicting Augustine as having cast a long shadow over the history of Western culture by denying humans the possibility to find pleasure in created life. Her book *Once Out of Nature. Augustine on Time and the Body* takes much broader aim than at sexuality alone. On her reading of Augustine, Adam and Eve's life in paradise did not even take place in ordinary time, since time, according to Augustine, only started after they were ejected from paradise. Adam and Eve's paradisaical selves were in a timeless state of transhuman existence, to be attained again when our created, mortal bodies will be transformed in heaven. Although sexuality comes in only indirectly for Nightingale, its role in Augustine plays out in three significant ways. First, it marks the rupture from life inside paradise, where Adam and Eve were transhuman and sex was passionless. Second, procreation affirms humanity's fall and therewith its ties to temporality and the food chain, that is, the afflicted way of life and death on this earth that Augustine would like to see suppressed.[50] Third, since transhumanism is humanity's original state in paradise and its final one in heaven, Augustine's aim for ordinary life must be to come as closely to it as possible, which makes him a sexually repressive advocate of asceticism. In line with her broader take on created life in Augustine, Nightingale states: "One must give praise for the natural world as God's creation but not settle down in it as a proper abode. The true dwelling for humans is elsewhere."[51] "Elsewhere" as a place of transhumanism would mean a world without sin and without sexuality.

AUGUSTINE AND GREGORY OF NYSSA: A COMPARISON

After this tour d'horizon it is hard to see Augustine's position on creation and gender as anything but deeply fraught. The gender hierarchy of Adam and Eve is fixed and driven by the urge for procreation rather than friendship. There seems to be no licensed enjoyment of human sexuality outside paradise, and even inside paradise sexuality seemed to be functional rather than pleasurable. The increasing drive for asceticism inside marriage reflects Augustine's desire to emulate that lost paradisical state.

Nightingale sees several theological factors at play in Augustine's negative position on nature and sexuality:

The incarnation and resurrection of Christ mark a triumph over nature and death. By mortifying his flesh through rigorous ascetic practices, Augustine looks forward to a perfect, unearthly body. As he claims, God will take all human bodily matter directly out of the food chain and use it to fashion the resurrected body. In short, God will create a transhuman body that dwells outside time and nature.[52]

Taking the incarnation likewise as my own point of departure, I want to cast Augustine's position on gender and creation in a rather different theological light. In doing so, I will forego the discussion of individual claims about Augustine, such as Clark's view that a marriage built on procreation can no longer be companionate, Nightingale's position that time only started outside of paradise and that Adam and Eve were transhuman, and Stone's dismay at Augustine's early infatuation with and subsequent dour suppression of sexual pleasure. I cannot help but think that Stone's problem stems in part from Augustine's unique position as a late antique author who wrote reflexively about his own sexuality, even if he did so in service of his developing view that sexuality, rather than, say, rationality, best defines the universal human condition. Given that Augustine's world was Roman, but also Christian, he developed a Christian sexual ethic for the entire world, though he was not able to wield political power and did not write in a prescriptive vein. Instead, I compare Augustine with Gregory of Nyssa to make clear how their respective assessments of the incarnation and its effects cause them to have a different take on the issue of marriage and virginity, with Gregory the more eschatological thinker and Augustine the earthlier and more political thinker. What sets them apart is not their position on institutional marriage or gender hierarchy *per se*, but rather Augustine's strong embrace of earthly life as the life to be lived by all Christians within the confines of a comprehensively Christian society. Augustine's horizontal and temporal conception of society, as differentiated from Gregory's vertically oriented ideal of eschatological perfection, distinguishes his view as one which Robert Markus aptly labeled his "defense of Christian mediocrity."[53]

What Gregory and Augustine share over and against the theological view attributed to Augustine by Nightingale is that they see incarnation (and resurrection) *not* as a triumph over nature *but* precisely as an embrace of it, the adoption of human nature by God. This is an important point insofar as neither thinker has a problem with materiality or with bodily physicality per se. But this shared point of unity is also where their views begin to diverge, whereby Gregory privileges the rational over the sensible. We get a good sense of Gregory's layered and finely calibrated anthropology, in which he combines the allegorical legacy of Origen with the incarnational theology of Athanasius of Alexandria, from a trio of works written closely together in the early 380s, i.e., his *On the Making of Man*, his *Treatise on Virginity* and his *Life of Macrina*. Subtext of all three treatises is his projection of an anti-Arian view of human life marked by the motif of the imitation of Christ, who was seen as fully divine but incarnated in a human body. To the extent that Gregory continues the allegorical reading of Genesis found in Philo and Origen, he clings to the symbolism—still found in Ambrose—whereby Adam represents the mind (*nous*) and Eve the senses (*aesthesis*). His androgynous humanity would through angelic multiplication have attained the perfect number of God-intended souls. When the fall, i.e., the rebellion of the sensible against the rational, derailed this mode of angelic multiplication, God gave humans corporeal bodies to procreate like the animals until the perfect number of souls would be reached.[54]

Through Christ's incarnation and subsequent resurrection humanity is redeemed, as Christ's embrace of human nature effectively affirms that nature. But there is more. Although Christ's redemption does not restore humanity's angelic mode of procreation, it empowers Christians to choose another lifestyle. In response to Christ's *descent* from divinity into humanity, i.e., his incarnation, ascetics can make a proleptic eschatological *ascent* and attain the passionless tranquility of the resurrected life. This is the meaning of virginity for Gregory, a life of virtue, in which the passions and turmoil of ordinary life are absorbed into a higher state of post-resurrection serenity. Inspired by his brother Basil of Caesarea's anti-Arian agenda, Gregory styled virgins as living testimonies to the resurrected Christ, whose presence would nourish and visibly sustain the Christian community.[55]

Although suspected of having been married himself, Gregory heaps exorbitant rhetorical praise on the ascetic life. By way of contrast to the serene life of virtue, he tenderly describes the all too real travails of married partners, who can be plunged into grief by the death of a child or of whom the older, male spouse can leave his young and inexperienced wife vulnerable to a mismatch upon his early death. Gregory clearly prefers virginity to marriage, both in terms of its otherworldly horizon and its avoidance of marital vulnerability. Contrary to Peter Brown, I see this preference in the end not as a defensive move to escape institutional marriage as tainted by mortality but as an added positive choice for Christians in the wake of Christ's resurrection.[56] Having made that choice, Gregory's sister Macrina proved indeed able to transcend her gender. When she was on her deathbed, she was the teacher in their final conversation, while Gregory succumbs to uncontrollable bouts of lamentation.[57]

Augustine's position on sin, gender, and sexuality differs from Gregory, insofar as he moves away from allegorizing of paradise, still found in Ambrose, thereby wiping out the complex Platonic metaphysical scheme supporting it. For him, Adam and Eve are gendered human beings who lived in a historical paradise, in which the normal rules of physics and biology were obtained, and no angelic multiplication was ever considered. The intellectual liberation lodged in Augustine's literal exegesis should not be underestimated. Stripped of its mythological allure, the creation of humanity became a new blank canvas on which Augustine could project the direct prehistory of his own Roman-Christian society. It is from that perspective that we find Augustine keenly interested in paradise in the *City of God*.

Augustine's attention to historical origin also changes the impact of incarnation. In Augustine Christ is consistently called the *mediator*, who connects heaven and earth, God and humanity. He is no longer the one whose descent generates an ascetic ascent, giving virgins the ability to overcome their gender and achieve angelic status. Instead, the incarnate Christ leads the way on the pilgrimage of life with all Christians in tow, married folk and virgins alike. As Augustine says in *On Holy Virginity* 28.28: "No doubt even married people can follow those footsteps; even if they do not put their feet exactly in the same footprints, at least they walk the same path."[58] Ascetics thus have a relative, not a qualitative lead over married Christians.

While Augustine adopts a celibate life for himself, he departs from Gregory (and also Ambrose, it would appear) in that he no longer considers the life of virginity the model Christian life. His is a different mindset, not animated by the *Song of Songs*, so starkly associated with the ascetic eros for the Bridegroom Christ, but with the fecund foliage of physical paradise. While in Gregory's *Life of Macrina*, she can be seen to have spiritual offspring, those are not the terms in which Augustine thinks. Fertility is the offspring God intended in Gen. 1: 28: "Go forth and multiply." As a mission rather than an imperative, it applies to humans as it does to the other animals, and as such connects marriage with procreation and creation. In *On the Good of Marriage*, Augustine was still uncertain about Adam and Eve's marital status in paradise, while Jerome famously changed his position to see their marriage take place in paradise but after rather than before the fall.[59] In *City of God*, Augustine considers their married status beyond dispute.

To see Adam and Eve as married in paradise legitimizes their union and sanctions any sexual relations they might have had there as an integral part of human sociality. They even might have had children, as a further sign that the human story is underway. Clearly, the fall has changed the nature of sexuality, such that Augustine is led to give a reversed, passionless description of sex-before-the-fall in paradise in *City of God* 14.23–24. But the procreative, sexual bond of Adam and Eve remains constitutive of their mini-society and as such also paradigmatic for human society at large. Since Adam and Eve are biologically human, the chasm between life inside and life outside paradise is less dramatic than in Gregory's scenario of a fall from angelic to animal status. Instead, their expulsion is experienced as displacement.

Keen on avoiding Pelagian circularity, whereby faith in Christ would restore Adam to a state of innocent freedom in paradise, Augustine holds that, after Adam's fall, no one is able to avoid sin. This is best considered an injunction to embrace earthly life in such a way that one's life merits sanctification. Sexuality becomes coopted as an essential part of the restraint that needs to be exercised in post-paradisaical life. The task of the pilgrim, of both man and woman in their married, hierarchical, and sexual relationship, is to jointly march onwards to the *civitas dei*.

CONCLUSION: BETWEEN EXEGESIS AND NATURALIZATION, WITH A COMMENT ON FOUCAULT'S LIBIDINIZATION

Yet the question remains why the story of Adam and Even in paradise, even if we see its precise meaning modulate over time from *On the Good of Marriage* to *The Literal Commentary on Genesis* to *The City of God*, seems to only gain in prominence for Augustine. Since it is bound to give rise to misunderstandings, the story keeps haunting our image of Augustine. The gender hierarchy of Adam and Eve and Eve's uncomfortably close association with her procreative role are an integral part of its problematic nature. To develop a concluding perspective on Augustine's attachment to the story, I will revisit the paradise vignette one final time.

One aspect of the story's endurance is no doubt its scriptural origin. In his article "Tyconius' Mystic Rules and the Rules of Augustine" in the volume *Augustine and the Bible*, author Robert Kugler sheds light on the different uses of scripture that set the former North-African Donatist Tyconius, author of the *Book of Rules*, apart from Augustine, who incorporated those rules at the end of the third book of his *On Christian Teaching*.[60] Their difference hinges on the meaning of prophecy. Whereas Tyconius treats the Bible as a live oracle as he discerns its prophetic message about those belonging to the one true church and those outside of it, Augustine treats the Bible as a privileged literary text, an objectified voice of God in need of hermeneutic interpretation for a church living in a mixed society (*civitas permixtum*).[61] As Brian Stock clarifies, Augustine is the first author whom we know to have converted based on reading (cf. "Pick up and read"), a command which led him to take up a scriptural text. There is a marked difference between how Saint Antony converted, who heard the scriptures as he was walking by a church with its door ajar, and how Augustine did so.[62] Augustine, in the words of Stock, is a reader and insofar as that means that he interprets texts, he also fashions and reforms human self and society in and through narrative.[63]

Putting the comparison with Antony and Tyconius aside, I want to underscore how Augustine increasingly embraced the creation story in Genesis as a charter for Christians, a *magna carta* for the church as a pilgrimage community (*civitas peregrina*), with Adam and Eve as the progenitors of the human race and their relationship, which was meant to produce offspring according to the divine command in Gen. 1:28, a married and, while intimate, also hierarchical one. Given the overriding dominance of this larger framework, there is in Augustine, unlike in Gregory of Nyssa and other patristic authors, no qualitative privileging of virginity. Neither is there the same deep erotic drive associated with the perfectionism that is inherent in the ascetic ideal. Ambrose may serve as an interesting counterpoise to Augustine here. He embodies the same ideals of virginity we encountered in Gregory, couched in the erotic language of the *Song of Songs*. But as a bishop he was faced with the stark reality that his attempt to coopt virgins for his episcopal retinue was not as successful as he might have hoped, which prompted him to make the odd and rather self-contradictory statement that the more virgins will gather around the bishop, the more the land will be blessed with offspring.[64] Such acrobatic moves are no longer found in Augustine, who strives for a unified Christian church that can encompass and accommodate the entire human race. This is aptly summarized by Markus:

> His reflection on human sexuality was prompted by meditating on the text of Genesis, and it provided the paradigm in which he diagnosed the rupture between God and man and within man himself in his fallen state. This involved a rehabilitation of the flesh. The whole person, body and soul, restored from revolt to concord, was to exhibit holiness. And finally, this involved a rehabilitation of marriage: never again would it be possible, after Augustine's rebuttal of the charge of Manicheism, to write of marriage in the manner of Jerome. Equally, however, it would be harder to write of virginity in the manner of Ambrose or Gregory of Nyssa.[65]

Markus's view of the rehabilitation of the flesh in Augustine as the opposite of Nightingale's idea of incarnation as a triumph over nature indicates the plight of the pilgrim church. Yet even if we see the paradise vignette as a *magna carta* that keeps open the possibility of a redeemed life, it is important to realize that Augustine's retrospective take on paradisaical marriage gives us a chastened view, one that befits the church as a pilgrim in the world. The obvious tension between what some modern interpreters imagined should be a sex life of near-unlimited pleasure in paradise before the fall and Augustine's version of a married yet largely chaste paradisaical life requires further comment.

I see two contemporaneous historical circumstances weighing down on any kind of presumed innocence of biblical paradise in Augustine. First, Virginia Burrus holds that naming the horizon of human becoming in the terms of Father, Son, and Holy Spirit, and to do so after Nicea's foregrounding of Christ as "begotten, not made," constructs both "an idealized masculinity and a masculinized transcendence." It also leads to an erasure of the female.[66] To this we may, next, add Elizabeth Clark's claim that the work of fourth century biblical exegetes who tried to integrate asceticism and marriage had an adverse impact on the hierarchy within marriage:

> Those commentators who unify the Old Testament and the New, the Hebrew past and the Christian present, also link marriage and ascetic renunciation on a continuum of Christian practice. Yet if marriage is here "redeemed," "difference" has been displaced onto a hierarchy within marriage, a hierarchy that ranks husband over wife.[67]

It strikes me as eminently plausible that the hierarchy of man and wife became similarly solidified in Augustine. As the indissolubility of marriage as a New Testament counsel is added to Genesis' goal of procreation, paradisaical marriage takes on an ever more paradigmatic and inflexible character.

Augustine never strays far from the book of Genesis, as the paradise motif continues to accompany him. There are other important aspects to the gender discussion in Augustine, such as that women are considered less the image of God than men in his Trinitarian thought,[68] but these can be countered by more positive views and do not seem decisive. Among Augustine's positive distinctive features is the idea that human beings retain the character of both God's image and likeness after the fall, whereas in the Origenist tradition the likeness would only be restored after the resurrection. The reason is apparently not Augustine's different notion of sin or grace, but rather his sense that an image without likeness is not credible, even if both image and likeness need reform after the fall.[69]

Although Augustine models married life on Adam and Eve in paradise, it is as if with their expulsion from paradise any memory of a state of pleasure has evaporated. Partly in response to Pelagius, Augustine concentrates increasingly on the need of the *civitas peregrina* to use life outside paradise as a time for growth and sanctification, with the aspects of time and history taking center stage, including humanity's lack of control over it. Nightingale's claim that Augustine wants to subject fallen human life to an ascetic suppression of desires may be too strong, but the moderation with which the Christian pilgrim must style her life according to the values of the City of God weighs down increasingly on that life. It is here that I see the tensions around gender difference in Augustine play out. They flare up not just because the wife must humbly obey her spouse in an increasingly habituated Christian polity, but also because in his later texts Augustine sees an increasingly diminished role for sexuality, thereby further endangering spousal intimacy. While sexuality was never itself the cause of the fall, concupiscence becomes operationalized in the fall and once deployed, overshadows the role of sexuality after the fall. Its effects range far beyond sexuality alone, for the earthly city as a whole sighs under the dominion of the lust to dominate (*libido dominandi*).[70] Insofar as these effects can be traced back to sexual concupiscence, they further conflate the story of paradise and the fall with the ills of fallen human society.

To the extent that sexuality intersects with other types of libidinous behavior, as Augustine's *City of God* makes abundantly clear, its portrayal in paradise falls in more and more with a *naturalization* of marriage, the impact of which is increasingly seen as morally charged. That is, Augustine's retrospective view collapses into a prescriptive view of the kind of married life he would like to see adopted by Christians around him and ahead of him.

This raises again the question of Christian eschatology as one on which our final judgment of Augustine may hinge. Does he indeed submit the world to a repressive sexual regime through his imposition of otherworldly values on this life, or does the disciplined conduct through which Augustine aims at moderation point to a temporal way forward for Christians living in the mixed society while still conveying eschatological hope? In his *Confessions of the Flesh*, Michel Foucault zooms in on marriage in Augustine as an area for juridical relations. He does so based on Augustine's operationalization of sexual concupiscence, which for him makes Augustine focused on the *use* of marriage. While Foucault has elsewhere been criticized for overlooking the importance of eschatology,[71] that is not the note on which I want to close. Neither do I disagree with his sense of the libidinization of sexuality, as Foucault rightly calls out Augustine's thought in *City of God* as providing a theoretical matrix for future developments.[72]

Foucault states that "with the idea of concupiscence as an evil, it was possible to combine, under the same theme of spiritual combat, the exercise of virginity and the practice of marriage." While I concur with Burrus that patristic thought after Nicea became increasingly focused on the male and with Clark that the telescoping of marriage and asceticism in the fourth century leads to greater hierarchy within marriage, I do not see the role of virginity in Augustine as quite on a par with marriage. The archetypal motif of Adam and Eve as married partners in paradise regulating the life of spouses in the *civitas peregrina* has no exegetical counterpart in a founding vignette of the ascetic life.[73] Although Augustine adopted celibacy for himself, without solid roots in the exegesis of Genesis its eschatological charge is reduced, and its theological eroticism is lessened. Instead, we see him follow a pastoral-political path that accommodates the life of Christians inside the *civitas permixta*, as he instructs them on their pilgrimage without undue regard for (ecclesial or imperial) hierarchy or privileged lifestyle.

NOTES

1. One of the first such studies on Augustine of a more general nature is Kim Power, *Veiled Desire: Augustine on Women* (New York: Continuum, 1994).

2. See Elizabeth A. Clark, *Jerome, Chrysostom, and Friends* (New York and Toronto: Edwin Mellen Press, 1979), esp. ch. 2 "Friendship Between the Sexes: Classical Theory and Christian Practice," 35–106.

3. The scholars whose work I discuss, Elizabeth Clark and Kari Børresen, worked to my knowledge independently, respectively in late antiquity and theology. Nevertheless, their work gravitates to similar conclusions.

4. See Kari Elisabeth Børresen, *Subordination and Equivalence: The Nature and Role of Woman in Augustine and Thomas Aquinas* (Kampen: Kok Pharos, 1995). See p. 133 for Augustine on marriage, p. 281 for Thomas on the sacrament of marriage, and pp. 304–5 for a conclusive statement on Thomas. Børresen appears to argue that Augustine sets a tone that also obtains for Thomas, but that in Thomas there is more equivalence between marital partners due to the remedial function of the sacrament. For Thomas, as for Augustine, marriage remains on the lowest sacramental rung.

5. See, respectively, Bernadette Brooten, "Nature, Law, and Custom in Augustine's *On the Good of Marriage*," in *Walk in the Ways of Wisdom: Essays in Honor of E. Schüssler-Fiorenza*, ed. S. Matthews, C. Briggs Kittredge, and M. Johnson-Debaufre (New York: Trinity Press International, 2003), 181–93; and Andrea Nightingale, *Once Out of Nature: Augustine on Time and the Body* (Chicago: University of Chicago Press, 2011).

6. For Augustine's position on nature more broadly, see my chapter "Creation and the Hexaemeron in Augustine," in *Thinking Nature and the Nature of Thinking. From Eriugena to Emerson* (Stanford: Stanford University Press, 2020), 79–108.

7. I have analyzed what I call "the Augustinian surplus" in my article "Between Praise and Appraisal: Medieval Guidelines for the Assessment of Augustine's Intellectual Legacy," *Augustinian Studies* 43, no. 1 (2012): 201–18.

8. The best-known treatment of Augustine's view of time on *Confessions* 11 is Paul Ricoeur, *Time and Narrative, Vol. 1*, trans. K. McLaughlin and D. Pellauer (Chicago: University of Chicago Press, 1984), 5–30. For the most profound treatment of time in Augustine, including a criticism of Ricoeur, see M. B. Pranger, *Eternity's Ennui: Temporality, Perseverance and Voice in Augustine and Western Literature* (Leiden: Brill, 2010), 35–54.

9. See Peter Brown, *The Body and Society: Men, Women, and Sexual Renunciation in Early Christianity* (New York: Columbia University Press, 1988), 285–304.

10. Michel Foucault mentions that Gregory, Chrysostom, and Augustine all see the "image of God" linked to the soul and not the body. See Michael Foucault, *Confessions of the Flesh: The History of Sexuality, Vol. 4*, trans. R. Hurley (New York: Pantheon Books, 2021), 144 n. 39, citing *De Genesi ad litteram* 3.22.34 in

support. However, Augustine does not call the body "the mirror of the mirror," as does Gregory in *De hominis opificio* 12.10–11, nor does he see likeness (as in image and likeness) only restored at the end of time. See on this n. 67 and 68 below. Also, in *Confessions* 1.1.1 and elsewhere Augustine refers to himself as *aliqua portio creaturae tuae* ("a little piece of your creation"), and so could presumably any woman, bringing out the leveling effect of nature.

11. On the fact that Augustine did not write on nature other than through the genre of exegesis, which differentiates from Origen and others, and my subsequent claim that Eriugena's early medieval *Periphyseon* is best seen as the natural theology that Augustine never wrote, see Otten, "Creation and the Hexaemeron in Augustine," 84–89.

12. See Elaine Pagels, *Adam, Eve, and the Serpent* (New York: Random House, 1988), 125. Commenting on the dominant influence of Augustinian teaching throughout western Christendom, she states that "it is Augustine's theology of the fall that made the uneasy alliance between the Catholic churches and imperial power palatable—not only justifiable but necessary—for the majority of Catholic Christians."

13. See Nightingale, *Once Out of Nature: Augustine on Time and the Body*, 3: "In Augustine's view, humans are extraterrestrials who have 'fallen' on a land where they do not belong. For humans, earth is a place of unbelonging."

14. Elizabeth Clark, "Adam's Only Companion: Augustine and the Early Christian Debate on Marriage," *Recherches Augustiniennes* 21 (1986): 139–62.

15. See Augustine, *The Literal Meaning of Genesis*, in *On Genesis*, trans. Edmund Hill, O.P., vol. I/13 *The Works of Saint Augustine: A Translation for the 21st Century*, ed. John E. Rotelle, O.S.A. (Hyde Park: New City Press, 2002), 380.

16. For my own earlier takes on this theme, see "Augustine on Marriage, Monasticism and the Community of the Church," *Theological Studies* 59 (1998) 385–405; "The Long Shadow of Human Sin: Augustine on Adam, Eve, and the Fall," in *Out of Paradise: Eve and Adam and Their Interpreters,* ed. B. E. J. H. Becking and S. A. Hennecke (Sheffield: Sheffield Phoenix Press, 2010), 29–49, and "Women in Early Christianity: Incarnational Hermeneutics in Tertullian and Augustine," in *Hermeneutics, Scriptural Politics, and Human Rights Between Text and Context*, ed. B. de Gaay Fortman, K. Martens, and M.A. Mohamed Salih (New York: Palgrave Macmillan, 2010), 219–35.

17. Augustine was ordained a priest in 391CE and created bishop of Hippo Regius in North Africa in 395 CE. On the integration of the married and ascetic lifestyles, see below n. 66.

18. See Robert A. Markus, *The End of Ancient Christianity* (Cambridge: Cambridge University Press, 1990), 45–62.

19. *On the Good of Marriage* (under the new title *On the Excellence of Marriage*, derived from Augustine's *Retractations*, which I have not here adopted) and *On Holy Virginity* are both translated by Ray Kearney in *Marriage and Virginity*, vol. I/9 *The Works of Saint Augustine: A Translation for the 21st Century*, ed. John E. Rotelle, O.S.A. (Hyde Park: New City Press, 1999/2005). *On the Work of Monks* is not included in this collection but *On the Good of Widowhood*, written around 414, is.

20. See Augustine, *On the Good of Marriage*, 56–57. See further Clark, "Adam's Only Companion," 140 n. 5 on the papal encyclical *Casti Connubii* (1930) as structured around the three goods of marriage.

21. The anonymity of Augustine's partner has given rise to much speculation. For a complete perspective, see Margaret M. Miles, "Not Nameless but Unnamed: The Woman Torn from Augustine's Side," in her *Rereading Historical Theology: Before, During, and After Augustine* (Eugene: Cascade Books, 2008), 127–48. Miles's article has insightful comments on *On the Good of Marriage*.

22. Augustine, *On the Good of Marriage*, 3.3 and 15.

23. Clark, "Adam's Only Companion," 153.

24. See Otten, "Marriage, Monasticism and the Community of the Church," 399–400.

25. See on this also my discussion of Foucault in the conclusion below.

26. See Augustine, *On the Good of Marriage*, 24.32; 57: "The value of marriage, therefore, for all races and all people, lies in the objective of procreation . . ."

27. See Tertullian, *To His Wife* (*Ad uxorem*) 1.7. 4 and II.1, as well as my discussion in Otten, "Tertullian's Rhetoric of Redemption: Flesh and Embodiment in *De carne Christi* and *De resurrectione mortuorum*," *Studia Patristica* 65 (2013): 339–40.

28. Augustine, *On the Good of Marriage*, 1.1–2.2; 33–34.

29. See Augustine, *On the Good of Marriage*, 24.32; 57: "In this age, however, it is certainly better and holier not to have children physically, and so to keep oneself free from any activity of that kind, and to be subject spiritually to one man, Christ."

30. See Augustine, *The Literal Meaning of Genesis*, 9.5.9; 380.

31. See Clark, *Jerome, Chrysostom, and Friends*, ch. 2 "Friendship Between the Sexes: Classical Theory and Christian Practice," 35–106.

32. See e.g., *On the Dress of Women* (*De cultu feminarum*) 1.1, where Tertullian accuses Eve of bringing death into the world and encourages all women to tear their clothes and wear ashes on their head as a sign of mourning. See on this Otten, "Tertullian's Rhetoric of Redemption," 332.

33. See Augustine, *The City of God*, trans. and intro. William Babcock, vol. I/6–7 *The Works of Saint Augustine: A Translation for the 21st Century*, ed. Boniface Ramsey (Hyde Park: New City Press, 2012–13), 117–18.

34. Brooten, "Nature, Law, and Custom in Augustine's *On the Good of Marriage*," 181–93.

35. Augustine, *On the Good of Marriage*, 17.20.

36. Brown, *The Body and Society*, 15.

37. See Plutarch, *Advice to Bride and Groom*, vol. 2 *Moralia*, trans. Frank Cole Babbitt (Cambridge: Harvard University Press, 1928), 299–343.

38. See my "Women in Early Christianity: Incarnational Hermeneutics in Tertullian and Augustine," 228–32.

39. See Augustine, *City of God*, 22.30; 554. After the sixth age God will rest, and humanity will rest in him. The seventh day will then be followed by an eighth day consecrated by the resurrection.

40. There are beautiful passages in Plutarch but also more concerning ones, see e.g., ch. 14: "Just as lines and surfaces, in mathematical parlance, have no motion of

their own but only in conjunction with the bodies to which they belong, so the wife ought to have no feeling of her own, but she should join with her husband in seriousness and sportiveness and in soberness and laughter."

41. See Elizabeth Clark, ed., *St. Augustine on Marriage and Sexuality* (Washington, D.C.: Catholic University of America Press, 1996). Three of the four chapters with selections from Augustine's writings on marriage and sexuality interpret them in the context of, respectively, his anti-Manicheism, the ascetic debates, and his anti-Pelagianism.

42. See the "Introduction" by David Hunter to *Marriage and Virginity*, trans. Ray Kearney, vol. I/9 *The Works of Saint Augustine: A Translation for the 21st Century*, ed. John E. Rotelle, O.S.A. (Hyde Park: New City Press, 1999/2005), 24 n. 1.

43. See Augustine, *The Literal Meaning of Genesis*, 9.5.9; 380.

44. On Pelagius, see Peter Brown, *Augustine of Hippo: A Biography, A New Edition with an Epilogue* (Berkeley and Los Angeles: University of California Press, 2000), ch. 29 "Pelagius and Pelagianism," 340–53, and Markus, *End of Ancient Christianity*, 43: "For Pelagius and his followers Christianity is a demand for moral ardour and unceasing struggle with inertia: 'it is no better to do nothing than to do wickedly.'"

45. See Geoffrey R. Stone, *Sex and the Constitution: Sex, Religion, and Law from America's Origins to the Twenty-First Century* (London and New York: W.W. Norton & Company, 2017), 17–18.

46. Stone does not say outright that Augustine saw sex as the cause of the fall but by collapsing cause and consequence he implies it with statements as the one cited. On the danger of this, see Foucault, *Confessions of the Flesh*, 273. It bears repeating that the sin of Adam and Eve was disobedience out of pride, and the infliction with concupiscence and hence sexual lust was the consequence of their fall and could so become what Foucault terms a medium for actualizing the original sin in every man.

47. Stone, *Sex and the Constitution*, 23. Stone is remarkably light on Paul's condemnation of same-sex acts and does not discuss Plutarch's *Praecepta conjugalia*. He engages Augustine through general secondary literature.

48. The paradise story is Augustine's most powerful narrative vignette indicative of human brokenness. He uses other tropes as well such as the restless heart or life in the region of unlikeness, which is derived from the parable of the prodigal son.

49. See Augustine, *City of God*, 11.12; 14.

50. On the fall and earthly time see, Nightingale, *Once Out of Nature*, 38–42.

51. Nightingale, *Once Out of Nature*, 6.

52. Nightingale, *Once Out of Nature*, 7.

53. Markus, *End of Ancient Christianity*, 45.

54. For a detailed exposition of how Gregory parses the exegesis of Gen.1:27, see J. Warren Smith, *Passion and Paradise: Human and Divine Emotion in the Thought of Gregory of Nyssa* (New York: Crossroad, 2004), 28–47.

55. On Basil's anti-Arian program, see Brown, *Body and Society*, 285–304.

56. Contrary to Brown I do not see the negative upshot of marriage and mortality as driving the choice for virginity but see it as a positive reaction to Christ's (incarnation and) resurrection emerging from Athanasius's incarnational theology. For a fascinating comparison between Judith Butler's gender performativity and

Gregory's virginity, see Sarah Coakley, "The Eschatological Body: Gender, Transformation, and God," in *Powers and Submissions: Spirituality, Philosophy and Gender* (Oxford: Blackwell, 2002), 153–67. Coakley considers Butler more tied to gender binaries in her attempt to subvert them than Gregory but sharing with him a push for an eschatological horizon. In Gregory's case, this leads to a submission of desire whereby gender roles are upended, and the ascetic life generates a process of self-transformation in the divine.

57. See Gregory of Nyssa, *The Life of Saint Macrina*, trans. Kevin Corrigan (Eugene: Wipf and Stock, 2001), 39–44. On the fascinating Cappadocian family relations between Basil, Gregory, and Macrina, with repercussions for the reading of various of their texts, see Philip Rousseau, *Basil of Caesarea* (Berkeley: University of California Press, 1994), 1–26.

58. Augustine, *On Holy Virginity*, 85–86.

59. Pagels, *Adam, Eve and the Serpent*, 93–94.

60. See Robert A. Kugler, "Tyconius' Mystic Rules and the Rules of Augustine," in *Augustine and the Bible*, ed. and trans. Pamela Bright (Notre Dame: Notre Dame University Press, 1986), 129–48. For a more elaborate take on Tyconius's prophetic rules, see Pamela Bright, *The Book of Rules of Tyconius: Its Purpose and Inner Logic* (Notre Dame: Notre Dame University Press, 1989).

61. See Kugler, "Tyconius' Mystic Rules and the Rules of Augustine," 142–43.

62. I was first made aware of this by Charles Hallisey, "The Surprise of Scripture's Advice," in *Religious Identity and the Problem of Historical Foundation: The Foundational Character of Authoritative Sources in the History of Christianity and Judaism*, ed. Judith Frishman, Willemien Otten, and Gerard Rouwhorst (Leiden: Brill, 2004), 28–29, with reference to *Confessions* 8.6. Hallisey makes various points here, one that Augustine wants to have the direct impact of scripture as in Antony who hears it. Hallisey derives another point from W.C. Smith, *What is Scripture? A Comparative Approach* (Minneapolis: Augsburg Fortress Press, 1993), 34–35, about the capaciousness of premodern exegesis, which does not see the text as content but uses it as a lens to read the meaning of life more broadly.

63. See Brian Stock, *Augustine the Reader: Meditation, Self-Knowledge and the Ethics of Interpretation* (Cambridge: The Belknap Press of Harvard University, 1996), 101 (referenced in Hallisey, "The Surprise of Scripture's Advice," 29): "We proceed from one Life, which is a text to be read (*legendum*), to another, which is a life to be lived: the text informs the life, as discipline informs conduct."

64. See on this W. Otten, "Earthly Christianity between Divine Promise and Earthly Politics," in *Religious Identity and the Invention of Tradition*, ed. J.W. van Henten and A.W.J. Houtepen (Assen: Royal van Gorcum, 2001), 60–83, esp. 80–83 with reference to Ambrose, *De virginitate*, 7.36 and to Neil McLynn, *Ambrose of Milan: Church and Court in a Christian Capital* (Berkeley: University of California Press, 1994), 53–68.

65. See Markus, *The End of Ancient Christianity*, 62.

66. See Virginia Burrus, *"Begotten, Not Made:" Conceiving Manhood in Late Antiquity* (Stanford: Stanford University Press, 2000), 185, 189.

67. See Elizabeth A. Clark, *Reading Renunciation: Asceticism and Scripture in Early Christianity* (Princeton: Princeton University Press, 1998), 154. See on this also my article "Creation and Gender: A Theological Appraisal" in *The Cambridge Companion to Christianity and the Environment*, ed. A. Hampton (Cambridge: Cambridge University Press, 2022), 303–18.

68. See above n. 10. See also Power, *Veiled Desire*, 135–57.

69. See R. A. Markus, "Marius Victorinus and Augustine," in *The Cambridge History of Later Greek and Early Medieval Philosophy*, ed. A. H. Armstrong (Cambridge: Cambridge University Press, 1967), 360–61, referenced in Stock, *Augustine the Reader*, 17. Charles Kannengiesser has argued that the Origenist position does not hold for Athanasius. See C. Kannengiesser, "Athanasius and Traditional Christology," *Theological Studies* 34 (1973): 109, reprinted in idem, *Arius and Athanasius* (Hampshire: Variorum, 1991).

70. See Augustine, *City of God*, Preface. See further Brown, *Augustine of Hippo*, 326–27.

71. See Michel Senellart, "Michel Foucault: une autre histoire du christianisme?" *Bulletin du centre d'études médiévales d'Auxerre* | BUCEMA Hors-série n° 7 | 2013. Les nouveaux horizons de l'ecclésiologie: du discours clérical à la science du social, 1–17 at 3–7.

72. See Foucault, *Confessions of the Flesh*, 283.

73. The example comes to mind of the three men in the furnace in Dan. 3, kept cool and liberated by God, which Augustine cites in *Holy Virginity* 56.57; 105 and in *On the Work of Monks*, in *Saint Augustine: Treatises on Various Subjects*, trans. Sister Mary Sarah Muldowney, R.S.M. et al., vol. 16 *The Fathers of the Church*, ed. Roy J. Deferrari (Washington, D.C.: Catholic University of America Press, 1952/2002), 27.35; 381. See Otten, "Augustine on Marriage, Monasticism, and the Community of the Church," 397 n. 23.

PART III

Language, Speech, and Exegesis

Chapter 6

Beyond God the Father
Augustine's Feminine Images of God and His Concerns for Human Women

Jennifer Hockenbery

In 1973, Mary Daly published *Beyond God the Father: Toward a Philosophy of Women's Liberation.* The first chapter of this book begins:

> The Biblical and popular image of God as a great patriarch in heaven, rewarding and punishing according to his mysterious and seemingly arbitrary will, has dominated the imagination of millions over thousands of years. The symbol of the Father God, spawned in the human imagination is sustained as plausible by patriarchy, has in turn rendered service to this type of society by making its mechanisms for the oppression of women appear right and fitting. If God in "his" heaven is a father ruling "his" people, then it is in the "nature" of things and according to divine plan and the order of the universe that society be male-dominated.[1]

Daly's argument in this book was that patriarchy was bolstered by masculine images of the divine suggesting a universal order of male over female and a philosophy of power as strength and might that oppresses rather than nourishes.

Because Mary Daly's undergraduate major was in Latin, it can be assumed that she knew that in Augustine's Latin texts, he often presented an alternative image of God as a Mother in *her* heaven, cherishing *her* people and lifting them up to *herself.* To Daly's point, these images until recently were known only to the reader of Augustine's original Latin works, for the English translations obscured Augustine's use of feminine pronouns for God leading to ignorance of, or at best confusion around, Augustine's understanding of the divine's feminine attributes.[2]

This essay looks at Augustine's original Latin writings to uncover the feminine images for the divine that he used routinely and his discussions of human women. This is an essay in philology, an essay about Augustine's use of words and the images they invoke in the imagination. And, also, this is an essay that details Augustine's understanding of power and his social and political views about human women as mothers, leaders, philosophers, teachers, and marital and sexual partners. In the end, I do not expect to prove that the use of feminine images for God necessarily correlates to admiration and advocation for human women and women's power but only to demonstrate that both occur in Augustine. In doing so, I hope to show that attention to Augustine's language and his views of women are relevant even as we consider our 21st century American use of language for God and our views of human women.

AUGUSTINE'S IMAGE OF GOD AS MOTHER

While Daly did not point out Augustine's use of maternal images of God in her 1973 book or in the 1985 reprint where she wrote a re-introduction to the topic, Robert O'Connell had been doing so as early as 1969. In *St. Augustine's Confessions: The Odyssey of the Soul*, O'Connell paraphrased Augustine's account[3] of how he left his Manichean materialist view of God for a noetic understanding of the divine—an understanding that was given to him by the loving divine herself as she called him away from materialism and soothed his fevered mind. O'Connell explains:

> Back now he comes, content to climb upon her waiting lap; for one last protest he looks back upon the way on which he ventured forth so hopefully in the morning brightness. This is her moment: with tender maternal hand she caresses his fevered head, gently turns his eyes away from what has been the cause of his complaining, places his head against her breast.[4]

O'Connell knew this was a fitting paraphrase of the original Latin. He also knew that it would sound radical to the twentieth-century English reader. He reiterates the point often in his books. In 1986, the year following Daly's paperback release of *Beyond God the Father*, he explains in *Imagination and Metaphysics*:

> Not only Father and Doctor, He—or She: Augustine is even brave enough to raise that question—has been Mother and Nurse to us, lifting us up when we

could not walk, carrying us when we could not run, suckling and caressing, and anxious only that we be "little ones" enough to accept and confide totally in that maternal Care.⁵

Again he repeats, still using the rhetoric of surprise in 1994, "[F]or the God Whom we deserted never deserts us. He—or is it She?—is like a mother anxiously fretting over her straying child; her care pursues him tirelessly, stubbornly, no matter where he wanders."⁶

Yet, while Father O'Connell was repeating the news of Augustine's use of maternal imagery for the divine each decade, no reader of an English translation would have known that he was being literal in his reading of Augustine's text. Indeed, not until Sarah Ruden's 2018 translation did any English translator dare to translate Augustine's pronouns literally. Their failure to do so had consequences on those who read Augustine, even those who did read the Latin.

If I may, I will use my own experience as an example. As a graduate student in philosophy at Boston University in the 1990s, I had dedicated two and a half years of study to working on Augustine's *Confessions*. In fact, in the last year as I finished my dissertation, I had become so narrowly focused that it would be accurate to say I was studying *Confessions* VII.x.16. I was well familiar with O'Connell's writings because he was one of the few scholars who agreed with my premise that the key to understanding Augustine's philosophical conversion was understanding that Augustine's view of Truth was not that of a Platonic form but of Christ whom he believed personally and lovingly reached out to the seeker of Truth.

Yet, despite having spent a year focused solely on two paragraphs of the *Confessions* that detailed Augustine's own explanation of his intellectual conversion, I faced a moment of surprise when I stared at the Latin text in the middle of the night before the morning when my final draft of the dissertation was due. It was then that for the first time I saw suddenly and clearly *IPSA* and *EA* and *EAM* used repeatedly in the passage. I looked again. Was Augustine calling God "She" and "Her"? It couldn't be. I looked again. I rubbed my eyes. I looked at my Latin grammar book. I had taken eight years of Latin in high school and college. I had read Augustine in Latin seminars with Father Matt Lamb at Boston College. Yet, I suddenly worried I had forgotten the pronouns. Yet, my grammar book confirmed *Ipsa* is She; *Eam* is her. O'Connell wasn't being provocative. He was just noting the obvious.

I retranslated the passage that night. Suddenly everything in the passage felt transformed. The central point that Augustine's Truth was not a distant and disinterested Form (or Thought Thinking Itself) was more clear in the text than I had seen it before. Furthermore, Augustine's Truth wasn't a loving Father as I had previously written, but a loving Mother.

This section is a key passage in the *Confessions*. It is a recounting of Augustine's initial conversion to the metaphysics and epistemology of Christianity—to the ideas that Truth exists, that Truth is bigger than our opinion of it, and that our access to Truth comes from Truth who is God, herself.

To give a little context, Augustine is about 29 or 30 when this happens. He had left, after nine years of membership, the Manicheans—a dangerous gnostic cult that insisted on belief in absurd things. Manicheans, who attracted hearers by provoking skepticism in more main stream religious systems as well as natural science, soon demanded their hearers not trust the words of any other people outside the cult. They then persuaded members that they could not trust plain reason or even their own lived experience which all could be corrupted. They insisted that members rely only on the secret teachings of the cult, teachings which were only understandable to the smartest and most divine of people.

Augustine had left the cult, having at last seen through their conspiracy theories and lies. But then he felt groundless. They had convinced him not to trust others or his sense experience. As a young professor he was convinced he could never get to any truth and that he could only teach his students the art of rhetoric and persuasion, a vocation that seemed less fulfilling each day. At the lowest point of despair in his intellectual journey, Augustine sat down with some Platonic books that told him to investigate himself—to investigate his own mind. And so he was meditating to see what was in his *cogito*. Here is his account of what occurred:

> I had been told to return inward, so I entered my inner self with you leading and helping me. I entered and saw with the eye of my soul above the eye of my soul, an unchangeable light—not a common light like we see with eyes of flesh, nor something of the same type but greater. . . . No, She was not this, but another, another greater than all these. Nor was She above my mind like oil is above water nor like the sky is above the earth, but She was superior, because She made me, and I was inferior, because I was made by Her. Whoever knows Truth, knows Her, and whoever knows Her, knows eternity, Love knows Her. O eternal Truth and true Love and loving Eternity! You are my God, to you I sigh day and night. And when I first knew you, you lifted me up, so that I could see that there there was something to see and that I was not yet the one to see it. And you beat back the weakness in my eyes and radiated passionately around me. And I trembled with love and dread. . . . And you called from a long way off, "Truly I am who I am." And I heard just as it is heard in the heart.[7]

Before when I had read this passage, I imaged a bright Platonic Light shining down on Augustine—and then this Light appeared as an image of an almighty Father who created Augustine lifting him up. But looking at the Latin, I saw the image more closely as it likely was in Augustine's own mind. Truth was picking up Augustine like a *mother* picks up the unquiet child who cannot see over the counter of his own pride, like a *mother* she turns the light on for him because he is afraid of the dark. She shows him the truth of things and reminds him of her love. And then she whispers in his heart something no human mother can ever say: I am the Truth; I am who I am; I am the God of Moses; I am the Ground of Being itself.

The maternal imagery struck me powerfully, and so I started looking to see if this was the only time Augustine used these pronouns. Anyone who knows Latin knows that of course, this was not the only instance. Anytime Augustine spoke of God as Truth, Wisdom, or Light he was obligated by his Latin language to use feminine pronouns for these feminine nouns. But he was not obligated to use maternal images too. Yet, his images of the Divine Mother run through all of the *Confessions* and many other works and his sermons.

It is probably important to some readers to note that when Augustine speaks of God the Mother, he is usually speaking not of the first person of the Trinity who is often denoted as God the Father, but of Christ. Without getting too mired in details concerning the doctrine of the Trinity (a doctrine that takes Augustine a large number of pages to explain to his public only to conclude in the end that "we speak many things but do not arrive" at any real understanding[8]), let it suffice to say that, for Augustine, the God who is revealed for us is Christ, so it is Christ who is the Mother about whom Augustine speaks. There is a particularly lovely passage that makes this clear:

> Because the Word was made flesh, so that your Wisdom by which all was created might become milk for our infancy. . . . Indeed, your Word, the eternal Truth, surpassing even the most superior of your creatures, raises those who were cast down up to Herself.[9]

This image of Christ as our nursing mother picking up her wayward children certainly found its way into medieval European piety. One must note the work of Julian of Norwich in particular. But, for some reason it did not make its way into any of the English translations of the text. Indeed, English translators went to great lengths to insist on the maleness of Christ in this text, against his own words.

Perhaps the most ridiculous mistranslation comes from William Watts's 1631 translation which says, "For the Word was made flesh that by thy wisdom, by which thou createdst all things, He might suckle our infancy . . . For thy Word, the eternal Truth being so highly exalted above the highest of thy creatures, reaches up those that were cast down, unto Itself."[10] Therein, not only is the Word, the eternal Truth, referred to as a Platonic neutered "Itself," but Watts claims that the nursing breast belongs to a He. Even in 1631, people surely knew that men did not suckle infants. While I suppose one could call this a "queering" of the image, it seems more obviously to me to be simply an invisibilizing of the feminine.

While that is the most egregious of the mistranslations, it is worth noting that for the next 380 years all the readily available English translations followed suit in using verbal gymnastics to hide Augustine's maternal pronouns. Sheed, Ryan, Bourke, Pine-Coffin, Chadwick, and even Maria Boulding in her twenty-first-century translation reworded the text and changed the final *ipsam* at the end of the sentence into Himself rather than the literal Herself. Other English translators simply neutered the image.[11]

If Daly is correct the inability for translators to do their work accurately was deterred by the dominance of patriarchy that did not allow them to imagine the feminine God in the mind of the Father of the Western Church. But rather than dwelling on these mis-translations, let us return to the inverse of Daly's question. Would we think differently about human women if we had a female image of God front and center?

AUGUSTINE'S IMAGE OF MONICA AS TEACHER, HIS IMAGE OF CHRIST AS SCHOOL MISTRESS, AND HIS VIEW OF WOMEN IN ACADEMIC STUDY

To start that discussion, let us look at what Augustine said about women socially and politically.[12] Let us start with how how he treated his human mother. Of course, Augustine clearly dismissed his mother as a teenager—he ignored her advice routinely. He shacked up with a girlfriend she did not like, he joined a cult she warned him not to join, he snuck off to Rome behind her back. Yet, after his conversion experience of being lifted up by the great I Am to see the Truth, Herself, he began to credit his human mother, Monica, with giving him the ground of his knowledge for his conversion. Moreover, he honored her persistence in her love for him and claimed that she was his first and foremost human teacher in his life about the Christian God.

Indeed, throughout the rest of her life after his conversion to Christianity he made a point to value Monica's voice in his philosophical dialogues and emphasize her role as a teacher to him and to the group. In *De Ordine (On Providence)* in *De Beata Vita (On the Happy Life)* and in *Contra Academicos (Against Academic Skeptics)*, Augustine wrote the character of his mother as the character issuing the key lines that turned the group to the final conclusion. Furthermore, in *De Ordine (On Providence)* he insists to his mother, as she doubts her abilities, that her philosophy is important and pleasing to him.[13]

Perhaps his view of Monica as a teacher and philosopher was open to him because of his image of Christ as not only the divine *Magister* but also quite pointedly as a *Magistra*. In the same passage from the *Confessions* in which Augustine spoke of Christ, the Word, as our nursing mother, he also uses the word *Magistra*:

> I sought a way of gaining the strength that is necessary to enjoy you, but I did not find such a way until I comprehended the mediator between God and human beings, the human Christ Jesus, who is God over all . . . Indeed I, a humble one, did not hold my God Jesus who is the humble one, nor did I yet know the things his weakness would teach us as our Schoolmistress.[14]

There is a grammatical reason for Augustine to choose *Magistra* here. *Infirmitas* is a feminine word in Latin. So the weakness (or humility) of Christ that acts as our teacher takes a feminine pronoun and, thus, the feminine use of the word "Teacher." But the use of the word "*infirmitas*" itself seems to be chosen for its feminine grammatical status. In this passage, Augustine explains the Word as a nursing mother and a school mistress. Augustine is invoking deliberately feminine images of Christ for the reader and highlighting the attributes and virtues of Christ that are traditionally tied to feminine attributes and virtues: the ability to nourish, humility, acceptance of weakness, the desire to pick up the downcast.

Whether the image of God as a feminine teacher helped Augustine recognize the importance of women teachers or whether the teachings of his own mother helped Augustine recognize the feminine nature of the divine is an open question. Importantly, Augustine in all of his writings about epistemology insists on the point that all human *magisters* and *magistras* can only teach insofar as The Teacher who is Christ aids them. It is Christ who allows teaching and learning to happen. Importantly, Christ is able to aid any gender of teacher or student no matter what the culture or the law says. On this point, Augustine was insistent as he advocated for women teachers and students.

In 395, Augustine wrote a letter (Epistle 264) to a woman named Maxima who was nervous about entering public debate. He encouraged her and gave her rhetorical and Biblical advice on how to enter the arena of public speaking. Also, in 395 he wrote a letter (Epistle 266) to a shy young woman named Florentina whose parents had noted her intellectual gifts. They had begged Augustine to teach philosophy to her. Augustine's letter to her insists that he could not be her instructor but he could be a dialogue partner. He claimed to seek to learn from her not to teach her, although he did not know whether he would learn directly from her insights or whether together in dialogue they would both come to know what they did not know before speaking together.

Making the epistemological point that all Truth comes from God, in 412, Augustine wrote a letter (Epistle 130) to a woman named Proba, who had asked a pious question about prayer. His answer quoted Cicero and noted that Truth, herself, spoke through the skeptical philosopher as she speaks through all who speak any truths. On the same theme, in 413 he wrote Epistle 147 to Pauline. This letter is broken into 57 chapters in order to attempt to answer her very difficult philosophical question about how God is visible in the world to the bodily eye. All fifty-seven chapters center around the idea that Wisdom, herself, must teach each person internally. Thus all people, both men and women, are taught by Wisdom.

This epistemology allowed Augustine to encourage philosophical thinking and teaching in women as well as men. Importantly, his epistemology also inspired women to pursue philosophical study even in later cultures where women's work in philosophy and theology was prohibited. Notably, the twelfth-century German Hildegard of Bingen was inspired by a similar epistemology of illumination to pursue philosophy and theology in publishing and preaching. Additionally, scores of early modern European woman such as Anne Clifford and Elizabeth Isham kept Augustine's works on their shelves and used his *Confessions* as models for their own autobiographies. And even American suffragists may have found inspiration in his teachings, as alluded to by Harriet Beecher Stowe's reference to Sojourner Truth as a preacher with the African eloquence of Saint Augustine after she gave several speeches claiming that all human beings had a right to use the intellect to serve the common good.[15]

AUGUSTINE'S IMAGE OF LEADERS AND MOTHERS

In the year 423, Augustine wrote a letter to a community of North African women who did not want to marry or be mothers but who wished to live in a community where they shared their wealth while studying and praying together. This letter became known as "The Rule of St. Augustine." As "The Rule of St. Augustine," the letter was adapted and adopted by many communities, not only communities of women and not only by Africans, but also by communities of men all over the world. By the eleventh century, a standardized version of the rule was adopted in the Western church in Europe—and for the next millennium this version has served various global communities well.

Interestingly, the standard English version of the Rule reads as follows:

> The superior should be obeyed as a father with the respect due him so as not to offend God in his person, and, even more so, the priest who bears responsibility for you all.
>
> The superior, for his part, must not think himself fortunate in his exercise of authority but in his role as one serving you in love. In your eyes he shall hold

the first place among you by the dignity of his office, but in fear before God he shall be as the least among you. He must show himself as an example of good works toward all. *Let him admonish the unruly, cheer the fainthearted, support the weak, and be patient toward all* (1 Thes 5:14). Let him uphold discipline while instilling fear. And though both are necessary, he should strive to be loved by you rather than feared, ever mindful that he must give an account of you to God.[16]

The rule was adapted for men, and thus the English uses masculine pronouns and images. That is all well and good in its inclusivity. But it is worth repeating that the original Latin letter was for women, and used feminine pronouns and images.

In the original Latin letter, Augustine wrote:

Let your Superior be obeyed as mother, with honored service, lest God be offended in her; and even more readily should you obey the presbyter/priest who has care for all of your vested interests. Truly, let her not think to dominate with power, but may she think herself happy to serve with loving care. Before the heart of the people, let her have honor over you, before the heart of God, let her lie beneath your feet. Around all, let her be an example of good works. Let her correct the unquiet, console those with small and weak souls, support the infirm, be patient towards all, may she willingly have discipline and with fear put it forward. And although both are necessary, nevertheless, more from you to be loved should she seek than to be feared; always thinking that she will have to give an account for you to God.[17]

On one hand, although Augustine is writing to women, when the rule is adapted to men, it may seem obvious to simply the change the words. On the other hand, the words say something important about governance style that is tied to gendered understanding. When Augustine uses the word "mother," he was thinking about a certain type of leader. Of course, motherhood is a culture construct, so it is important to understand who was Augustine's mother and what was their social context.

Augustine credited Monica as teaching him about Christ, reading him the Bible, taking him to church, and preaching to him the Gospel throughout his life. He also spoke of her as protecting him from his father's crass secular Roman values and from his father's violent temper. Augustine feared his father, but he loved his mother. It was his mother who paid for his higher education. Monica prayed him through his nine year period in the dangerous and elitist cult of the Manicheans. Augustine insisted that she was constantly present for him, patiently smoothing his hair whenever he came back to her for comfort after disobedience. This image of such a mother he painted with such vivid words.

Yet, it is essential to note that the mother in the fourth-century ancient Roman Empire had no legal authority over her children. The father owned the child, made life and death decisions for the child. Many mothers feared the father; Augustine noted in many places how difficult family life was for women because of these laws. He saw this legal inequality as part of the broken order of the world after Eden. It was not the pains of childbirth that are so hard for women, he explained in his exegesis of Genesis, but the horrible reality that she always has "to turn to the man."[18] In short, in Augustine's world, the authority of the mother rested not on the power invested in her by the empire—but only in the gratitude and recognition of a child for his mother.

Yet, in the "Rule," the mother is the model superior and leader—one who does not rule with power but with love. One who may need to use discipline and even fear to keep her child in line, but only in order to help the child grow into the child God has created him to be. As a mother, she is motivated only by love.

Importantly, Augustine made it clear that his mother depended in everyway on God. It was God who filled her breasts with milk to care for him, who filled her minds with truths to teach him, who inhabited the space between her and him so that he could recognize the truths she spoke and the love she had. When Augustine praised the human leader who acted like a mother, he also reminded the reader that every human leader gets all her power from God. It is a credit to his mother, in his view, that she recognized this. Such humility is the foundation of true human leadership.

AUGUSTINE'S IMAGE OF GOD AS DIVINE MISTRESS AND HIS VIEW OF HUMAN SEXUAL RELATIONSHIP

While Augustine's encouragement of women to study philosophy and speak publically is admirable, while his creation of a Rule so that women could live together in community to study and pray is commendable, and while his praise of his own mother is noteworthy, there is likely to be raised a fair concern over his treatment of his own child's mother. Augustine divorced his long term lover, his concubine, his common law wife, and mother of his child after his conversion from Manicheanism during the period of academic skepticism. He claimed that he never loved her rightly even as he admitted that his heart was torn in two when she left. Then he took another concubine immediately, even as she remained returned to Africa to live as a celibate. Augustine himself had harsh words about his behavior toward his lover. He insisted that his treatment of her was not to be modeled. Indeed, his pathological melancholy after his divorce is a warning about the dangers of a Stoic skepticism that leads one to doubt one's heart.

While Augustine harshly rebukes himself for his behavior towards his concubine, it is worth noting that he does not ever chastise her. More interestingly, there is significant reason to think as deeply about the effect of her relationship on Augustine's piety as we did about Monica's. Augustine's feminine images of God do not only include God as Mother—but God as female lover as well. Let's push the Freudian analysis aside for a moment –there is something important in this imagery as well as provocative.

The twelfth-century theologian, Bernard de Clairveaux, wrote beautiful descriptions of piety invoking images of the soul as the bride and Christ as the groom. These carried much influence in medieval and modern mysticism and devotional piety. But for Augustine, when he invoked images of divine eroticism, Christ as Wisdom was portrayed as a beautiful woman. In the *De Libero Arbitrio (Freedom of the Will)*, he explained, "Truly people shout that they are happy when they embrace the beautiful bodies they deeply desire, the bodies of their wives or even the bodies of prostitutes. And should we doubt that we are happy in the embrace of Truth?"[19]

Augustine routinely used the rhetorical flourish of comparing the embrace of Truth, who is Christ, to the embrace of a lover. Moreover, if O'Connell was right in his thesis that "to understand Augustine, we must learn how to capitalize a number of key terms in his writings—especially the terms which are his code-words for the Eternal Christ: words like Philosophy, Reason, Intellect, Order, Truth and Wisdom,"[20] then the reader will find even more provocative images of Christ as female lover throughout his early dialogues where he claimed he was on fire and full of concupiscence for Philosophy whose breasts no one of any age can fear to be excluded.[21]

Indeed, Augustine clearly explained that his desire to see and hold his lover naked was analogous to his desire to know Wisdom, who is Christ. But in the *Soliloquies*, his reason asks him to consider what it is he is saying. "Now, we ask, what type of lover of Wisdom are you, who with the most pure view and embrace, desire to see and hold her as if naked, without the imposition of clothes?"[22] This is a key line. In Augustine's descriptions, especially in his early writings, the Christian seeker of Truth is a desiring male and God who is the Truth is a desired female. When viewed through the heteronormative lens, which was Augustine's lens, God who is Truth portrayed as a beautiful woman, is suddenly seen as the most desirable thing there is to the male lover. Still looking through the heteronormative lens, the whole heterosexual matrix is flipped upside down by Reason's question to Augustine. Who is Augustine to be God's lover? God is GOD, the most powerful, the ground of all Being. She is not an object to be won; she is not the one given value by the male gaze. God is God, the Value-maker, the Good by which all good things are made Good, the Truth by which all true statements are made true. Thus, in Augustine's metaphor of divine eroticism, it is the female lover who has the power, who names what will be, and who with her love bestows worthiness on her lover.

There is good evidence from Augustine's writings that this "groom's" mysticism affected his view of sexual relationship and marriage. First, as a young man the affect was problematic. If Augustine's metaphor of divine love is read literally instead of metaphorically—as if human erotic relationship is considered a mirror of the divine relationship—it glorifies the woman as the pure one who deserves more than the average human man can give her. This can lead to real problems in relationships for those who hold this literal theology. Some examples can be seen in how Abelard treated Heloise and how he wrote about her role in their relationship.[23] Later examples can be seen in Soren Kierkegaard's various pseudonyms who speak of women as if their innocence and purity makes any male lover unworthy and in Kierkegaard's personal journal entries about Regine Olson. Abelard forced Heloise into a convent and sought to convince her that he could not love her rightly thus she must turn to God. Kierkegaard famously ruminated over his need to break his engagement to Regine in order to protect her from himself and to obey a command from God. Indeed, Augustine's own life is too often explained as if it followed this trope, as if he divorced his concubine and later became celibate to spare her (and any wife he might have) the effects of his not being worthy of loving her as she ought to be loved.[24] But it was not faith that led Augustine from his lover, it was doubt. He divorced her during a period when he had decided to ignore his heart and follow Roman customs in order to gain human status, no longer believing that real satisfaction could ever be found.

Moreover, importantly Augustine denounced the view that divorce was permissible in order to pursue abstinence. He proclaimed that human relationship is human and that human men and human women are equal. In his Christmas sermons this is a particularly prominent theme, that because God has been born a man and because God has been born of woman, both sexes may be honored. Particularly of note, in the *Retractions* Augustine apologized for his florid metaphors for philosophy. Perhaps, he worried he might confuse a reader into making a category mistake in comparing human relationship with divine relationship. Just as he insisted that human student/human teacher relationships are always relationships of equality, so, too, Augustine insisted that in human romantic relationship both partners ought to give to each other equally and ought to treat each other's wills with equal respect. They must not confuse each other with the divine.

As evidence of this view of equality of human beings in relations, there are several letters he wrote as a pastor to women and to men refusing to condone divorcing a spouse to become a celibate unless the decision is mutual. If a husband wishes to become celibate but his wife wishes to remain in sexual relationship, Augustine insisted the husband must consent to her will—and vice versa.

Despite this, it became common practice in medieval Europe for men to divorce their wives claiming their wives had a spiritual vocation and then often re-marrying after putting their first wife in a convent. In the twelfth-century Hildegard of Bingen reasserted the Augustinian argument against this and demanded that men should not be allowed to put their wives in a convent and take a new wife. She reiterated, only if both spouses agree to take on spiritual vocations can one be released from the marital vows.

In the mature Augustine, mutuality is the key for all human erotic relationships. In his sermons, he routinely chastises men who expect chastity from their wives but not from themselves. He preaches especially to men who try to justify to the church their mistresses by saying that the mistress is not an adulteress because she is monogamous. Augustine retorts that she may not be an adulteress but the man is an adulterer. Augustine declares in no uncertain language that such behavior in men is to be condemned:

> So she serves you faithfully and she knows no one but you, and she is not disposed to know another. Therefore if she is chaste, why are you fornicating? If she has one, why do you seek two? This is not allowed. This is not allowed. This is not allowed. To hell they go. Here I am free. Here it is allowed for me to say what is true.[25]

There is to be no double standard for sexual morality—if women are expected to be chaste (and they are) than so are men.

In this, Augustine went against Roman culture and Roman law which allowed men to take concubines and mistresses, to divorce wives without their consent, to treat women and the children they bore as property. Augustine condemned these human laws and insisted vows between men and women in marriage and in sexual relationship generally are to be mutual.

AUGUSTINE'S UNDERSTANDING OF POWER

Also, going against Roman culture, Augustine firmly chastised men who beat their wives and advocated against parents and teachers spanking children. On one hand, Augustine may be rightly criticized for suggesting in several places that a gentle wife can change a violent husband, and thus unfairly blaming a beaten woman for not being gentle enough. On the other hand, in making this suggestion he is saying something Christian and revolutionary about the nature of real power.

Indeed, Augustine's praise of the gentle persuasion of women is a counter cultural declaration that love and gentleness are more powerful and more holy than the violent force of abusive men. Hildegard of Bingen took this word seriously, too. She confronted men such as the emperor Barbarossa with letters and treatises that declared that the devil puts faith in force and violence and Christ overpowers the world by gentleness and love. Of course, it is essential to note that Christ's power does not protect him from abuse, suffering, and finally death, but in Hildegard's view, Christ's suffering and death conquers death itself.

To a contemporary feminist, such words about power may feel like a pale substitute for real political change. While Augustine chastised the cruelty of Roman law concerning the father as an owner of the child and while he sympathized with the plight of women generally, he was awfully stoic about it. He did not himself become politically an advocate for legal changes. Even after the fall of the Roman Empire in Northern Africa which occurred in the same days as his death, there remained a marked legal power differential between fathers and mothers, limited access to education for women, and no norm of mutual relationship in marriage in the geographical areas influenced by the Western Church that considered him a Father and named him the Doctor of Grace.

CONCLUSION

So did Augustine's words about God and his frequent feminine images seriously challenge patriarchy in his time and help us to challenge patriarchy in ours? The answer goes back to Mary Daly's hypothesis. Does putting a feminine image of God, change the way the culture treats women? By using both masculine and feminine pronouns for the Divine and by using maternal and bridal images for Christ as a nursing mother, a school mistress, and as a value-creating lover, Augustine's language when translated literally forces a reader, especially an English reader who is un-used to these translations, to stop and think about who God is and what God wants in the world. When Augustine spoke of the mother as a model superior in an era in which a mother had no legal power but only the authority of love, the reader must re-consider how real leadership ought look.

Of course, Augustine certainly used masculine and neutral images for God: Dominus—Sir, Rex-King, Pater-Father, Verbum-Word, Cibum-Food, Bonum—the Good. That Augustine used feminine words and images only seems interesting perhaps because of English speakers' contemporary cultural context and centuries of English translations that minimized these. That it strikes a contemporary reader as noteworthy that the Ancient African Doctor saw the importance of having both men and women as scholars in philosophy and theology, that he stressed mutuality in sexual and marital relationship, and that he encouraged gentleness and love in leadership tells us perhaps far more about the current social context than his. Thus, whatever has happened in the past as readers praised Augustine, it is to our own theological imagination we now must turn and to our own social and political rules guarding gender that we must attend.

NOTES

1. Mary Daly, *Beyond God the Father: Toward a Philosophy of Women's Liberation* (Boston: Beacon Press, 1973/1985), 13.

2. For an in depth look at the mis-gendered translations of Augustine's works, see Jennifer Hockenbery, "The He, She, and It of God: Translating Saint Augustine's Gendered Latin God-talk into English," *Augustinian Studies* 36, no. 2 (2005): 433–44.

3. All quotations from the *Confessions* are my translations from the Latin text Augustine, *Confessiones,* ed. J. J. O'Donnell (Oxford: Clarendon, 1992). This scene is Augustine, *Confessiones*, VII.xiv.20: "My mind had imagined for itself a god extended through all space to infinity and it thought that this was you and enshrined this in its heart. And once again, it was made into a temple of idols which were abominable to you. But afterward, unknown to me, you soothed my head and closed my eyes so that they should not look upon vanities and I stopped for a little while and slept away my madness. I awoke in you and saw that you were infinite in another way. This came to me but not as a vision of the flesh."

4. Robert O'Connell, *St. Augustine's* Confessions*: The Odyssey of the Soul* (Cambridge: The Belknap Press of Harvard University Press, 1969), 36.

5. Robert O'Connell, *Imagination and Metaphysics* (Milwaukee: Marquette University Press, 1986), 23.

6. Robert O'Connell, *Soundings in St Augustine's Imagination* (New York: Fordham University Press, 1994), 93.

7. Augustine, *Confessiones*, VII.x16: "*Et inde admonitus redire ad memet ipsum, intravi in intima mea duce te, et potui, quoniam factus es adjiutor meus. Intravi et vidi qualicuque oculo animae meae supra eundem oculum animae meae, supra mentem meam, lucem incommutabiliem: non hanc vulgarem et conspicuam omni carni, nec quasi ex eodem genere grandior erat, . . . Non hoc **illa** erat, sed aliud, aliud valde ab istis omnibus. Nec ita erat supra mentem meam, sicut oleum super aquam nec sicut caelum super terram, sed superior,* **quia ipsa** *fecit me, et ego inferior, quia factus ab* **ea.** *Qui novit veritatem, novit* **eam,** *et qui novit* **eam***, novit aeternitatem. Caritas novit* **eam***. O aeterna veritas et vera caritas et cara aeternitas! Tu es Deus meus, tibi suspiro die ac nocte. Et cum te primum cognovi, tu assumpsisti me, ut viderem esse, quod viderem, et nondum me esse, qui viderem. Et reverberasti infirmitatem aspectus mei radians in me vehementer, et contremui amore et horrore; . . . et clamasti de longinquo, 'Immo vero ego sum qui sum.' Et audivi, sicut auditur in corde[.]*"

8. Augustine, *De Trinitate*, in *Opera Omnia: Patrologiae Latinae Elenchus*, ed. J. P. Migne (Paris: n.p., 1841–1845), XV.xxviii.332, http://www.augustinus.it/: "*Multa, inquit, dicimus, et non pervenimus.*"

9. Augustine, *Confessiones*, VII. xviii.24: "*quoniam verbum caro factum est, ut infantiae nostrae lactescaret sapientia tua, per quam creasti omnia . . . verbum enim tuum, aeterna veritas, superioribus creaturae tuae partibus supereminens, subditos erigit ad se ipsam.*"

10. William Watts, *St. Augustine's Confessions with an English translation by William Watts* (London: William Heinemann, 1631), 389, https://archive.org/details/confessionswithe01augu/page/388/mode/2up.

11. For a full analysis of each of these translations see Hockenbery, "The He, She, and It of God."

12. See the section on Augustine's influence on women in theology in Jennifer Hockenbery, *Wisdom's Friendly Heart: Augustinian Hope for Skeptics and Conspiracy Theorists* (Portland, Cascade, 2020), especially 113–19.

13. Augustine, *De Ordine*, in *Opera Omnia: Patrologiae Latinae Elenchus*, ed. J.P. Migne, (Paris: n.p., 1841–1845), I.xi.31, http://www.augustinus.it/. For more on Augustine's relationship with Monica as teacher see Catherine Conybeare, *The Irrational Augustine* (Oxford: Oxford University Press, 2006), 61–138.

14. Augustine, *Confessiones*, VII xviii.24: "*Et quaerebam viam comparandi roboris quod esset idoneum ad fruendum te, nec inveniebam donec amplecterer mediatorem dei et hominum, hominem Christum Jesum, qui est super omnia deus. . . . Non enim tenebam deum meum Iesum, humilis humilem, nec cuius rei **magistra** esset eius infirmitas noveram.*"

15. Harriet Beecher Stowe, "Sojourner Truth, the Libyan Sibyl," *Atlantic*, April 1863.

16. Augustine, *The Rule of St. Augustine*, trans. Robert Russell, O.S.A., Brothers of the Order of Hermits of Saint Augustine, Inc., 1976, based on the critical text of Luc Verheijen, O.S.A., *La regle de saint Augustin*, in *Etudes Augustiniennes* (Paris: n.p., 1967).

17. My English translation of Augustine, *Epistolae*, in *Opera Omnia: Patrologiae Latinae Elenchus*, ed. J.P. Migne (Paris: n.p., 1841–1845), 211, http://www.augustinus.it/: "*Praepositae tamquam matri obediatur, honore servato, ne in illa offendatur Deus: multo magis presbytero qui omnium vestrum curam gerit. Ut ergo cuncta ista serventur, et si quid servatum non fuerit, non neglegenter praetereatur, sed emendandum corrigendumque curetur, ad praepositam praecipue pertinet, ita ut ad presbyterum qui vobis intendit, referat quod modum vel vires eius excedit. Ipsa vero non se existimet potestate dominante, sed caritate serviente felicem. Honore coram hominibus praelata sit vobis; timore coram Deo substrata sit pedibus vestris. Circa omnes se ipsam bonorum operum praebeat exemplum. Corripiat inquietas, consoletur pusillanimes, suscipiat infirmas, patiens sit ad omnes, disciplinam libens habeat, metuens imponat. Et quamvis utrumque sit necessarium, tamen plus a vobis amari appetat quam timeri; semper cogitans Deo se pro vobis redditoram esse rationem. Unde magis obediendo non solum vestri, verum etiam ipsius miseremini; quia inter vos quanto in loco superiore, tanto in periculo maiore versatur.*"

18. My English translation of Augustine, *De Genesi ad litteram libri duodecim*, in *Opera Omnia: Patrologiae Latinae Elenchus*, ed. J.P. Migne (Paris: n.p., 1841–1845), XI.xxxvii.50, http://www.augustinus.it/: "*ad virum tuum conversion tua.*"

19. My English translation of Augustine, *De Libero Arbitrio*, in *Opera Omnia: Patrologiae Latinae Elenchus*, ed. J. P. Migne (Paris: n.p., 1841–1845), II.xiii.35, http://www.augustinus.it/: "*An vero clamant homines beatos se esse, cum pulchra corpora magno desiderio concupita, sive coniugum, sive etiam meretricum amplexantur; et nos in amplexu veritatis beatos esse dubitabimus?*"

20. Robert O'Connell, *Images of Conversion in St. Augustine's* Confessions (New York: Fordham University Press, 1996), 34.

21. See Augustine, *Contra Academicos*, in *Opera Omnia: Patrologiae Latinae Elenchus*, ed. J. P. Migne (Paris: n.p., 1841–1845), II.ii-II.iii, http://www.augustinus.it/.

22. My translation of Augustine, *Soliloquia*, in *Opera Omnia: Patrologiae Latinae Elenchus*, ed. J. P. Migne (Paris: n.p., 1841–1845), I.xiii.22, http://www.augustinus.it/: "*Nunc illud quaerimus, qualis sis amator sapientiae, quam castissimo conspectu atque amplexu, nullo interposito velamento quasi nudam videre ac tenere desideras.*"

23. See, for example, Abelard's insistence that he had abused Heloise by seducing her in the *Historia Calamitatum* and Heloise's insistence in *Letter 1* that she found the greatest joy and even holiness in their love: *The Letters of Abelard and Heloise*, trans. Betty Radici (New York: Penguin, 1974), 66–67; 110–18.

24. See, for example, Jostein Gaarder's fictionalized account of a letter from Augustine's concubine which centers around the theme that Augustine left her in order to save his soul: Jostein Gaarder, *Vita Brevis: A Letter to St. Augustine*, trans. Anne Born (London: Phoenix, 1997).

25. My translation of Augustine, *Sermones*, in *Opera Omnia: Patrologiae Latinae Elenchus*, ed. J.P. Migne, (Paris: n.p., 1841–1845), 224.3, http://www.augustinus.it/: "*Sed servat tibi forsitan fidem, et non novit nisis te unum, et non disponit nosse alium. Cum ergo illa sit casta, tu quare fornicaris? Si illa unum, tu quare duas? Non licet, non licet, non licet. In gehennam eunt. Vel hinc sim liber. Vel hinc liceat mihi dicere quod verum est.*"

Chapter 7

Women's Talk

Silent Voices and Inarticulate Cries— Augustine on Conceiving and Giving Birth to the Word

Carol Harrison

Women are generally silent or silenced in the early centuries of the Church.[1] Rarely is a female voice heard, and when it is, it is usually quickly muted.[2] Women had no voice, because their social, cultural and religious identity was one that was shaped and formed by a medical and philosophical understanding in which femininity was defined by a lack of masculinity: women were intellectually and physically weaker than men; they possessed minds which were too feeble for education or public office; bodies which were not strong enough for physically demanding activity; voices that were thin, shrill, high-pitched and singsong.[3] It was held that, although women's bodies lacked the vital heat of their male counterparts, their relative coolness and moistness made them ideal for childbearing; that although they lacked the power of a ruling masculine reason, they were naturally inclined to submission and to maintaining the social order by marrying, creating a family, bringing up children, spinning and weaving—and in more well-off households, supervising servants and running a household. Their social sphere was the private one of the home; their cultural role was as a wife and mother; their religious role was to be faithful, charitable, modest, obedient and above all, silent. With a few notable exceptions, then, women in the early Church were domesticated, placed behind closed doors, and remained unseen and unheard.

All of this is so counterintuitive; so inherently unacceptable and offensive for men and women in the twenty-first century, that we academics struggle to confront it—even when we are able to take account of the social, cultural and religious norms which made it well-nigh natural and inevitable to both men and women in antiquity. We cannot but try to mitigate the extremes, to find glimmers of what we would now recognise as normative and desirable, and to concentrate on the exceptions who broke the mould—the female ascetics, martyrs and saints. But try as we might—and there is, in fact, a good deal that can and has been said, especially in a Christian context—we can only go so far.[4]

What I would like to do in this paper is to suggest that women's silence is not necessarily to be thought of as a bad thing; that their silence can, in fact, be understood as a sort of silent thunder; a presence rather an absence; heavy with meaning and mystery, and that on the occasions when it does break and the air cracks and lightning flashes, it communicates far more than reasoned male discourse or eloquence.[5]

In particular, I would like to think about Augustine's understanding of how we human beings know; how that knowledge is present to our minds; how it is apprehended and reflected upon; and finally, how it is expressed.[6] The language and analogies he often deploys in this context are those of conception, gestation, pregnancy, birth: a word is conceived in the mind and memory; it dwells there silently, without verbal formulation; it is born of cogitation, before it is brought forth in sound or words. He describes this process in *The Trinity* as follows:

> All these things then that the human consciousness knows by perceiving them through itself or through the senses of its body or through the testimony of others, it holds onto where they are stacked away in the treasury of memory. From them is begotten a true word (*gignitur verbum verum*) when we utter what we know, but a word before any sound, before any thought of sound. For it is then that the word is most like the thing known, and most its image, because the seeing which is thought springs direct from the seeing which is knowledge, and it is a word of no language, a true word from a true thing, having nothing from itself, but everything from that knowledge from which it is born (*de illa scientia de qua nascitur*).[7]

As we will see, he also describes the silent word that has been conceived within as being brought forth spontaneously and inexorably, just as a pregnant woman must give birth to the child that is growing in her womb—often with difficulty and hard labour, accompanied by groans, moans, and sighs.[8]

That Augustine's language and imagery here are drawn from the uniquely female process of conception, pregnancy, gestation, and childbirth is probably not hugely significant, however. Many ancient authors, classical and Christian, use the same analogies and they are, to a large extent, obvious ones. But I do think they do tell us something about the nature and working of the voice that effectively gives women a voice, even if—indeed because—it is sometimes a silent or inarticulate one.

To begin to explore the nature of this voice we must begin, however, not with male and female, but with God Himself (or Herself or Itself?),[9] for in the Christian tradition the Godhead is understood to be eternally generative: the Son is eternally begotten of the Father; the Holy Spirit, proceeding from the Father and the Son, unites the Trinity in love. Beginning with the Prologue of John's Gospel, the generative nature of the Godhead was more often than not expressed in terms of words: the Word of God, eternally begotten of the Father before all ages, is the one through whom all things come to be; the one who was conceived in the womb of the virgin Mary, of the Holy Spirit, and brought forth for our salvation.

I don't intend to unravel the theological complexities of the preceding paragraph. It is there to remind us that before we speak about human words and voices, we must remember that any theological account of them is inevitably informed by a theology of the Word of God and of the Incarnation. In fact, I think we might well argue that one mutually informs and shapes the other: that a theory and practice of language informed a theological articulation of the Word of God and that a theology of the Word informed the theory and practice of words/language. That this must remain at the level of analogy, and that we must constantly remind ourselves, as Augustine constantly reminds his listeners and readers, that it is a very limited analogy, which reflects the limitations of human knowing and powers of expression before a transcendent and ineffable Godhead, goes without saying.[10]

Nevertheless, it is a useful one, and citing John's Prologue, Augustine makes clear how a correct understanding of the inner word in our mind and of how it is brought forth as a spoken word, can help us avoid misunderstanding the eternal Word of God:

> What is in a word? (*quid est verbum?*) What is so great about a word? It makes a sound and vanishes. It lashes the air, strikes the ear, then ceases to be." Listen to a bit more: *The Word was with God* (*Verbum erat apud Deum*); it was abiding, not making a sound and then vanishing. Perhaps you are still belittling it: *The Word was God* (Jn 1:1). Within you, my good man, when a word is in your heart, it is something other than a sound; but for the word which is in you to reach me, it seeks a sound as a vehicle . . . the sound of the syllables carried your thought to my ears, your thought climbed down through my ears into my heart, the sound which acted as intermediary flew away. But that word, which took on sound, was with you before you uttered it; because you did utter it, it is now with me, and has not left you. Pay attention to that, whoever you are, you scrutinizer of sounds; you belittle the Word of God, you who do not understand the word of a human being![11]

My point in wading into these deep theological waters is simply (if that is possible!) to note the important point that when we think about the female voice in early Christianity, and especially in Augustine, this profound theological matrix cannot be ignored. Human words and voices were understood both in relation to and in contrast to the Word of God—not least, for our purposes, when early Christian theologians came to consider the Annunciation and Incarnation of the Word to Mary.

Mary is arguably the archetypal female voice. This is first of all because she is a pre-eminent example of the sort of faithful listening that gives rise to an inward conception which communicates the mysteries of the faith. Of course, it might be argued that Mary is not only archetypal but unique, and that the fact that she happens to be a woman is neither here nor there, but this is not how she is presented by Augustine.

In a series of homilies on the feast of John the Baptist, in which John, the forerunner, is described as the "voice" who prepares the way for Christ, the "Word,"[12] the contrast between the doubting and suspicious response of John's father, Zechariah, to the angel Gabriel's promise of a son; and the humble and obedient response of Mary to Gabriel's annunciation that she will conceive the Word of God by the Holy Spirit, is one that Augustine deploys to demonstrate what it is to listen in faith. He observes: "But because *nothing is impossible for God* (Lk 1:37), the promise of a son was made to a man who didn't believe it. The father had his voice taken away because he lacked faith; it had already been written, after all, *I believed, therefore I spoke* (Ps 116:10). He didn't believe, and he didn't speak."[13]

Elsewhere, he contrasts conception in lust with conception in faith. Christ's conception is one "inaugurated" as Augustine puts it, in *The Trinity*, "by the spirit not the flesh, by faith not lust" (*cuius conceptum spiritus, non caro; fides, non libido praevenit*); Mary's 'holy virginity conceived by believing not by embracing'(*credendo non concumbendo*).[14] In another sermon on the Feast of John the Baptist, he writes:

> Finally, listen to how this shall come about: *The Holy Spirit will come upon you, and the power of the Most High will overshadow you.* Such shade knows nothing of the heat of lust. *For that reason, because the Holy Spirit will come upon you, and the power of the Most High overshadow you* (Lk 1:35); because you are conceiving by faith, because you will have a child in your womb by believing, not by lying with a man, *for that reason, the holy child that will be born of you shall be called the Son of God.* (Lk 1:35)[15]

Conceiving the Word in faith, therefore, the word dwells within Mary; she carries Him within her womb until she brings Him forth, so that He can be communicated to others, and so that they too may believe and the Word enter their hearts. What Augustine describes is effectively the process by which he thinks all human communication works: what we conceive within ourselves when we hear, think or become aware of what is in our hearts and minds, is an inner word, which dwells within us without sound, without a voice, without words, until we must find words in order to bring it forth, so that we can communicate it to the heart and mind of another.[16] As he observes to his congregation:

> Here you are, you've been wanting to say something; this very thing you want to say has already been conceived in the heart, it's being held by the memory, got ready by the will, kept alive in the intelligence (*tenetur memoria, paratur voluntate, vivit intellectu*). And this very thing you want to say is not yet in any language. The thing itself that you want to say, that has been conceived in the heart, is not in any language, neither Greek, nor Latin, nor Punic, nor Hebrew, nor the language of any nation. The thing has simply been conceived in the heart, ready to come out (*Res est tantum corde concepta, parata procedere*). So there you have a word, already formed, already complete, abiding in the heart; it seeks to come out, in order to be uttered to the hearer.[17]

In this passage, Augustine is thinking about how Christ the Word can be said to *precede* John the voice: for Christ must be conceived by John in faith, as an inner word, before he can bring Him forth and witness to Him for others to hear. In this sense, John is like the patriarchs and prophets, apostles and preachers, or indeed any devout soul who hears, conceives and then brings forth God's word. As Augustine comments:

> John was cast in the role of the voice, but symbolically, in a mystery; because he wasn't the only one to be the voice. Everybody, you see, who proclaims the Word is the voice of the Word. What the sound from our mouths is, you see, to the word we carry in our hearts, that every devout soul that proclaims it, is to that Word, of which it is said, *In the beginning was the Word, and the Word was with God, and the Word was God; this was in the beginning with God*. (Jn 1:1–2)[18]

As he stands before his congregation as preacher, Augustine includes himself among the devout souls who become voices by conceiving and giving birth to the Word:

> So in me, as though on the threshold of my heart (*tamquam in cardine cordis mei*), as though in the cabinet room of my mind, the word preceded my voice. No voice has yet sounded in my mouth, and the word is already in my heart. But in order that what I have conceived in my heart (*quod corde concepi*) may come out to you, it requires the service of the voice.[19]

As his sermon is to celebrate the feast of John the Baptist, Augustine unsurprisingly identifies John as the archetypal conceiver and bearer of the Word:

> So gather together all the voices which preceded the Word as into one man, and lump them all together in the person of John. He was cast in the symbolic role of all of them, he alone was the sacred and mystical representative or person of them all. That's why he is properly called the voice, as the sign and sacrament of all voices (*tamquam omnium vocum signaculum atque mysterium*).[20]

But why, we might ask, does Augustine not assign this role to Mary, who literally as well as spiritually conceived and brought forth the Word? Surely she, even more than John, is the "sacred and mystical representative . . . the sign and sacrament of all voices"? But Augustine—perhaps predictably here, given the context (the feast day of John the Baptist) and the fact that no one in his time could begin to imagine a female voice with such weight and authority—opts for John.

We will return to the nature of Mary's voice, but before we do this, we need to think further about the significance of the inner Word, whom Mary conceived and carried, hidden within herself, silently and mysteriously, before she brought Him forth, voiced Him, and communicated Him to others. As Augustine asks in his sermon on John the Baptist, "So what was Christ for Mary? The hidden Word" (*Quid ergo Christus ad Mariam? Verbum occultum*).[21] Mary's hidden word is, of course, no ordinary inner word, but the Word of God. However, I think that Augustine's point here is that any devout soul who hears and believes God's Word is like Mary; they, too, conceive his Word within themselves.

As will have become apparent, even in this short essay, Augustine tends to revert to the process of human thinking and communication whenever he reaches for an analogy to illustrate and expound the truths of the faith. As the texts that we cited at the beginning of this essay demonstrate, the inner word, or *uerbum mentis*, is one that does a lot of work in demonstrating how we can believe, comprehend, and reflect on the truths of the faith without ever needing to resort to spoken words. In an early work entitled *The Teacher* he identifies the inner word with the presence of Christ, the inner teacher or *magister interior*, who speaks directly to our hearts and minds, and subsequently repeatedly directs his congregation to listen to Him, rather than to his own preaching and teaching:

> But I have introduced these points, even if we are not up to examining all the twists and turns of such a great mystery, either for lack of capacity, or of time. You will be taught much better by the one who speaks in you (*Melius vos docebit qui loquitur in vobis*) even when we aren't present; the one whom you think

loving thoughts about, whom you have taken to your hearts, whose temple you have become.²²

Interestingly, he makes the same point specifically in relation to female correspondents. Writing a letter in response to Paulina's question about whether God can be seen with the eyes of the flesh, Augustine responds that she should attend to the inner teacher, not to his words:

> Receive, then, the words of understanding in accord with the interior self. ... Lift up, then, the spirit of your mind, which is renewed in the knowledge of God according to the image of him who created it, where Christ dwells in you through faith, where there is neither Jew nor Greek, neither slave nor freeman, neither male nor female. ... Once you are raised up in your interior self, pay attention and see what I am saying. I do not want you to follow my authority so that you think that it is necessary for you to believe something because I said it. Rather, either believe the canonical scriptures if there is something that you do not as yet see is true, or believe the truth who teaches interiorly (*interius demonstranti veritati*) in order that you may see this clearly.²³

This is especially the case for the realities which transcend our human understanding, which the inner teacher makes present to us within, and which our outward, sounding words can never adequately express, but simply serve to admonish us towards. As Augustine observes in *The Teacher*:

> But on the subject of the realities (*universis*) which we understand, it is not a word that resonates without, but the Truth that presides within the spirit itself that we consult (*intus ipsi menti praesidentem consulimus veritatem*), admonished perhaps by the words to consult it. Now the one we consult is the one who teaches, Christ, of whom it is said that he lives in the inner man, that is the immutable and eternal Wisdom of God.²⁴

Indeed, describing the inward understanding/word that he enjoys directly, wordlessly and intuitively within, Augustine laments the indirect and counter-intuitive struggle to find words with which he might convey it to his listening congregation: much better, he reflects, to simply listen to God speaking within. As he writes to the priest Deogratias, who had asked for advice on how to improve his own lacklustre preaching:

> I am nearly always dissatisfied with the address that I give. For the address I am eager to offer is the superior one which I enjoy again and again in my inner being before I begin to formulate it in spoken words. And when I find that my actual address fails to express what I have before my mind, I am depressed by the fact that my tongue has been unable to keep up with my intellect. For all the insight that I have I want to pass on to my hearer, and I become aware that,

speaking as I am, this is not going to happen, mainly for the reason that that insight floods the mind as with a sudden flash of light (*rapida coruscatione*), whereas speech is slow-moving and drawn-out and of a very different nature.[25]

When he reflects on the nature of prayer, Augustine likewise observes that it is the silent, non-verbal movement of the inner word; the "voice" or "tongue of the heart," toward God, which best articulates our prayer and stretches us out in desire and longing towards God, so that we become more capable—not of grasping or comprehending God, but—of receiving and participating in Him.[26] So, preaching on psalm 3:5, "*With my voice I have cried to the Lord*," he comments:

> That is, not with the voice of my body (*corporis uoce*), which is produced with the noise of reverberating air (*strepitu uerberati aeris*), but with the voice of the heart (*uoce cordis*), which is unheard by other people but makes a noise which to God is like shouting. It was by speaking in such a voice that Susanna was heard. The Lord himself taught that it was with such a voice that prayer should be made behind the closed doors of one's bedroom, that is to say, in the recesses of the heart, without any noise (*sine strepitu*).[27]

In short, the inner word, conceived within, is the presence of the Word within us, speaking without words, directing what is in our mind and heart towards God, because (as we will see), like the presence of the Word in Mary's womb, it is no more and no less than the presence and movement of God within us.

The intuitive, wordless, silent conception of the inner word is one that is not only characteristic of Mary but of all human beings, men and women. Men, as well as women, can conceive the word in faith, so that it dwells within their minds and hearts, but it is significant that it is not only the imagery of conception, pregnancy and birth that is gendered, but that what it expresses is the ability of men *and* women to apprehend the truths of faith in a manner that subverts the usual gender stereotypes of Augustine's age: of ruling male intellect and reason and submissive female obedience; of masculine eloquence and female silence; of masculine public power and female private domesticity. Here, the silent, inward, submission of faith to God's gracious Word, paradigmatically demonstrated by Mary, is held to be the model of faithful listening, comprehension and above all, of prayer, for all devout Christians, men and women. For as Augustine urges:

> A person of interior life, one in whom Christ has begun to dwell through faith, must cry to the Lord with his own true voice, not with the noise of the lips but with the affections of the heart (*non in strepitu labiorum, sed in affectu cordis clamet ad Dominum*). God does not hear where humans hear. . . . [Y]our inner

thoughts are your clamor in the Lord's hearing (*cogitatio tua clamor est ad Dominum*).[28]

So, Mary, who sat at Christ's feet and listened to him intently, while her sister Martha busied herself about the household, is said by Christ to have chosen the better part. As Augustine observes in a sermon on this passage: "Mary, you see, was absorbed in the sweetness of the Lord's words. Martha was absorbed in the matter of how to feed the Lord; Mary was absorbed in the matter of how to be fed by the Lord. Martha was preparing a banquet for the Lord, Mary was already reveling in the banquet of the Lord."[29]

This dramatic subversion—and I don't think we can overemphasize just how dramatic it is—is based, first and foremost, not just on an understanding of how human communication works (that was shared with many ancient thinkers, who similarly spoke in terms of an inner word and an uttered word),[30] but on how God communicates to us. In other words—at least in Augustine—it is based on a conviction that the inner word, its conception, its gestation and its coming forth is from God, through God and toward God. It is something we are given—a grace; it is not something we merit or achieve through rational insight, discursive intellectual reflection, or rhetorical persuasion, either as men or women. Our hearing and believing; conception, gestation and bringing forth of the word, are all, Augustine insists, of grace—and perhaps, precisely because the women of Augustine's day had no claim to authority, to understanding, to even to a voice, they are the best witnesses of this: what they conceive and what they bring forth can only be given by God. Rhetorically questioning our Lady about her role in the incarnation, Augustine captures this conviction in a rather bewildered way in *Sermon* 291.6:

> "What are you, that are due to give birth later on? How have you deserved this? Where have you received it from? Where from, that the one who made you will be made in you? Where, I repeat, does such a great good as this come to you from?"
>
> I appear to be questioning the virgin rather impudently, and knocking somewhat rudely at her modest ears with this voice of mine. But I can see the virgin, modest indeed, and yet answering me and giving me some advice:
>
> "You are asking me where all this comes to me from? I am rather shy of telling you in reply about my own blessings; listen to the angel's greeting, and acknowledge in me your salvation. Believe the one whom I believed. You are asking where all this comes to me from? Let the angel answer:
>
> Tell me, angel, where did Mary get all this from?

"I have already said where, when I greeted her: *Hail, full of grace.*" (Lk 1:28)[31]

What is happening here is that the classical preoccupation with public speaking, displays of rhetorical prowess, the authority of reason, and the power of persuasion—which were all, of course, regarded as the essential markers of masculinity[32]—are being rather shockingly subverted and replaced by a very different sort of voice: the voice of the devout faithful, among whom Augustine not only includes the patriarchs and prophets, John the Baptist, apostles and preachers, but all men *and* women who have conceived the word of God in the silence of their hearts and minds. Their struggles to voice/bring forth the Word in temporal, faltering, evanescent human words, so that it can be conveyed it to the minds and hearts of listeners, are the antithesis of classical male eloquence, power and prestige. Preaching on John the Baptist's assertion that "It is necessary for him to grow, but for me to diminish," Augustine reverts to this distinctive understanding of the voice:

> I take hold of my voice, and with the voice I've taken hold of I speak to you. The sound of my voice conducts to you the understanding of my word; and when the sound of the voice has conducted to you the understanding of the word, the sound is indeed over and done with; but the word which the sound conducted to you is now in your mind, and hasn't departed from mine. So the sound, having conveyed the word to you, doesn't the very sound seem to you to say, *It is necessary for him to grow, but for me to diminish*? The sound of the voice rang out to perform its service, and departed, (*Sonus vocis strepuit in ministerium, et abiit*) as if saying, *This joy of mine is now complete* (Jn 3:30.29). Let us hold on to the Word, let us not lose the Word conceived in the very marrow of our minds (*verbum medullitus conceptum non amittamus*). Do you want to see the voice disappearing, and the divinity of the Word remaining?[33]

Albeit temporal and fleeting, the sound of the voice therefore has an important role. As Augustine puts it here: "The sound of the voice rang out to perform its service." But this voice is most definitely not, for Augustine, the voice of manly, rhetorical persuasion. It is the humble, submissive, obedient and self-effacing sound of devout believers, who, like Mary or John the Baptist—and, ideally, like all Christian teachers and preachers—speak only to convey the Word that they have conceived in their own hearts and mind to the hearts and minds of their listeners, and who then humbly efface themselves. In one sense this is an impossible task, if what they have conceived by their listening and humble obedience[34] is the eternal, immutable Word of God, who has deigned to dwell in them through faith. Their spoken voices are, by contrast, as Augustine repeatedly observes, temporal, fleeting, and unable to do more than gesture to a truth which can only be found silently, within, in what he describes as "the ineffable voice of the heart": "But any who have risen beyond even these words, and begun to think worthily of God as far as human beings are permitted to will find a silence that is to be praised by the inexpressible voice of the heart (*ineffabilis corde uocis*)."[35] Augustine's contrast between voice and Word is one that draws on a long-standing classical distinction between the inarticulate voice (*uox confusa*) and the articulate voice (*uox articulata*).[36] The former was generally used to describe nonverbal, irrational, meaningless noise, such as the sounds made by animals; the latter to describe verbal, rational, meaningful speech, such as human beings use to communicate with each other. Reflecting on the vast gulf which separates created human beings from their eternal Creator, however, Augustine appears to relegate all human utterance to the category of "voice" or "sound," as in the quotation from *Sermon* 293 above, in contrast to the silent, eternal, divine "Word." *All* voices, he seems to be suggesting, whether inarticulate or articulate, are merely fleeting sounds that can do no more than gesture and admonish toward a truth that they can never fully express. He is therefore insistent that all we have, as human beings—men and women, John the Baptist and Mary, preacher and congregation—is voice; and that "voice" only becomes "Word" when God speaks to, in and through us, giving meaning to our voiced utterances, enabling them to communicate what cannot be fully expressed or understood in human voices, to the mind of another, thus enabling the Word to be conceived and to dwell—silently and wordlessly—in their minds.

Unsurprisingly, Augustine often describes the temporal and fleeting voice by which the Word we have conceived within is communicated to others, not in terms of articulate human words but in terms of an inarticulate "cry."[37] Reverting to the analogy of conception, gestation and birth, he describes the process by which we give utterance to the Word that dwells within us as like the process of giving birth; the Church is/we are like a pregnant woman who must bring forth the child that is growing within her; her groans and cries of labor turning to shouts of joy when the child is born.[38] Similarly, when what wells up within the heart overflows, Augustine likens the cry of joy (*jubilus*) to that of a pregnant woman on the point of giving birth, who must bring forth what she has conceived.[39] When the fullness of love spills over in ineffable delight; and when the voice of the inner man can no longer keep silence, then it erupts in full-throated, resonant waves of rhythmic, wordless sound: the sound of jubilation:

> Words fail us, but love does not . . . when we cannot articulate our thoughts, we must shout for joy. God is good, but what kind of good he is, who can tell? We cannot put it into words, but we are not allowed to remain silent. This is our problem: we cannot find words, but our sheer joy does not permit us to be silent; so let us neither speak nor hold our tongues. But what are we to do, if we can neither speak nor keep silence? Let us shout for joy. *Let us shout for joy to*

> *God, our salvation; shout with joy to God, all the earth* (Ps. 94.1; 99.1). What does that mean: *Shout for joy*? Give vent to the inarticulate expression of your joys, belch out (*eructate*) all your happiness to him. What kind of belching will there be after the final feasting, if even now after a modest meal our souls are so deeply affected?[40]

Augustine likewise describes the practice of reading and preaching on Scripture as one in which we conceive its joys and labour to bring them to birth, so that they might be born in the ears and minds of those who hear us. Preaching to his congregation, he therefore urges them to "provide my sermon with a nest" in themselves.[41]

Once again, what we find here is a voice which subverts articulate, literate, rational utterance and replaces it with inarticulate, illiterate, irrational cries. It is a voice that expresses the limitations and constraints of human utterance; its inability to fully capture or comprehend what it is bringing forth; its reaching after the inexpressible with inarticulate cries of suffering, joy—and, of course, praise—and once again, it subverts the established classical understanding of what constitutes an articulate voice.[42]

The limitations of human words to capture and confine the eternal Word are also demonstrated in the human life of the incarnate Word Himself, which Augustine similarly describes, in an extraordinary passage of the *Confessions* as a "cry": each stage of the His life becomes a cry, a shout or "voice of thunder," calling us back to the eternal Word that dwells within:

> He who is our very life came down . . . and summoned us in a voice of thunder to return to him (*et tonuit, clamans ut redeamus hinc ad eum*) in his hidden place, that place from which he set out to come to us when first he entered the Virgin's womb...[43] from there he came forth . . . impatient of delay he ran, shouting by his words, his deeds, his death and his life, his descent to hell and his ascension to heaven, shouting his demand that we return to him (*clamans dictis, factis, morte, vita, descensu, ascensu, clamans ut redeamus ad eum*). Then he withdrew from our sight, so that we might return to our own hearts and find him there.[44]

When he comes forth from the Virgin's womb, however, the eternal Word holds back his shouts to first becomes an infant without speech (*infans*—speechless)[45]—and it is clear to Augustine that it is precisely in Christ's humility and speechlessness that we first learn who he is. In a Sermon preached on Christmas Day he observes: "Thus by his very coming in this sort of way he is silently exhorting us, as effectively as if he shouted it aloud, to learn *to be rich in the one who became poor for us* (2 Cor 8:9)."[46]

The incarnate Word's inarticulate speechlessness and silence, which then gives way to thunderous cries, is evidence, for Augustine, of both his humanity and of his divine humility or self-emptying. In another sermon preached on Christmas Day, he therefore exclaims: "O manifest infirmity and wondrous humility in which was thus concealed total divinity!"[47] Although Christ is the Word of God he became an infant without words; although he is the Eternal Word he became a human being whose words and deeds were, like those of Mary, John the Baptist, and of all devout Christians, no more—and no less—than a voice, a cry or a shout, admonishing us to return to the Word who dwells within.

This emphasis on the humble voice is one that must have been a challenge for Augustine, the former professional rhetor, who had made a career educating others in the art of public speaking and, as municipal rhetor of Milan, in making speeches himself. His ambivalence, and the lasting difficulties he experienced in reconciling his past with his present life as a Christian bishop, is one that lies close to the surface of the many uneasy, self-conscious reflections on the role of the Christian speaker, and a Christian use of rhetoric, in letters, sermons and treatises such as *De Doctrina Christiana* Book 4. This was not least because he had to face the unavoidable fact that Jesus and his disciples represented the antithesis of classical culture's ideal of masculine authority: like the majority of Augustine's congregation they were low born, poor, simple and uneducated; their speech was plain and unpolished.[48] As he often observes, God chose fishermen, not orators.[49] Their faith rested on a humble submission to Christ (and later, to the authority of the Church), not on learning or reasoned, philosophical reflection. As Augustine puts it:

> The weak things of this world he chose, in order to disconcert the strong; and the foolish things he chose, in order to disconcert the wise; and the low-born things of this world God chose, and the things that are not (that is, they don't count), as though they were, that the things that are might be rendered vain' (1 Cor 1:27–28). He had come, you see, to teach humility and overthrow pride; God had come in humility.[50]

In short, in classical terms, those whom Jesus called possessed what we have identified as the voice of the devout faithful; a voice that subverted the classical ideal of masculinity but possessed all the traits which were customarily attributed to women in classical antiquity. This is, of course, a voice that Augustine first encountered in his own devout, uneducated mother, Monnica, who, on a number of significant occasions in his works, voices the truth in a simple, direct manner that rests on faith rather than reason; a humble submission to authority rather than intellectual debate; on God rather than herself.[51] Reflecting on his wayward adolescence in the *Confessions,* Augustine asks: "Do I dare to say that you were silent, my God, when I was straying from you? Were you really silent to me at that time? Whose, then, were the words spoken to me by my mother, your faithful follower? Were they not your words, the song you were constantly singing into my ears?"[52] At this stage Augustine would not listen; His mother's words, he comments: "Seemed to me mere woman's talk (*monitus muliebres*), which I would have blushed to heed. In truth they came from you, but I failed to realize that, and assumed that you were silent and she alone was talking. By using her you were not silent to me at all; and when I scorned her I was scorning you."[53]

This voice also becomes, for Augustine, the voice of the Church, the Bride of Christ,[54] who conceives believers in faith, carries them in her womb and gives birth to them in baptism.[55] Above all, it becomes the voice of the Church, the Body of Christ (*totus Christus*), in whom and through whom He speaks and prays, uniting her with Himself, as the Head of the Body. Again, the imagery is feminine; the emphasis is on obedience and submission; humility and faith; and most especially, on grace.

In his subversion of the classical stereotypes of the male and female voice, in which masculine eloquence, authority and public power are replaced by a silent, humble, inward, submission of faith to God's gracious Word; and in his radical rethinking of the classical distinction between the confused voice and the articulate voice, so that all voices, confused *and* articulate, are judged to be no more than fleeting and inadequate gestures towards the Eternal Word who is found in the ineffable voice of the heart, Augustine offers us an understanding of the voice that simultaneously confirms and subverts gender stereotypes. It is one that is characteristically (in classical terms) feminine rather than masculine; plain rather than eloquent; humble, obedient and submissive rather than controlling; weak rather than strong; based on faith rather than reason; self-effacing rather than self-assertive; given rather than acquired; gesturing beyond itself rather than to itself. In other words, it is, in terms of Augustine's day, a voice which is thoroughly feminine; one for which the most fitting analogy he can find is that of pregnancy, gestation and birth; and the best example (besides his own mother) that of Mary, the Mother of Jesus, at the Annunciation.

NOTES

1. The project is funded by the Polish Minister of Science and Higher Education within the program under the name "Regional Initiative of Excellence" in 2019–2022, project number: 028/RID/2018/19.

2. Eg. 1 Cor. 14:34. See Mary Beard, "The Public Voice of Women," *Women's History Review* 24, no. 5 (2015): 809–18.

3. See Peter Brown, *The Body and Society: Men, Women and Sexual Renunciation in Early Christianity* (New York: Columbia University Press, 1988). For texts

on the female voice in contrast to the male voice in classical musical theorists, see Andrew Barker, *Greek Musical Writings, vol. 2 Harmonic and Acoustic Theory* (Cambridge: Cambridge University Press, 1989), 80–84; 88–89; 105–8. On the role of the rhetorical voice in defining masculinity, in contrast to the 'effeminate' voice see Maud Gleason, *Making Men: Sophists and Self-Presentation in Ancient Rome* (Princeton: Princeton University Press, 1995) and E. Gunderson, *Staging Masculinity: The Rhetoric of Performance in the Roman World* (Ann Arbor: Michigan University Press, 2000).

4. No one has contributed more to the study of women in early Christianity than Elizabeth Clark and Gillian Clark. For the former's reflections on the limitations of what can be achieved see "Holy Women, Holy Words: Early Christian Women, Social History, and the 'Linguistic Turn,'" *Journal of Early Christian Studies* 6, no. 3 (1998): 413–29 and note 10 for references to her other relevant works. For the latter's nuanced reflections on understandings of gender see the collection of essays in *Body and Gender, Soul and Reason in Late Antiquity* (Farnham: Ashgate, 2016) and *Women in Late Antiquity: Pagan and Christian Lifestyles* (Oxford: Oxford University Press, 1993).

5. For a collection of essays on the significance of the female voice in Greek literature see, André Lardinois and Laura McClure, eds., *Making Silence Speak: Women's Voices in Greek Literature and Society* (Princeton: Princeton University Press, 2001).

6. All translations are from Augustine, *The Works of Saint Augustine: A Translation for the 21st Century* (Hyde Park: New City Press, 1990–) unless otherwise noted.

7. Augustine, *The Trinity*, trans., intro., and notes Edmund Hill, O.P., vol. I/5 *The Works of Saint Augustine: A Translation for the 21st Century*, ed. John E. Rotelle O.S.A. (Hyde Park: New City Press, 2012), 15.4.22.

8. See notes 39 and 40 below.

9. As Jennifer Hockenbery observes, "Augustine never used exclusive language. For Augustine God is not a He, a She, or an It. These pronouns correspond with the words which denote God, not with God qua God. Because the Latin writer is forced to change the gender of the pronoun with the gender of the word to which it corresponds, the Latin reader is less likely to pin a gender on God and more likely to see such gender roles as part of the language rather than the metaphysics of the divine being." See "The He, She and It of God: Translating Saint Augustine's Gendered Latin God-talk into English," *Augustinian Studies* 36, no. 2 (2005): 440/ 433–44.

10. Augustine, *The Trinity*, 15.4.24

11. Augustine, *Homilies on the Gospel of John*, trans. and notes by Edmund Hill, O.P., vol. III/12 *The Works of Saint Augustine: A Translation for the 21st Century*, ed., intro., and notes, Allan Fitzgerald O.S.A. (Hyde Park: New City Press, 2009), 37.4.

12. See Tim Denecker and Gert Partoens, "*De uoce et uerbo*. Augustine's exegesis of John 1:1–3 and 23 in sermons 288 and 293A auct. (*Dolbeau* 3)," *Annali di Storia Dell'Esegesi* 31, no. 1 (2014): 95–118.

13. Augustine, *Sermons (1–400)*, trans. and notes Edmund Hill, O.P., vol. III/1–10 *The Works of Saint Augustine: A Translation for the 21st Century*, ed. John E. Rotelle O.S.A. (Hyde Park: New City Press, 1990–95), 289.1.

14. Augustine, *The Trinity*, 13.5.23. His point here is that Christ was conceived without the inheritance of original sin.

15. Augustine, *Sermons*, 291.5.

16. This understanding of human communication was a commonplace of philosophical reflection on language. See Jaap Mansfeld, "'Illuminating What is Thought:' A Middle Platonist *Placitum* on 'Voice' in Context," *Mnemosyne* 58, no. 3 (2005): 358–407 for references (and to the analogy of pregnancy to describe how the voice gives birth to what is welling up in the mind see p. 374).

17. Augustine, *Sermons*, 288.3.

18. Augustine, *Sermons*, 288.4.

19. Augustine, *Sermons*, 288.3.

20. Augustine, *Sermons*, 288.4.

21. Augustine, *Sermons*, 289.3.

22. Augustine, *Sermons*, 293.1.

23. See Augustine, *Letters (1–270)*, trans., intro., and notes Roland J. Teske, S.J., vol. II/2 *The Works of Saint Augustine: A Translation for the 21st Century*, ed. Boniface Ramsey (Hyde Park: New City Press, 1997–2005), 147.2; cf. 147.44. Similarly in a letter to Florentina he writes, "You must hold most firmly what he who is the interior teacher of the interior human being will teach you. For, even if through me you can come to know something conducive to salvation, he shows you in your heart that what is said is true, because *neither he who plants nor he who waters is important, but God who gives the increase* (1 Cor 3:7)." See Augustine, *Letters,* 266.4. Referred to by Mark Vessey, "Response to Catherine Conybeare, 'Women of Letters,'" in *Voices in Dialogue: Reading Women in the Middle Ages*, eds. Linda Olson and Kathryn Kerby-Fulton (Notre Dame: Notre Dame University Press, 2005), 86–87.

24. Augustine, *The Teacher*, in *The Teacher; The Free Choice of the Will; Grace and Free Will*, trans. Robert P. Russell, O.S.A., vol. 59 *The Fathers of the Church* (Washington D.C.: Catholic University of America Press, 1968), 11.38.

25. Augustine, *Instructing Beginners in Faith*, trans., intro., and notes Raymond Canning, vol. V *The Works of Saint Augustine: A Translation for the 21st Century*, ed. Boniface Ramsey (Hyde Park: New City Press, 2009), 2.3; cf. 10.14: "What we perceive silently with our minds brings us greater delight and holds us more tightly, and we do not want to be called away from it to the world of noisy speech, which is a vastly different place"; and 10.15: "What is imbibed by the mind in one swift draught takes long and convoluted by-ways as it comes to expression on our lips of flesh, and, because our utterance differs greatly from our insight, we find that speaking palls and we would rather remain silent."

26. Augustine, *Homilies on the First Epistle of John*, trans., intro., and notes Boniface Ramsey, vol. III/14 *The Works of Saint Augustine: A Translation for the 21st Century*, ed. Daniel E. Doyle, O.S.A. and Thomas Martin O.S.A. (Hyde Park: New City Press, 2008), 4.6.

27. Augustine, *Expositions of the Psalms, Vol. 1–6*, trans. and intro. Maria Boulding, O.S.B., vol. III/15–20 *The Works of Saint Augustine: A Translation for the 21st Century*, ed. John E. Rotelle, O.S.A. (Hyde Park: New City Press, 200–04), 3.4; cf. 102.2, 119.9, 125.6; cf. Cyril of Jerusalem *Procatechesis* 14: "The unmarried

women should be kept together in the same way, either singing or reading silently, so that their lips move inaudibly, 'for I do not allow a woman to speak in church.' Married women should observe the same practice, praying and moving their lips silently, so that Samuel can come and your barren soul can conceive salvation, for God will hear you, which is what the name Samuel means" in Edward Yarnold, *Cyril of Jerusalem* (London: Routledge, 2000), 84.

28. Augustine, *Expositions of the Psalms*, 141.2.

29. Augustine, *Sermons*, 104.1. Augustine often uses the analogy of eating, rumination and (sometimes) belching forth the word of God alongside that of conception, gestation and birth. See Augustine, *Expositions of the Psalms,* 21.i.27: "*The poor shall eat and be satisfied.* The humble, those who despise this world, will eat, and they will imitate me, for being so nourished they will neither strive for this world's plenty, nor fear its want. *And those who seek the Lord will praise him*, for the praise of the Lord is the belching (*eructatio*) out of that fullness. *Their hearts will live for ever and ever*, for that food nourishes the heart" (emphasis mine). Similarly, Augustine describes John, the beloved disciple, who leant on our Lord's breast at the Last Supper and drank in the mystery of the Word, as then belching it forth when he began to write his Gospel. See Augustine, *Sermons*, 341.5 and *Homilies on the Gospel of John*, 1.7: "In the beginning was the Word. . . ."

30. See references in Mansfeld, n. 16 above.

31. This passage is redolent of many later Syriac verse homilies and hymns on the Annunciation by the likes of Jacob of Sarug or Ephrem the Syrian. See Susan Ashbrook Harvey, "Spoken Words, Voiced Silence: Biblical Women in Syriac Tradition," *Journal of Early Christian Studies* 9, no. 1 (2001): 105–31.

32. See Gleason, n. 5 above.

33. Augustine, *Sermons*, 293.3; cf. *Confessions*, trans. and intro. Maria Boulding, O.S.B., vol. I/1 *The Works of Saint Augustine: A Translation for the 21st Century*, ed. John E. Rotelle O.S.A (Hyde Park: New City Press, 1997/2005), 11.6.8, where Augustine reflects on how God made heaven and earth by his eternal Word and contrasts this with words spoken in time by the voice: "The mind would then compare the words sounding in time with your silent Word in eternity (*cum aeterno in silentio verbo tuo*), and say, 'These are something different, totally different. They are far below me and have no being, since they are fleeting and ephemeral; but the Word of my God is above me and abides for ever.'" The most well-known passage is, of course, *Confessions* 9.10.25 and the Vision at Ostia, in which the various levels/voices of created reality gradually fall silent so that Augustine and his mother, Monnica, are able fleetingly to touch the eternal Word itself.

34. *Obaudire* (to obey); *audire* (to hear).

35. Augustine, *Sermons*, 341.16.

36. See Mansfeld n. 16 above; Carol Harrison, "Confused Voices: Sound and Sense in the Later Augustine," in *The Intellectual World of Christian Late Antiquity*, eds. Lewis Ayres, Michael Champion, and Matthew R. Crawford (Cambridge University Press, Forthcoming); Mark Payne, *The Animal Part: Human and Other Animals in the Poetic Imagination* (Chicago: University of Chicago Press, 2010).

37. Most famously, Augustine, *Confessions*, 10.27.38; cf. 1.6.8; 13.29.44.

38. See Augustine, *Expositions of the Psalms*, 101.i.2: "I think that the barren Sarah must have been happy even in her groaning as she was giving birth ((*laetam gemuisse cum pareret*); and from our fear of you, Lord, we, like Sarah, have conceived and brought forth the spirit of salvation' (*concepimus et parturivimus spiritum salutis*);" *Sermons*, 216.7: "Look, mother Church is in labor, see, she is groaning in travail to give birth to you, to bring you forth into the light of faith (*ecce ut te pariat, atque in lucem fidei producat, laborat in gemitu suo*). Do not agitate her maternal womb with your impatience, and thus constrict the passage to your delivery."

39. Augustine, *Expositions of the Psalms*, 137.4: "Our heart is pregnant, on the point of giving birth, and searching for a place to bring forth its adoration" (*Gravidum cor nostrum parturit, et ubi pariat quaerit*); cf. 32.ii.8; 65.2: "The sound of a heart labouring to bring forth into its voice its happiness over what it has conceived" (*quasi parturientis et parientis cordis laetitiam in vocem rei conceptae*).

40. Augustine, *Expositions of the Psalms*, 102.8; cf. 134.3; 146.11.

41. Augustine, *Sermons*, 37.1.

42. There are exceptions to this position in classical thought and writers who held that non-verbal sound communicates meaning. These are considered by James I. Porter, *The Origins of Aesthetic Thought in Ancient Greece: Matter, Sensation and Experience* (Cambridge: Cambridge University Press, 2010) esp. ch. 6 "The Music of the Voice"; "Rhetoric, Aesthetics and the Voice" in collected volume 92–108. There is also a focus on the sound of the voice as conveying meaning in rhetorical reflection on the art of delivery, where the voice, gesture and facial expression are all held to be communicative. See Cicero, "*Orator,*" in *Cicero: Brutus and Orator*, trans. Robert A. Kaster (Oxford: Oxford University Press, 2020), 184–88; Quintilian, *The Orator's Education* 11.3, ed. and trans. Donald A. Russell, Loeb Classical Library 494 (Cambridge: Harvard University Press, 2001), 84–185.

43. This is reminiscent of Ignatius, who speaks of the virginity of Mary and the birth and death of Jesus as "three mysteries for crying out that were wrought in the silence of God." See Ignatius, *Letter to the Magnesians*, in *The Apostolic Fathers: Greek Texts and English Translations*, trans. and ed. Michael W. Holmes, 2nd ed. (Grand Rapids: Baker Academic, 2007), 6.1–9.2.

44. Augustine, *Confessions*, 4.12.19.

45. Augustine, *Sermons*, 184.3: "The one who holds the world in being was lying in a manger; he was simultaneously speechless infant and Word." As Jean Louis Chrétien in *Saint Augustin et les actes de parole* (Paris: Presses Universitaires de France, 2002), 102 comments: "Far from being an occasion for sentimentality or emotion, Christmas invites us to consider the abyssal movement of the Word depriving itself of speech: the centre of the meditation is Christ's *kenosis*" (translation mine).

46. Augustine, *Sermons*, 192.3.

47. Augustine, *Sermons*, 184.3.

48. Augustine, *Sermons*, 341.4.

49. Augustine, *Sermons*, 341.4: "And so it was safer and sounder for the Lord to gain an orator through a fisherman than a fisherman through an orator."

50. Augustine, *Sermons*, 341.4.

51. Augustine, *The Happy Life*, in *Trilogy on Faith and Happiness*, trans. Roland J. Teske, S.J., Michael Campbell, O.S.A., and Ray Kearney, vol. I/3 *The Works of Saint Augustine: A Translation for the 21st Century*, ed. Boniface Ramsey (Hyde Park: New City Press, 2010), 10; 16; 27. See also *On Order (Divine Providence and the Problem of Evil)*, in *The Happy Life; Answer to the Skeptics; Divine Providence and the Problem of Evil; Soliloquies*, trans. Robert. P. Russell, O.S.A., vol. 1 *The Fathers of the Church* (New York: Cima Publishing Co., Inc, 1948), 2.1. Cf. *On Music*, in *The Immortality of the Soul; The Magnitude of the Soul; On Music; The Advantage of Believing; On Faith in Things Unseen*, trans. Robert Catesby Taliaferro, vol. 4 *The Fathers of The Church* (Washington D.C.: Catholic University of America Press, 1947), 6.17.59; *Against the Academics (Answer to the Skeptics)*, in *The Happy Life; Answer to the Skeptics; Divine Providence and the Problem of Evil; Soliloquies*, trans. Denis J. Kavanagh, O.S.A., vol. 1 of *The Fathers of the Church* (New York: Cima Publishing Co., Inc, 1948), 3.19.42; *On Order* 2.26–30; *On the Greatness of the Soul (The Magnitude of the Soul)*, in *The Immortality of the Soul; The Magnitude of the Soul; On Music; The Advantage of Believing; On Faith in Things Unseen*, trans. John J McMahon, S.J., vol. 4 *The Fathers of The Church* (Washington D.C.: Catholic University of America Press, 1947), 7.12; See also *On the Usefulness of Belief*, in *On Christian Belief*, trans. and notes Edmund Hill, O.P., Ray Kearney, Michael G. Campbell and Bruce Harbert, vol. I/8 *The Works of Saint Augustine: A Translation for the 21st Century*, ed. Boniface Ramsey (Hyde Park: New City Press, 2005), where he emphasises the priority and necessity of faith, hope and love in contrast to reason:

52. Augustine, *Confessions*, 2.3.7.

53. Augustine, *Confessions*, 2.3.7.

54. Augustine, *Teaching Christianity*, trans. and notes Edmund Hill, O.P., vol. I/11 of *The Works of Saint Augustine: A Translation for the 21st Century*, ed. John E. Rotelle, O.S.A. (Hyde Park: New City Press, 1995), 1.16.15; *Sermons*, 341.19.

55. Augustine, *Sermons*, 228.1–2. See Robin Jensen, *Living Water: Images, Symbols, and Settings of Early Christian Baptism* (Leiden: Brill, 2010), 248–50, for references to this common motif in the early Church. She notes that it was especially popular in North Africa.

Chapter 8

Variations on Eve

Karmen MacKendrick

Augustine tells us that when he was young, he dismissed Christianity in part based on its texts, which seemed to him to tell stories fit for children and not for serious thinkers. As a young adult, he was drawn instead to the richly complicated philosophy of the Manichaeans, finding it less offensive to his intelligence. In fact, one reason that he finally abandoned Manichaeism was his dissatisfaction with the argumentative abilities of those supposed to be its best thinkers. The stories of the Hebrew Bible and associated Christian scriptures only became interesting to him after he heard the interpretations that the bishop Ambrose of Milan gave in his sermons, interpretations informed by Platonic philosophy and offering the layers of complexity that Augustine had previously missed. After his own rather drawn out and convoluted conversion to Christianity, he became another tireless scriptural exegete.

Late ancient and medieval exegesis is fascinating in its own right, and for many reasons. It is often intensely philosophical, drawing on both Greek philosophies and their Roman derivatives. It can be dizzyingly intertextual. And it wanders among genres in a way that has become distant from us now. Augustine is exemplary here, offering argumentative textual analyses, sermons, and prayers (sometimes from the midst of analysis, as in the *Confessions*). Most intriguingly, he alludes to scriptural myth to develop myths of his own, which can serve their own interpretive function, a practice he shares with other early Christians, not all of whom make it into orthodoxy. He is also like other exegetes of his time in being drawn repeatedly to the biblical book of Genesis, so much so that he devotes multiple entire volumes to it, along with significant parts of several others. In the course of these extensive discussions, the figure of Eve appears both analytically and mythically, and the latter adds both complication and nuance to the former. I would like here to read the myth and analysis into each other.

The analytic exegeses are not entirely consistent, which is less of a problem than one might think. In the *Confessions*, Augustine envisions readers arguing over the meaning intended by Moses, whom he believes to be the author of the early books of the Hebrew Bible. Rather than insisting on one interpretation over another, he asks, "Why not rather say both, if both are true?"[1] This generous approach reappears in *On Christian Teaching*, his work most focused on interpretation, where Augustine explains that multiple interpretations may be "in harmony with the truth," even intended by "the Holy Spirit," whose inspiration he believes is behind scriptural texts, "For what more liberal and more fruitful provision could God have made in regard to the Sacred Scriptures than that the same words might be understood in several senses . . . ?"[2] He does caution that readings dissonant with other parts of Christian scripture or teaching are still a problem, but otherwise, he encourages a generosity of interpretation. In the *Confessions*, he remarks that if he had been so privileged as to have written Genesis under divine inspiration, he would hope "that if, in the light of the truth, another exegete saw a different meaning, that also would not be found absent from the meaning of the same words."[3]

This generosity and multiplicity may serve us well in reading through Augustine's interpretations of Eve. She is caught up in the wider range of his thoughts on gender, and there seems to be a consensus that Augustine ultimately determines that women must be inferior in *some* way to men— "women *qua* humans were created in God's image, but women as specifically female were not," as E. Ann Matter summarizes.[4] But the consensus is hardly complete, as Matter also notes, and his ideas about women are as complex as any of the "theological concepts with which he struggled in his long and eventful life."[5] The complexity of Eve shows up from the beginning, as Augustine works his way through the Genesis stories of creation—and returns to begin over and over again.

IN OUR IMAGE, IN OUR LIKENESS

Augustine raises his optimistic question about interpretation as he begins, in the penultimate book of his *Confessions*, to work through chapter one of Genesis. He doesn't make it very far, despite previous efforts in his books on Genesis and in, among others, *On Christian Teaching* and the massive volumes *On the Trinity* and *City of God*. Sometimes he makes it as far as chapter three, when he considers the stories of humanity's exile from Paradise and the complicated consequences that follow. He finds that the truths keep unfolding. Human creation gets complicated quickly, since the first and second chapters of Genesis offer different and not quite compatible accounts as to how it happens.

The first of these stories is brief: "Then God said: 'Let us make humankind in our image, according to our likeness. . . . ' So God created humankind in his image, in the image of God he created them; male and female he created them."[6] This passage is long enough, though, to give Augustine particular trouble—he even abandons his first effort at a full exegesis of Genesis when he reaches it.[7]

The verses gain added importance from their role in Augustine's intellectual history. His early contempt for Christian stories was not only about style; the Manichaeans were dismissive of what they saw as the claim that God has a material body.[8] What else, after all, could be meant by insisting that humans are God's image? After he heard Ambrose, Augustine also began to hear a way past the flat-footed Manichaean reading. That he could get past it, however, does not quite mean that he knew where to go from there. His *Unfinished Commentary* on Genesis actually offers two readings, added at different stages of the project.

The earlier is Christological. Since he is dealing with material beings who are somehow in the divine image, it makes sense to him to consider the materialized, or incarnate, version of God in the person of Christ. Perhaps humans could be in God's image insofar as they are like God the Son. Even though he is considering the enfleshed version of divinity, Augustine argues that the resemblance is not physical; instead, "the rational substance" of the human mind "was made both through and to the likeness," and "the likeness of God to which man was made can be understood as the very Word of God, that is, the only-begotten Son."[9] Despite the masculinity of the Son, this first reading is largely indifferent to gender: the rational substance that belongs to every human is created in the image of God's likeness; that is, of the Word that is credited in the fourth Christian gospel as a co-creative persona of God.[10]

Eventually Augustine adds two more paragraphs, before abandoning the book.[11] He does not undo or discount his earlier interpretation. Now, however, he focuses more on the "us" and "our" in the scriptural citation: "Let *us* create," "in *our* image, according to *our* likeness." This suggests that the original reflected by the image cannot be singular, as the Son is. On the updated interpretation, it is still the human mind that is the image of God. Now, however, that mind is understood to be the image of the Trinity of Father, Son, and Spirit.[12] It is never entirely clear how this image works, but then, it is imperfectly clear how the Trinity itself works. In *On the Trinity*, Augustine again parallels the mind to the Trinitarian God, though he is somewhat anxious to make it clear that the human mind can never approach the stature of divinity. He understands the mind as having the faculties of memory (corresponding to the Father), understanding (corresponding to the Son), and will or desire (corresponding to the Holy Spirit).[13] As he helpfully suggests, "if this cannot be grasped by the understanding, let it be held by faith. . . ."[14]

In neither of these versions—the mind in the image of Christ, the mind in the image of the Trinity—does Augustine immediately worry about whether the image belongs more or less to a particular gender.[15] That the plural God who makes "in our image" creates plural humans, "male and female," interests Augustine, but not as a problem. It is true that he seems sometimes to assign gender to different mental faculties, the inferior active and the superior contemplative: "Thus let man be made to the image and likeness of God, male and female, that is, intellect and action."[16] He acknowledges the intellectual sophistication of some women while still suggesting that most are not men's intellectual equals—but he keeps circling back to insist that the image of god is human, regardless.[17] He considers whether woman might be the image only as a part of humanity; that is, in combination with man—but the same would then be true for man.[18] That is, perhaps the image is male-and-female because it needs both to be a proper image of God. Today, we might be discouraged by the limitation of seeing only humans in the divine image, or by the gender binary. But it remains encouraging to see that Augustine does not exclude any humans from being in the image of the God who makes them. The first story of Eve sets her on a largely equal footing with her consort, both images of God, though the image is something of an abstraction.

A HELPER, AS HIS PARTNER

Matters become less encouraging when Augustine tries to reconcile the Genesis account with a verse from Paul's first letter to the Corinthians, which depends in turn on the second story of human creation.[19] Paul argues that men are disgraced by praying or prophesying with their heads covered, and women by doing the same with their heads uncovered. His explanation is not altogether clarifying: "A man ought not to have his head veiled, since he is the image and reflection of God; but woman is the reflection of man. Indeed, man was not made from woman, but woman from man."[20] In taking up this verse, Augustine necessarily takes up as well the second story of human creation. There, the first *man* is created from earth enlivened with God's breath; the first *woman* is created later, from the man's animate flesh, in order to be a companion who alleviates his loneliness.[21]

The effort to reconcile Genesis 1 with Genesis 2 and Paul leads Augustine into great convolutions of thought, and to a focus on yet another part of the brief first story: from image, to us and our, and now to male-and-female. These considerations appear especially in *On the Trinity* and the two books of another Genesis account, *Genesis Against the Manichaeans*. Ultimately,

Augustine retains his earlier ideas that the part of the human that is properly said to be in the image of God is the mind, that the mind is the image of the Trinity, and that the likeness of mind to God holds irrespective of gender—though we have already seen that he is imperfectly consistent about this. He decides now that the distinction between "male and female" in creation is at the level of body: "A common nature, therefore, is recognized in their minds, but in their bodies a division of that one mind itself is figured."[22] This also allows him to see the second creation story as simply an elaboration of the first.

In his considerations in *Genesis Against the Manichaeans*, Augustine does not at first differentiate bodies by gender. Instead, he argues that the uprightness of the human body is part of our greatness, showing that "our minds are rightly raised to higher things."[23] Matters become less promising near the end of the text, where Augustine turns more specifically to Eve's creation. Here he uses bodily difference to justify subordination:

> For there was still need to bring it about not only that the soul rule over the body, because the body has the position of a servant, but also that virile reason hold subject to itself its animal part, by the help of which it governs the body. The woman was made as an illustration of this, for the order of things makes her subject to man.[24]

Both *The Literal Interpretation of Genesis* and the *Confessions* also place women's presumed inferiority in the flesh rather than in the image. In the former, Augustine writes, "Now women are not excluded from this grace of renewal and this reformation of the image of God, although on the physical side their sexual characteristics may suggest otherwise, namely, that man alone is said to be the image and gory of God."[25] In the latter, he suggests that women's physicality creates a naturally subordinate position; though like both God and man "in the mind of her rational understanding," in body woman "should be . . . subject to the sex of her husband."[26] *On the Trinity* suggests something similar, with an emphasis on the universality of the divine image among humans, but a suggestion that women considered in their bodies are lesser than men in theirs.[27] So it seems that humans, irrespective of gender, are spiritually and intellectually in the divine image, but that women's bodies are somehow inferior to men's. This consideration does not arise in the first creation story, where even the separation of "male and female he created them" reads as a division that is not a hierarchization. (It has even been read to suggest an androgynous god.) The second creation story takes on its importance less on its own than as an element of Paul's arguments, which are more evidently misogynist than the Genesis passages that ground them. Read through Paul reading the second chapter of Genesis, woman is inferior as secondarily created, as made to help man (though the help seems to be through companionship), as dependent on the man for her flesh. As divinely created, flesh is good. We cannot quite escape the realization, though, that there is a scale of goodness, and male flesh seems to be better than female. The second story of Eve seems to vacillate about her equality with Adam; both are good, and here the goodness includes flesh. Her flesh often appears to be somehow subordinate and even inferior to his, though, however equal their minds.

AND TO DUST YOU SHALL RETURN (AND COME BACK AGAIN)

Bodily inferiority would not matter if bodies didn't. But believing as he does in a good creator, Augustine refuses to see material creation as an evil—and happily, his division of better and lesser flesh is less stable than it might seem. Another Genesis story is the most famous scriptural source for claims about Eve; in it, we read not of the creation of humans but of their fall from their early status as close to their God. The pair of the first humans to be created is allowed to eat anything growing in their garden Paradise, except the fruit of one tree.[28] That fruit will give them a breadth of knowledge that could make them like gods, provided they were also to eat the fruit of immortality.[29] Tempted by a serpent, the humans eat the fruit of the tree of knowledge anyway; when their creator finds out, he angrily exiles them from Paradise—before they can gain immortality and become too much like gods themselves. Though there are many oddities that draw exegetes to these stories, Augustine is concerned with two points in particular: just how to understand the act of disobedience, and just what the effects of the exile are for subsequent generations.

That this original sinful act is passed on to all humans, and that the blame falls chiefly on Eve, are both points of dogma widely attributed to Augustine. The first of these is well supported; the second is less so. It's easy to see how that reading arises from the story. Eve eats first, then persuades her consort to do the same; he, in turn, blames her the moment they are caught by their creator. (To be fair, she then blames the serpent, so no one really comes across as an exemplar of courage.) When Augustine blames Eve, it is usually to highlight the contrasting figure of Mary. The pair shows up often in his sermons: "Man was ensnared through a woman administering poison; let man be restored through a woman administering salvation;" he writes, or "It was a woman who sold us death; a woman who bore us life." The sentence preceding this last one offers a parallel comparison, "Now therefore, let everyone, having been condemned in the first man, pass over to the second [Christ]."³⁰ Augustine is fond of these contrasting pairs. One of the most inventive opposes Eve not to Mary the mother but to Mary Magdalene as she tells the other, skeptical disciples that she has seen Christ's empty post-resurrection tomb: "A woman brought the news of death to her man in paradise; and women too brought the news of salvation to men in the Church."³¹ More elaborately: "When Eve reported what the serpent had said, she was listened to straightaway. A lying woman was believed, and so we all died; they didn't believe women telling the truth so that we might live."³² Augustine and other church fathers love to contrast "the first man" to "the second," calling Christ a "new Adam," emphasizing the beginning over.³³ Eve may be blamed, but not more than her consort.

One reason that the popular imagination holds on to Eve as the guilty party has to do not with her ability to persuade the first man, but with the stubbornly lingering association between the first sin and sex—both intercourse and desire. This sin must be her fault, since women are famously the sorts of creatures who tempt otherwise rational men into carnal lust. We can at least feel relieved that Augustine says nothing of the sort. It is not even true that sexual desire remains for him the root of all sin, though he does find it a particularly powerful and persistent temptation. The first sin is disobedience, and although this affects sexual desire, it does not arise from that desire. In fact, he sometimes argues that prior to disobedience, there was sex in Paradise (at least between the humans, and one can imagine among the other animals there as well), and it was mutually pleasurable and good, if a little too rational to be universally appealing.³⁴ Augustine tends to see punishments as built into sins, rather than being subsequently imposed; the penalty for disobedience is disobedience. When the humans turn their wills and desires away from God as their object and from harmonizing with God as their intent—that is, when they disobey—they break the will's original harmony.³⁵ In a ripple effect of consequence, humans find themselves both distant from God and inwardly inharmonious. Their own wills disobey them, so that they harbor conflicting desires. Their bodies disobey their wills—and as Augustine points out, this is nowhere so evident as in the seeming self-will of the genitals, though he thinks that we have lost a great many other skills and pleasures in being unable to harmonize our flesh more perfectly with our wishes.³⁶ So the first sin is disobedience, and the result is our inability to obey both God and our own best selves. Disharmony is passed along not because sexual reproduction is a sin, but because the homunculi of the first man's sperm have been altered, in Lamarckian style, by his actions.³⁷ Eve is relevant to the sin, but not so much to its inheritance, though admittedly for rather androcentric reasons.

The lingering effect of that first sin is the tendency to keep sinning; that is, to turn away from the good. *Concupiscence*, often interpreted as lust, has a broader sense for Augustine: we inherit a tendency to make the wrong choices; not so much to love evil as to be distracted from or mistaken about the good.[38] We do the wrong things because we want the wrong things.

And this turns us to the role of that contrasting, redemptive pair of humans, and ultimately to resurrection. Christ's incarnation and self-sacrifice allow humankind to overcome death completely, though only after dying once, as Christ did. In Augustine's version, risen bodies are even better and more beautiful than they were in Eden. When bodies are perfected for their heavenly lives, he says, they will retain their sexes, because being female is not, in fact, a defect.[39] This claim sits oddly with the notion that women are inferior by virtue of body. If there is nothing defective about one kind of body, how can that kind of body be inferior to another?

An important aspect of bodily perfection is sinlessness. Augustine distinguishes three options. In our fallen, inharmonious state, we cannot avoid sin. The first couple could have, though they didn't.[40] Risen bodies cannot sin. This sounds alarming; surely only the most mind-numbingly pious among us could imagine that such restricted ability is a thing of joy. But resurrected bodies see divinity and beauty everywhere; "see" not as a reasoned abstraction, but as an incarnate act. "It will not be as now, when the invisible realities of God are apprehended and observed through the material things of his creation," writes Augustine. Rather, "He will be seen in every body by means of bodies, wherever the eyes of the spiritual body are directed with their penetrating gaze."[41] All that the resurrected perceive is God, and so their desire and attention is necessarily well directed. They cannot sin not because their wills are constrained, but because everything available to desire is good. They cannot be distracted from their delight in God because it is God's beauty that they see in all things.

Risen bodies remain themselves.[42] But they are themselves in their best versions, with their damage and imperfections mended, their proportions made pleasing, and their abilities harmonized with their wills. Even those pesky genitals become cause for the praise of divinity: "All the members and organs of the incorruptible body, which now we see to be suited to various necessary uses, shall contribute to the praises of God; for in that life necessity shall have no place, but full, certain, secure, everlasting felicity," Augustine writes. Every bit becomes "part[] of the bodily harmony."[43] The harmony extends from the parts of the body to its animation. We cannot even imagine the kind of movement of which risen bodies are capable, Augustine says exuberantly, but, "One thing is certain, the body shall forthwith be wherever the spirit wills, and the spirit shall will nothing which is unbecoming either to the spirit or to the body."[44] In *On Christian Teaching*, Augustine distinguishes the *use* that most of the world has from the *enjoyment* that we rightly take in God; in this post-resurrection world, enjoyment characterizes every encounter, as it should, when all we encounter is divine.[45] Augustine cites Paul's declaration

"That God may be all in all," explaining, "He shall be the end of our desires who shall be seen without end, loved without cloy, praised without weariness. This outgoing of affection, this employment, shall certainly be, like eternal life itself, common to all."[46] So bodies of any gender will be desirable in the same way that God is, because, again, all that there is to desire is God, who is all in all. Desire is re-unified even when its objects seem to be many, and the scattering created by the original sin is undone.

The first creation story left us with a largely egalitarian, if disembodied, sense of humankind. The second offers much more of an opportunity to argue that women should be subordinate by virtue of bodily dependence and thus inferiority. The story of the first punishment seems to strengthen the argument, since Eve eats the fruit first and persuades her consort to do the same. The original sin, though, is patrilineal. When the story of which it is part reaches its culmination—from the sin, to the exile into mortality, to the redemption by Christ, to bodily immortality—Augustine is specific about the equal glory of all bodies. All of his readings tend to be ambivalent, ambiguous, or vacillating about women's place and value, but his final vision is one of universal good, and the third Eve is risen into perfection. That good comes, he says consistently, through the sacrifice made by the "second Adam." He is far less consistent about the "second Eve," who seems to have multiple identities—Mary the mother and Mary Magdalene at least. Let us give her one more.

A NEW EVE

As I have noted, Augustine, like some other late ancient thinkers, takes up scriptural myths to work variations on them. This is a different kind of exegesis than we are used to now, requiring a more poetic kind of attention. In particular, his *Confessions* is full of variations on biblical stories, often caught up into his ostensibly autobiographical descriptions. A duo of famous examples can make this clear. In book two, he describes stealing pears, just for the sake of doing so. His description of his own sinfulness seems absurdly exaggerated—after all, he only stole some pears, not even a great many, and not, so far as we know, from someone in urgent need of them. But the drama makes sense as a variation on the primal sin of plucking the wrong fruit. Augustine describes his error, like that one, as a mistaken desire for freedom—the first humans desire to make their choices in defiance of God's; Augustine turns his desire toward peer approval rather than toward divinity.[47] The theft is minor; the parable is not. The second famous instance comes from his final conversion to Christianity, in another garden full of trees. He listens not to the whispering hiss of a serpent but to a child's voice ("take up and read") and a convenient text (Paul's letter to the Romans). And his scattered desires, his various clinging "old loves," are gathered together into a desire for good.[48] The shattering and dispersal of desire that marks the first sin is undone, if only for a moment, in the surpassingly peaceful instant of turning desire to God. The story of the pears re-creates the original sin, where the real freedom of perfect accord is lost in the brief, distracting pleasure of rule-breaking among friends. The conversion by voice and book reverses the story, returning desire from distraction. Even when his exegesis is indirect, he keeps approaching the pair of creation and sin from new angles.

Both of these are quite male stories. Augustine's rowdy adolescent companions all seem to be boys, and in the garden, he is joined by his devout friend Alypius. The *Confessions* holds at least one more story revisiting both human creation and original sin, though. In it, the feminine role is not that of a mediating seducer, herself drawn and drawing her consort away from God to the serpent and sin, but of a figure whose role is better than the man's, and very nearly the best of all.

This story is succinct, and much of it occurs offstage. Moving on from his pear-stealing years, Augustine becomes a teacher of rhetoric. In those years, he says, "I had one," a feminine one who remains unnamed. Augustine says that he "found her in my state of wandering desire," but that they were faithful to one another—a faith that lasted about fifteen years and saw the birth of a son.[49] Whatever drama and unhappiness Augustine faces in those years, hers is a steady presence. Though she does not play a role like that of Alypius in encouraging Augustine's conversion to Christianity, there is also no indication that she leads him into temptation, even to something as small as stealing fruit (he does not even accuse her of enticing him into their relationship).

Much of Book 6 of the *Confessions* involves another group of boys and other kinds of peer pressure. Augustine is met in Milan by his friends Alypius, who "attached himself to me with the strongest bond," Nebridius, whose "single motive was to live with me," and Romanianus, an "intimate friend" who is also, usefully, rich.[50] The group plots their lives together, with Augustine breezily remarking that one of them should be able "to obtain the governorship of a minor province," for which "It would be necessary to marry a wife with some money . . ."[51] He will later disparage his own desires for "honours, money, marriage,"[52] but not before they are encouraged by his mother, who seems delighted by the possibilities. She procures the promise of a child from a good family who will, if all goes according to plan, mature into a suitable bride.[53]

In a strikingly passive construction, Augustine says that as part of this plan, "The woman with whom I habitually slept was torn away from my side because she was a hindrance to my marriage."[54] The passivity, like the banishment, seems horrifyingly casual. So too does the lustful incontinence that turns Augustine, after her departure, to what he suggests is rather indiscriminate sex. She, on the other hand, responds with perfect virtue, "She had returned to Africa vowing that she would never go with another man."[55] Between her exile and his promiscuity comes perhaps the most striking part of the description: "My heart which was deeply attached was cut and wounded, and left a trail of blood." While he seeks out more partners, describing himself as "frigid but desperate," that wound, "inflicted by the earlier parting, was not healed. After inflammation and sharp pain, it festered."[56]

These are intensely allusive paragraphs. Danuta Shanzer has argued persuasively against scholars' tendency to read Augustine's behavior here as a demonstration, through the consort's namelessness and his consent to her exile, of the low value that he places on women, however close they may be to him. She points out that "the language of the passage is a heady and significant mixture of the biblical and the medical. Augustine invites one to read a world of emotional, and indeed theological, significance into the trauma" of his partner's departure.[57]

Perhaps the most evident allusion is to the second creation story. Shanzer points out that though Augustine's description joins the couple as intensely as the humans in the Genesis story, it also inverts that story: "instead of a pair being created by something torn from someone's side, a pair is split up. Rather than the man 'cleaving,' to the woman, the woman 'clove' to his heart."[58] In Genesis, the division is only precedent to a joining together, a bond of flesh to flesh, that holds as tightly beyond Paradise as within it.[59] In the *Confessions*, a longstanding bond is cut apart, and "instead of emerging miraculously intact from the process, [Augustine] is left with a bleeding wound that will not heal."[60] The male superiority that Augustine has suggested as a reading of the Genesis story certainly does not hold here; the man is damaged both in body and in virtue by the absence of the virtuous woman.

The wound is allusive to further stories, both in and beyond scripture. Augustine "constantly uses *de latere* ('from the side') for *de costa* ('out of a rib')," Shanzer writes. "Needless to say, *latus* also enables a desirable ecclesiological typology with Jesus' wound . . ."[61] As Virginia Burrus elaborates:

> Augustine shifts away from the biblical language of "taking one of his ribs" (*tulit unam de costis eius*) and replaces it with the language of "drawing from his side" (*in latere, unde illa detracta . . . est*). It may not be too much to suggest that, in so doing, he layers the gospel representation of Jesus' pierced and fondled "side" (*latus eius*: John 19.34, 20.25, 20.27) onto the figure of Adam.[62]

Augustine, declaring his side wounded, describes an unwilling *imitatio Christi*. The act of imitation reminds us of the image so central to the first story of human creation and to Augustine's readings of it. Augustine's own imaging or imitation is distinctly imperfect. He does not willingly participate in this image; despite his eagerness for higher office, he would not have chosen to be wounded. His conflicted will—his set of incompatible desires—highlights his fallen state, and the woman's actions further highlight the imperfection by contrast. She better imitates Christ's self-control, maintaining her chastity and devotion. She is even cast as the sacrifice for an ungrateful man. It is not Adam who finds a second, Christic form here.

Augustine the exegete moves from understanding the divine image in Christological terms to seeing it as Trinitarian. His exiled companion in the *Confessions* embodies the mind as it mirrors the Trinity: she does not forget him, it seems, at any time, past or now or to come; she does not misunderstand what is valuable in the world, nor does she throw away that value for the lesser good of wealth or office; she does not turn away or break her will or her love. The desire that turns away is always an echo of the first sin, of human desire turned from pure divine love. Shanzer points out the resonance and inversion between Augustine's sin and that of the first man: "Adam claims to have followed his woman into sin, Augustine . . . admits that he did not follow her into virtue."[63] Augustine, once he has first turned from her, finds his own desire scattered all over, among women he does not number for the reader. Like Adam, he is miserable in his inability to return to that singular desire that was always satisfiable. All sins mirror the first, the unwillingness to devote desire without distraction. "You were with me, and I was not with you," Augustine writes of his earlier search for God's presence; in the woman's choice of chastity, she remains with him, and he—sending her away, seeking worldly honors, casting about for other sexual partners—is not with her.[64] Her desire does not waver, nor does she choose separation.

Just as the first, selfishly misdirected desire to disobey introduces death to humankind, so Christ's obedient sacrifice of his own desire in favor of God the Father's—"not my will but yours be done"—returns the possibility of embodied life without death.[65] Humanity's misdirection of desire smudges the divine image in humankind, and the God of which humans are supposed to be an image has to become human to restore clarity to it. Just as the sinful humans' desires scattered into inharmonious distraction, so too do Augustine's. Being wounded in his side, torn in his heart, Augustine may echo the sacrificial moment of the crucifixion, but he halts there, unable to proceed to resurrection because he cannot redirect his desire, distracted as he is first by status and then by sexual urgency. Only his unnamed partner continues into the saving reunification of desire, chaste in flesh and continent in love. Though also torn (from his side), she takes the next step.

Augustine is not going to be so blasphemous as to present any human being as the second coming, and despite his better moments, it seems unlikely that he would be willing to consider the possibility that the messiah might reappear as a woman.[66] But Christ as the second Adam is fascinatingly mirrored by this second Eve—neither one of the Marys, but torn like the first Eve from the side of a man with whom she was paired.[67] The first Eve initiates the heritage of human distractedness; this Eve is appears untempted by distractions and multiple desires; in Trinitarian manner she is steadfast in love, memory, and so far as we can tell, understanding. She even returns home from their extended exile, back to Africa from Milan. Even the absence of her name, which seems so careless, is shared with the prelapsarian Eve, who gains her name only after the exile from Paradise (Gen. 3:20).

Augustine's desires to understand and to be truthful often have him revisiting and complicating his earlier texts, and the results are not always quite compatible as logical arguments. With the principle of charity, we can read them as multiple truths—which is sometimes more about poetry than about matters of fact. In the more clearly exegetical passages, Eve's participation in humanity as a Christological or Trinitarian image is valued, but slightly undermined too, usually by her embodiment. The unnamed woman of the *Confessions* shows mythically how that image is redemptively taken up in embodied desire. Augustine tells divinity obliquely, as he thinks that one must.[68]

Augustine *wants* to imitate Christ, but he repeatedly casts himself as the imperfect model, as Adam. He needlessly steals fruit; he is briefly at perfect peace in a garden; his desires scatter thoughtlessly even when he knows that they shouldn't. He abandons the one who satisfied him and remains with him. She does not turn away, even when her love is rejected, and does not give in to distractions. It would be blasphemous for Augustine to declare a new Eve, but obliquely, without name, she appears as Eve's most intriguing variation.

NOTES

1. Augustine, *Confessions*, trans. Henry Chadwick (Oxford: Oxford University Press, 1991), 12.31.42.

2. Augustine, *On Christian Doctrine*, in *St. Augustine's City of God and Christian Doctrine*, trans. James Shaw, series 1, vol. 2 *Nicene and Post-Nicene Fathers*, ed. Philip Schaff (Buffalo: Christian Literature Publishing, 1886), 3.27.38.

3. Augustine, *Confessions*, 12.26.36.

4. E. Ann Matter, "The Undebated Debate: Gender and the Image of God in Medieval Theology," in *Gender in Debate*, ed. Clare Lees and Thelma Fenster (New York: Palgrave, 2002), 41.

5. Matter, "Undebated," 43; E. Ann Matter, "Augustine and Women," in *Augustine Through the Ages: An Encyclopedia*, ed. Allan D. Fitzgerald (Grand Rapids: William B. Eerdmans, 1999), 890.

6. Gen. 1:26–27; all Biblical translations NRSV. The ellipsis omits a very problematic passage about human dominion over the rest of the earth—obviously important, but not essential to the present gender-focused reading.

7. Augustine, *On the Literal Interpretation of Genesis: An Unfinished Book*, in *St. Augustine on Genesis*, trans. Roland Teske S.J., vol. 84 *The Fathers of the Church*, ed. Ludwig Schopp et al. (Washington, D.C.: Catholic University of America Press, 1991), 143–90.

8. See Teske, "Introduction," in *St. Augustine on Genesis*, trans. Roland Teske, S.J., vol. 84 of *The Fathers of the Church*, ed. Ludwig Schopp et al. (Washington, D.C.: Catholic University of America Press, 1991), 10, with reference to *Confessions* 6.3–4 and the early dialogue *De Beata Vita* 1.4. See also Augustine, *Genesis Against the Manichees*, in *St. Augustine on Genesis,* trans. Roland Teske, S. J., vol. 84 *The Fathers of the Church*, ed. Ludwig Schopp et al. (Washington, D.C.: Catholic University of America Press, 1991), 1.17.

9. Augustine, *Unfinished*, chs. 60–62.

10. Augustine returns to the opening lines of this book, the Gospel of John, nearly as often as he does to Genesis, and for similar reasons—he wants to begin at the beginning. The book opens with a poetic prologue, which credits the *Logos* as God, with God, and that through which everything is made.

11. Teske, "Introduction," 6.

12. Augustine, *Unfinished*, ch. 61.

13. Augustine, *On the Holy Trinity*, trans. Arthur West Haddan, series 1, vol. 3 *Nicene and Post-Nicene Fathers*, ed. Philip Schaff (Buffalo: Christian Literature Publishing, 1886), 15.23. See also 15.20: "Which three things, if any one intelligently regards as by nature divinely appointed in his own mind, and remembers by memory, contemplates by understanding, embraces by love, how great a thing that is in the mind, whereby even the eternal and unchangeable nature can be recollected, beheld, desired, doubtless that man finds an image of that highest Trinity."

14. Augustine, *On the Holy Trinity*, 7.12.

15. In the later, finished literal commentary, Augustine will make the more complicated argument that the human creation in Genesis 1 is of the potential for humanity, and in 2 its realization. This does not alter the gender considerations set forth here. See *The Literal Meaning of Genesis, Vol. 1 and 2*, trans. John Hammond Taylor S. J., vol. 41/42 *Ancient Christian Writers: The Works of the Fathers in Translation*, ed. Johannes Quasten, Walter J. Burghardt, and Thomas Comerford Lawler (New York: Paulist Press, 1982), 6.5.8, 6.6.10.

16. Augustine, *Genesis Against the Manichees*, 1.25.43. Augustine also suggests in other texts that women are not usually men's intellectual equals. See, e.g., *The Happy Life*, trans. Ludwig Schoop, in *The Happy Life, Answer to Sceptics, Divine Providence and the Problem of Evil, Soliloquies*, vol. 5/1 *The Fathers of the Church*, ed. Ludwig Schoop et al. (New York: Cima Publishing, 1948), 2.10 and *Genesis Against the Manichees*, 2.11.15.

17. Augustine, *On the Holy Trinity*, 12–13; see especially 12.7.12. See also E. Ann Matter, "Christ, God, and Woman in the Thought of St. Augustine," in *Augustine*

and his Critics, ed. Robert Dodaro and George Lawless (New York: Routledge, 2000), 167.

18. Augustine, *On the Holy Trinity*, 12.7.10.

19. See Augustine, *Genesis Against the Manichees*, 2.26.40; *Unfinished*, ch. 61; *On the Holy Trinity*, 12.7.

20. 1 Cor 11: 7–8.

21. Gen. 2:7, 2:21–22.

22. Augustine, *On the Holy Trinity*, 12.7.13.

23. Augustine, *Genesis Against the Manichees*, 1.17.

24. Augustine, *Genesis Against the Manichees*, 2.11.

25. Augustine, *Literal Meaning of Genesis*, 3.22.

26. Augustine, *Confessions*, 13.33.47.

27. Augustine, *On the Holy Trinity*, 12.7.10.

28. Gen. 2:16–17.

29. Gen. 3:22–23.

30. Augustine, *Sermons* 51.3, 184.2, in *Essential Sermons, Part III: Homilies*, trans. Edmund Hill, vol. 25 *The Works of Saint Augustine: A Translation for the 21st Century*, ed. Daniel Edward Doyle (Hyde Park: New City Press, 2007).

31. Augustine, *Sermons*, 51.3; see John 20:1–18.

32. Augustine, *Sermons*, 322.3.

33. The inspiration for this comparison is Romans 5:12–21 and 1 Cor. 15:22, 15:45.

34. Margaret Miles, "Sex and the City (of God): Is Sex Forfeited or Fulfilled in Augustine's Resurrection of Body," *Journal of the American Academy of Religion* 73, no. 2 (June 2005), 307–27, at 316 noting Augustine, *City of God*, 14.24. As Elizabeth Clark points out, Augustine's views on the question of sex in Eden evolved, not always in the direction of clarity. See Elizabeth A. Clark, "'Adam's Only Companion': Augustine and the Early Christian Debate on Marriage," in *The Olde Daunce: Love, Friendship, Sex and Marriage in the Medieval World*, ed. Robert R. Edwards and Stephen Spector (New York: State University of New York Press, 1991), 15–31, at 19, 22.

35. See Augustine, *City of God*, 2.36.

36. Augustine, *City of God*, 13.13.

37. Augustine, *City of God*, 13.14; "On Merit and the Forgiveness of Sins," trans. Peter Holmes and Robert Ernest Wallace, series 1, vol. 5 *Nicene and Post-Nicene Fathers*, ed. Philip Schaff (Buffalo: Christian Literature Publishing, 1887), chs. 10–11. Gillian Clark points out some of Augustine's stranger and more complicated language, in which he writes of "Adam's womb" as a source of humankind, perhaps as indicating that Eve and Adam are "one flesh." Clark, "Adam's Engendering: Augustine on Gender and Creation," *Gender and Religion* 34 (1998), 21–22.

38. Augustine, *City of God*, 12.8: "For its defections are not to evil things, but are themselves evil; that is to say, are not towards things that are naturally and in themselves evil, but the defection of the will is evil . . ."

39. Augustine, *City of God*, 22.17. Augustine is aware of intersex bodies, which he calls hermaphroditic (see e.g. *On the Holy Trinity*, 12.7). He does not discuss them in his descriptions of resurrection, where every body rises as a perfected version of

itself. Though I admit that I am reading him optimistically, it does seem at least possible that these bodies too might rise in their own perfection; Augustine is adamant that risen bodies retain sexed characteristics as part of their beauty, and not for reproductive use.

40. Augustine, "On Rebuke and Grace," trans. Peter Holmes and Robert Ernest Wallace, series 1, vol. 5 *Nicene and Post-Nicene Fathers*, ed. Philip Schaff (Buffalo: Christian Literature Publishing, 1887), ch. 26.

41. Augustine, *City of God*, 22.29. "It is possible, it is indeed most probable, that we shall then see the physical bodies of the new heaven and the new earth in such a fashion as to observe God in utter clarity and distinctness, seeing him present everywhere and governing the whole material scheme of things by means of the bodies we shall then inhabit and the bodies we shall see wherever we turn our eyes." Cf. "the eyes of the body will see God," 22.30.

42. For ways in which this identity is complicated by the interchange of matter, see Virginia Burrus and Karmen MacKendrick, "Bodies without Wholes: Apophatic Excess and Fragmentation in Augustine's *City of God*," in *Apophatic Bodies: Negative Theology, Incarnation, and Relationality*, ed. Chris Boesel and Catherine Keller (New York: Fordham, 2010), 79–93; and Karmen MacKendrick, "Glorious Return: Resurrected Bodies," in *Material Mystery: The Flesh of the World in Three Mythic Bodies* (New York: Fordham, 2021).

43. Augustine, *City of God*, 22.30.
44. Augustine, *City of God*, 22.30.
45. Augustine, *On Christian Doctrine*, 1.22.20.
46. 1 Cor 15:28; Augustine, *City of God*, 22.30.
47. Augustine, *Confessions,* 2.4.9–12.
48. Augustine, *Confessions*, 8.12.26–29.
49. Augustine, *Confessions*, 4.2.2.
50. Augustine, *Confessions*, 6.10.16, 6.10.17, 6.14.24.
51. Augustine, *Confessions*, 6.11.20–6.12.21.
52. Augustine, *Confessions*, 6.6.9.
53. Augustine, *Confessions*, 6.13.23.
54. Augustine, *Confessions*, 6.15.25.
55. Augustine, *Confessions*, 6.15.25.
56. Augustine, *Confessions*, 6.15.25.

57. Danuta Shanzer, "*Avulsa a Latere Meo*: Augustine's Spare Rib: *Confessions* 6.15.25," *The Journal of Roman Studies* 92 (2002), 159.

58. Danuta Shanzer, "Augustine's *Anonyma I* and Cornelius's Concubines: How Philology and Literary Criticism Can Help in Understanding Augustine on Marital Fidelity," *Augustinian Studies* 48, no. 1–2 (2017), 208–9.

59. See Genesis 2:24; cf. Virginia Burrus, "'Fleeing the Uxorious Kingdom': Augustine's Queer Theology of Marriage," *Journal of Early Christian Studies* 19, no. 1 (Spring 2011), 13.

60. Shanzer, "*Avulsa*," 159.
61. Shanzer, "Augustine's *Anonyma I*," 207–8.
62. Burrus, "'Fleeing the Uxorious Kingdom,'" 7.

63. Shanzer, "Augustine's *Anonyma I*," 208–9.
64. See Augustine, *Confessions*, 10.27.
65. Luke 22:42; cf. John 6:38.
66. See Augustine, *Sermons*, 51.3, where he writes of Christ "appearing as a man—and I agree he had to be that;" and explains, "So he came as a man to show his preference for the male sex."
67. Neither couple is officially wed, but both are effectively so. Burrus, "'Fleeing the Uxorious Kingdom,'"13 with reference to Shanzer, "*Avulsa*," 176.
68. Augustine, *Sermons*, 117.5: "if you can grasp it, it isn't God."

PART IV
Education and Community

Chapter 9

Promise and Peril

Maggie Ann Labinski

Western philosophy has argued on behalf of the pedagogical value of erotic desire from its earliest beginnings. One might recall Plato's dialogue about Eros at a famous symposium[1] or Aristotle's observation that "humans by nature desire to know."[2] Such traditional accounts suggest that the erotic is the condition of the possibility of education—i.e., an invaluable force that propels students in their intellectual pursuits. It is a theory that has been widely corroborated by lived experience. While fear, competition, or even shame can coerce a certain level of participation, nothing compares to the learning that is possible when a student is motivated by their own longings.

Unfortunately, we live at a time when it is difficult to trust erotic desire. Movements like #MeToo have made it painfully clear that the violent misuse of these desires is no rarity. The list of individuals accused of manipulating the erotic for the sake of their own sexual prerogatives continues to grow,[3] and this list includes prominent figures within the field of academia. Campuses are struggling to respond to the weaponization of desire in the classroom. These cases challenge teachers and students alike to reevaluate whether the erotic should have any role to play in the context of education.

INTERPRETIVE LENS

The tension between the promise and the peril of erotic desire has been well analyzed by feminist scholars.[4] Feminists were among the first to document the educational cost of erotic violence (e.g., sexual harassment, propositioning, etc.), especially its impact on students.[5] The majority of these studies concluded that the cultivation of desire is risky business.[6] Passion is a formidable thing,[7] and when abuse does occur, the injury inflicted is often irrevocable.⁸ It is hard to imagine any scenario that would justify exposing students to such terrible consequences.

At the same time, feminists have argued against reducing the meaning of the erotic to the terms of this abuse.⁹ The irruption of desire *can* take the form of sexual misconduct. However, it can also unfold in ways that support students in their educational journeys. As Audre Lorde explains, to access these gifts one must differentiate between the breadth of erotic desire and the narrower scope of sexual activity:

> The erotic is a measure between the beginnings of our sense of self and the chaos of our strongest feelings. It is an internal sense of satisfaction to which, once we have experienced it, we know we can aspire. For having experienced the fullness of this depth of feeling and recognizing its power, in honor and self-respect we can require no less of ourselves.¹⁰

To be in touch with the erotic is to recognize the most intimate parts of the self. When students are encouraged to seek out these parts, they are given access to a unique "power"—i.e., an inner strength that inspires learning by holding them accountable to their own deepest longings. A classroom that unlocks these desires is one that centers students as the true "measure" of any and all educational success.

QUESTION

My question, thereby, is largely practical. How might teachers invite erotic desire into the classroom responsibly? Can we acknowledge the benefits articulated by philosophers like Plato and Aristotle without ignoring the dangers exposed by #MeToo? More specifically, I wonder about the advantages of following the both/and methodology offered in feminist scholarship. Such an approach not only allows for a balanced understanding of the erotic. It also focuses attention on the student. It is students who have the most to lose when the erotic goes awry, and it is students who have the most to gain when these yearnings are taken seriously. As a result, it would seem that any meaningful analysis of this phenomenon should be oriented around them—should insist that students have desires too.

To this end, I would like to explore how one teacher attempted to negotiate the erotic in his classroom: Augustine of Hippo. Augustine's thought has been criticized regularly by feminist scholars.¹¹ So, too, his reputation might lead one to believe that he would be opposed to the messiness of desire.¹² However, in the early dialogue *De ordine* (On Order), Augustine offers a compelling both/and narrative of his pedagogical struggles with the erotic.[13] In what follows, I will begin by giving a brief introduction to *De ordine* that highlights Augustine's description of his own desires. Next, I will unpack Augustine's response to the desires of two of his students: Licentius and Monica. I will argue that the differences between these interactions suggest a shift in Augustine's understanding of the erotics of pedagogy. It is a change that, ultimately, encourages readers to reconsider the gendered dynamics of the classroom. I will conclude by gesturing towards the implications of *De ordine* for contemporary higher education.

DE ORDINE

Frustrated with his teaching post in Milan, Augustine retired to Cassiciacum to seek the truth and practice philosophy.[14] While there, he built a school of sorts—an educational community that was both inspired by, and distinct from, the schools of rhetoric he left behind. In particular, Augustine's school[15] placed a special emphasis on the use of rigorous debates (*disputationis*) and the perspective of a Christian worldview.[16] Augustine's courses had no open enrollment policy. A select group of friends and family accompanied him out of Milan and took on the role of students. Augustine purports to have had some of their more fruitful conversations transcribed, and scholars have come to call these the "Cassiciacum Dialogues"[17]—i.e., *Contra Academicos* (Against the Academicians), *De beata vita* (The Happy Life), and *De ordine*.

While most scholars doubt that these dialogues reflect actual conversations held between Augustine and his students,[18] their educational framework is undeniable.[19] These texts have been an important resource for those who wish to understand Augustine's philosophy of education.[20] Of the Cassiciacum Dialogues, *De ordine* is the most explicitly educational in content. Within its pages, Augustine's primary task is to clarify the 'order' of the disciplines—i.e., the progression of studies essential to liberal education. Augustine's analysis arises in response to a broader philosophical/ theological problem. By way of introduction, Augustine explains that he wrote the piece to help its recipient (an old friend by the name of Zenobius) wrestle with the seeming contradiction between their shared belief in the divine order of the world and the lived experience of disorder:

> There is an order to be found, within things and between them, which binds and directs this world. . . . [But] no sooner does one lift one's head enough to pay attention to the obstacles and difficulties of life, then it comes natural to ask how it is that on the one hand God takes care of human affairs, and on the other these same affairs are shot through with so much evil.[21]

A significant part of the conclusion of *De ordine* is that one can gain the right perspective about this apparent disconnect by studying the disciplines.[22] George Howie explains:

> It is held that the liberal arts demonstrate in a very clear manner the existence of fundamental order in a universe, whose obvious imperfections and shifting standards might seem to the superficial observer to demonstrate the opposite conclusion. It follows that, if man is to perceive law and order in the world, he must expand his understanding according to what Augustine calls "the right order of instruction" (*ordo eruditionis*).[23]

Augustine's decidedly Christian version of liberal education arises, in other words, as a way to rethink the "problem of evil." The details of his account have had undeniable influence, from the early stages of the *triviuum* and *quadrivium* to the core curricula utilized at many universities today.[24]

AUGUSTINE

However, Augustine's pedagogical interests in *De ordine* are not limited to the generation of the disciplines. The very first pages of the dialogue suggest that he is also eager to consider the nature of desire and its presence in the classroom.[25] In fact, it is Augustine's own desires that set the stage for all that is to come. As the text opens, it is the middle of the night and Augustine cannot sleep. The reason for his apparent insomnia is not what we might initially suppose. It is not because the pressures of organizing his school have gotten the best of him. It is not because he is feeling guilty for having abandoned his post in Milan. Augustine lies awake because he is consumed with amorous desires: "Out of love (*amore*) for truth I had got into the habit of spending about half the night awake, thinking. For urgent matters it would be the earlier part, otherwise the latter."[26] Despite the conversations he has been having with his students, Augustine's hunger has not been appeased. He is left wanting more—more of his beloved truth. Led by this erotic attachment, Augustine extends the borders of the classroom into his bedroom and "thinks" rather than sleeps.

Augustine's late-night practice suggests that his desires are insatiable. Such sessions may have been necessary back in Milan—at those schools that Augustine believed were uninterested in the truth.[27] However, here at Cassiciacum, Augustine can structure each day around his love. Even he is forced to admit that his ritual is extreme. For example, Augustine notes that while he expected much of his students, he did not require that they join him in the evening: "As they worked a lot during the day, it would have seemed excessive to expect them to go on working during the night."[28] One can only assume that Augustine's companions appreciated the reduction in their workload. Yet, for Augustine—for someone with his unwavering passion—these midnight soirees would appear to be no work at all.

Augustine's erotic inclinations lead to a particular kind of "thinking." First, Augustine is inspired to wonder (*mirare*). This wondering is directed at even the most mundane of objects. On the night in question, Augustine is drawn to wonder about a sound. He explains, "I was awake, as I said, when I could hear the sound of water just behind the bathrooms. On becoming aware, I paid more attention."[29] In these moments, the world presents itself as pure opportunity. Even the simplest of sensory experiences serves as a chance for Augustine to tend to the truth. He declares: "What wouldn't lovers of truth and beauty be eager to see and search out? Isn't any such occasion good enough to bring the beauty of reason to bear on things known and unknown, and let it attract its followers wherever and however it can? Cannot signs of it be seen anywhere and coming from everywhere."[30] Second, Augustine's desires prompt him to question. More specifically, Augustine is drawn to questions about causality: "What struck me was that the same water, on rushing against the stonework, produced an alternatively loud and soft sound. Much as I thought what the cause (*causa*) of it might be, I could not make it out."[31] Augustine's yearnings beget a thinking that well reflects his general hope for Cassiciacum. By highlighting the activities of wondering and questioning, Augustine offers a picture of how the desire for the truth might lead one to philosophy.

It is a beautiful account of what it means to allow the erotic into our educational spaces. Augustine is a model academic. There is something appealing—if not idyllic—about the idea of being so enticed by the truth that even sleep seems uninviting. In addition, there is much to like about the vision of philosophy that follows from Augustine's desires. His description of wondering and questioning likely resonates with many of us who live and move in the discipline today. However, questions remain. While Augustine's desires seem picturesque, they are also isolated. Augustine is very much alone in his thoughts. There is no one else, no other erotic inclinations, that he is obliged to take into consideration. By extension, there are no alternative forms of thinking, different ways of doing philosophy, that might challenge the way Augustine expresses his desires. One wonders how someone in this consuming state would respond to others? The stakes, after all, are high: for lest we forget, though Augustine is alone in his thoughts, he is not alone at his school. Augustine may have his desires, but those passions are set to unfold within a broader pedagogical community.

LICENTIUS

As the dialogue continues, readers are introduced to one of the most cherished members of this community, a young student by the name of Licentius. Augustine clearly loved Licentius, and their intimacy plays an important role throughout the Cassiciacum Dialogues. Many of the conversations that comprise these texts provide a poignant display of their mutual friendship. It is an affection that would seem to be deepening as Licentius advances in his studies. Augustine states: "A strong bond of friendship (*amicum*) was also developing between the two of us, for after despairing of his education, all of a sudden he had burst into the very core of philosophy."[32] This is, arguably, the dream of many a teacher. Licentius has fallen hard for his teacher's beloved. Like Augustine, he finds himself enamored with the truth.

Unfortunately, while the two desire the same beloved—while Augustine is clear that Licentius is committed to philosophy—they are not responding to her in the same way. Readers are given some indication of this conflict in the lines that follow. The evening progresses, and Augustine hears Licentius shuffling around nearby. Recognizing that his student is awake, Augustine cannot resist going against his word and asking Licentius to "work into the night." He summons Licentius to join him in his philosophical efforts: "I see that your Muse has lit the lamp for night work. Have you noticed the ups and downs of the sound of this water pipe?"[33] Licentius responds that he has, indeed, heard the sound. However, he is not convinced that it is a matter of any consequence. Unlike his teacher, Licentius dismisses the noise as nothing more than the possibility of unfavorable weather.[34] In other words, Licentius notices the water, but he feels no erotic pull, no passion that might call him to think about it. Instead, he suggests that if anything is tempting him to wonder and question, it is the realization that his teacher would focus on something so silly in the first place: "[B]ut I greatly wonder (*mirari*) at you now. . . . That you marvel (*miratus*) at such things. . . . Please leave me alone; I have other things to think about."[35]

Augustine is taken aback. His faith in his own desires, and the intellectual acts they incite, appears to intensify. He replies that the problem does not rest with him. The real issue is that Licentius seems to be suffering from an impoverished kind of desire. His snub suggests that he does not long for the truth with the same wild abandon of his teacher. This has allowed him to become distracted by inferior versions of thinking, watered-down examples of philosophy. More specifically, Augustine contends that, like those back in Milan, Licentius has let himself be wooed by poetry: "That's why you [do] not wonder (*mirabaris*); your poetry [keeps] you entertained."[36] Augustine maintains that, while Licentius is usually more than willing to follow him, tonight he is sadly preoccupied with his own substandard contemplative practice. The words of the poets offer an infinite stream of enticing sounds. These sounds have curtailed Licentius's ability to be lured by anything else, including a (presumably) very exciting water pipe.

To better express his frustration, Augustine takes recourse in a poetic image—an attempt, perhaps, to fight fire with fire. He reminds Licentius of the tragic pining of Pyramus and Thisbe.[37] As the story goes, Pyramus and Thisbe were so smitten with each other that they would spend their time whispering through a crack in the wall that separated their homes. They eventually agreed to elope. However, the two died by suicide before they could run off. Augustine proposes that Pyramus and Thisbe mirror Licentius's relationship with his own beloved: "I feel sorry for your singing and howling these verses of yours in all kinds of rhythms. They are erecting a wall, between you and the truth of things, thicker and more impenetrable than the one that divided the lovers Pyramus and Thisbe you are crooning about. At least they could whisper to each other through a crack."[38] According to Augustine, poetry is little more than an unnecessary barrier—a "wall" that will create nothing but distance between Licentius and the truth. Augustine argues that the desires he and his student share call for a specific kind of philosophy, one that does not include thinking about poetic verse.

Licentius, understandably, reels from the imagery. He asks his teacher if he might not be more precise. What is it, exactly, that Licentius is supposed to do? Augustine's response sends his student back to the scene of the crime:

> Return to the Muses. . . . You were about to relate the point when Thisbe kills herself over Pyramus' half-dead body, who had fatally wounded himself in error. At that point, the emotional climax of the story, you have your opportunity. Consider the curse of that unclean lust and poisoned passion as the basis for that miserable end. Then turn to praising that clean and sincere love by which disciplined characters made beautiful by virtue are raised up by a philosophical mind.[39]

Augustine reasons that there is one way in which poetry might serve his young friend. The emotional grief that Licentius experiences when he remembers the "unclean lust and poisoned passion" depicted by the poets can be used to propel him to the "clean and sincere" desires of those like his teacher—i.e., those with a genuine "philosophical mind." By feeling the misery of such tragic choices, Licentius might better appreciate the wretchedness of his current situation.

Augustine's advice demonstrates that he considers Licentius's predicament to be an erotic tragedy in the fullest sense of the phrase. It also indicates that he sees only one route forward: Licentius must get in line and embrace the method of philosophy modeled by his teacher. Augustine's practice of wondering and questioning may be open to a wide array of possible objects—invitations from "anywhere" and "everywhere." Nevertheless, this openness does not extend to poetic verse. For Augustine, there remains a sharp line between poetry and philosophy.[40] To love the truth authentically is to know the difference.

Augustine's assessment may be justified. Perhaps the practice of philosophy is incompatible with poetry.[41] Perhaps Licentius does not yet know how to dote on his beloved properly. Regardless, the erotic paradigm Augustine models with his student raises serious pedagogical questions. Augustine's personal relationship with the truth dominates this exchange. Rather than humoring the possibility that Licentius's passion for the poets is a legitimate extension of his love, he accuses his student of harboring false desires. He implies that if Licentius really desired the truth, he would imitate his teacher's method of late-night thinking. Augustine demands an erotic sameness—one where the goal of educative community is to create uniformity across its members. Ironically, such demands would hardly seem necessary in the present case. For, again, this teacher and student have much in common. As Augustine has admitted, Licentius loves the truth. He has already "burst into the very core of philosophy." Surely a teacher as skilled as Augustine could find some parallel between his own fascination with the sound of running water and his student's attraction to the sound of poetic verse. Is it so inconceivable that a poem might serve as yet another avenue into the wondering and questioning which has brought both of these men to Cassiciacum? Regrettably, such possibilities are buried beneath Augustine's erotic intractability.

As such, this exchange would seem to nuance the otherwise positive nature of Augustine's boundless love. While his longings may serve *him* well, it is not clear that Augustine's desires play well with others. It is a shortcoming of which Augustine seems only too aware. Though Licentius is the first student Augustine meets in *De ordine*, he is not the last. As the story unfolds, readers are introduced to yet another of Augustine's best and brightest. This time, he is compelled to take a radically different approach.

MONICA

Augustine and Licentius fall asleep. Daylight brings fresh demands and new difficulties. More importantly, the new day brings the formal introduction of other students. Among them is Augustine's mother, Monica. The scope of Monica's influence over Augustine cannot be overstated.[42] It was Monica who first introduced her son to Christianity and whom Augustine credits with his spiritual conversion. Despite this, like many of the women that materialize in Augustine's texts, locating the "real" Monica is no easy task. Readers are given only her son's side of the story, and Augustine is hardly an unbiased commentator. Consequently, many scholars have argued that the best readers can do is catch glimpses of the woman hidden behind her son.[43]

The glimpses provided in *De ordine* are provocative. When Monica enters the scene, the cohort at Cassiciacum is already immersed in their morning discussions. Monica asks the group how their lessons have progressed.[44] In response, Augustine insists that the question she raised be recorded, as was their policy.[45] Monica, however, appears confused by her son's request. She asks: "What are you doing? I have never read of women entering into such debates in any of your books."[46] One can only imagine how Monica would have delivered the line. Was her question genuine or tongue in cheek? Did she furrow her brow or roll her eyes? At any rate, her remarks lead Augustine to address the traditional Western assumption that women should be excluded from the classroom.[47]

Augustine begins by offering brief remarks about his own theory of gender. He argues that gender is an external facet of human experience. Monica is a woman, in other words, because her physical body looks like one. The problem, Augustine submits, is that this externality makes gender ripe for social/political manipulation. In the same way particular articles of clothing are used to indicate an individual's position in the world, gender can be used to rank people into hierarchies. Augustine infers that some teachers have no problem structuring their classrooms around such markers. By contrast, Augustine declares that he is primarily interested in his students' internal qualities—i.e., those mental and spiritual components that best define "human" life. As such, Augustine concludes that Monica's gender would never prevent her from studying with him: "I don't give two hoots about the judgment of the proud and the ignorant. They rush into reading books as into kowtowing to men. They pay no attention to human qualities, but to clothes, pomp, and the ephemeral circumstances of well-being."[48]

Augustine argues that, because these "human qualities" reside within, they are difficult to observe. Still, he submits that the time he has spent with his mother has proven that she is more than worthy of joining them. In fact, Monica is an exceptional example of what Augustine considers to be the most important quality—i.e., the ability to desire the truth. Augustine describes Monica as uniquely skilled in erotics. For example, Monica's longing for her beloved is so intense that it has not only changed her life. It has rewritten her relationship to death: "You love it so much, indeed, that neither setbacks of any kind nor death itself holds any terror for you."[49] Monica's desires have enabled her to live without fear—no easy thing for a fourth/fifth-century parent whose child just quit his job to meander around the countryside. Augustine contends that to reach such a point is an achievement of the highest order. So, too, he maintains that Monica's desires have given her a rare aptitude for philosophy: "Living with her for so long, I had had occasion to observe her keen mind and burning love for things divine. On the celebration of my birthday with some friends we held a debate on some important matter, later put down in writing. There I verified the greatness of her mind, so that no other person seemed to me fitter for true philosophy."[50] The "burning" nature of Monica's desires, her dedication to philosophy, confirms that she is more than suited for Augustine's vision at Cassiciacum.

Nevertheless, and like Licentius, Monica's approach to philosophy differs in meaningful ways from her son's. Augustine explains that while it is clear that Monica is a philosopher, her method of thinking is not what one might expect. He suggests that, as remains the case today, what is allowed to count as philosophy is often dictated by those emersed in *academic* philosophy. The structure of Augustine's own school—his preference for debate and his sentimentality about the country—reflects the "Ivory Tower" perspective of his time. Augustine's approach to his beloved truth, in other words, is not neutral. He pursues her through a particular lens. Monica makes this lens visible. More pointedly, she confirms that one's relationship with the truth cannot be circumscribed by such a limited framework. Augustine continues: "The writings of many learned men contain stories of shoemakers given to philosophy, and of men of even lowlier station. . . . And there will be some, believe me, who will find my talking with you here more pleasing than finding platitudes or high-brow stuff. There were plenty of philosopher-women in ancient times, and I rather like your philosophy."[51] Monica's longings suggest that erotically inspired thinking can take a variety of forms and follow a range of trajectories. There is a "pleasingness" to her philosophy that clashes with the "high-brow stuff" expected in Augustine's "learned" (and male) world. Accordingly, her philosophical acts not only call into question the terms of Augustine's practice. They also challenge the politics of academia, the otherwise un-seen formalities that can curtail one's ability to recognize a genuine but contextually atypical pursuit of the truth.[52]

Given the nature of his earlier exchange with Licentius, Augustine's reaction here is striking. Despite the obvious dissimilarities between mother and son, Augustine does not imply that Monica is a threat to his erotic existence. Nor does he declare that her desires are somehow inadequate or indicative that she needs to work harder at imitating him. Instead, Augustine suggests that Monica's approach to philosophy compels all those present, including himself, to look within—i.e., to reassess their own erotic leanings and the intellectual practices they encourage. For Augustine, this process leads him to concede that he does not desire perfectly. To be fair, Augustine is not so bold as to share the details of his shortcomings. Perhaps there are still certain "setbacks" in life that bring him anxiety? Perhaps death continues to cause fear? What Augustine does disclose is that Monica's erotic skills complicate his authority in the classroom. Turning to his mother, he says: "Should I not therefore be *your* willing disciple."[53] Augustine allows Monica's desires to restructure the very fabric of their pedagogical community. He concludes that the differences between them are not to be downplayed or ignored. Rather, they are to confirm who is to be called teacher at Cassiciacum: Monica. It is yet another affront to the traditional Western politics of the "Ivory Tower." Monica's new position defies the gender-based sexism that would otherwise refuse a woman the right, not only to exist in the classroom, but to lead it.

Augustine is adamant that his words are no attempt at maternal flattery. He argues that if Monica did not desire as she does, if she failed to exhibit this most human of human qualities, he would have no choice but to "despise" her in his writings.[54] One wonders if Augustine could have pulled off such disavowal. The gift of Monica's presence throughout his life would seem to render this an impossible choice. Fortunately, it is a choice that Augustine will not have to make. He declares that it is not the son's love of the mother that Monica's longings call into question. It is the mother's love for the son. Augustine contends that Monica is such an exceptional philosopher that her desire for the truth—her love of wisdom—even exceeds her love of him: "I would not despise you, however, were you to love it even half-heartedly. Much less would I do such a thing if you loved wisdom as much as I do. As a matter of fact you love it far more than you love me."[55] Monica's desires are so remarkable that they push Augustine to reevaluate both their pedagogical and familial relationships. It is a maternal nudge that, once again, strikes a political chord. Monica's preference for the truth complicates conventional conceptions of the intersection of education and the family. It casts doubts upon the long-standing notion that women do not belong in the classroom because their desires should be directed toward their children alone.

Though many of us would likely have serious concerns about the definition of gender that Augustine used to arrive at this conclusion, there is something to be said about the fact that he arrived here at all.[56] Augustine's decision to place a female student at the center of his classroom is a rare move for the Western tradition. It is also a surprising change of pace for the man who had previously allowed his own desires to dominate. Augustine's interaction with Monica models a willingness to prioritize the passions of his students. Like Licentius, Monica has her own contemplative projects, ones that include philosophizing in new ways. This time Augustine is prepared to let those projects shape his own. As a result, the limits of his erotic headship are brought into relief. While Licentius was berated into submission, now it is Augustine who submits—who yields his erotic power to a woman and shares the reigns of his classroom.

IMPLICATIONS

What might it mean to embrace the pedagogical benefits of the erotic in a world that continues to struggle with widespread abuse? How can teachers summon such forces in ways that do not endanger the members of our campuses? Feminist scholars have argued that such a both/and question requires, first and foremost, that we give precedence to the desires of students—that we support their passions and give them the room to claim them as their own. Augustine would seem to agree. At the very least, his encounters with Licentius and Monica suggest a significant change in his sense of the erotic. It is a transformation that leads him to privilege his students' longings and rethink his definition of philosophy. By extension, Augustine's experiences shed important light on how readers might understand the remainder of *De ordine*—i.e., the ordering of the disciplines that the interlocutors are just now ready to explore. For the rest of the dialogue, Augustine will argue for a rather rigid progression through the arts and sciences. Taken by itself, this might imply that he held a top-down theory of liberal education—a version rooted in the knowledge and authority of teachers. However, the space Augustine gives Monica shows that, at least in his classroom, such traditional academic hierarchies need not have the final word.

While one can only speculate as to how Augustine would have us grapple with this complexity in the twenty-first-century classroom, it would seem that readers might tease out a few pieces of concrete advice. First, and most generally, Augustine compels us to recognize the consequences of our erotic attachments upon the lives of others. While we, too, may enjoy the occasional evening alone with our beloved truth, such desires do not exist in a vacuum. As communal beings, as communal teachers and learners, we do not have the luxury of solipsistic insatiability. Augustine suggests that, if the erotic is to serve the classroom, the social dimension of desire must be acknowledged. As Jyl Lynn Felman explains, the risk of the erotic is greatest when it is allowed to emerge as a one-dimensional monologue. When at its best, desire exists as "a back-and-forth, an exchange of ideas."[57] To invite the erotic with care, in other words, is to invite a dialogue—one, perhaps, like *De ordine*.[58]

Secondly, Augustine encourages us to embody a more malleable approach to the intellectual practices that follow from our desires. It is easy to assume that our ways of thinking are absolute. By contrast, Augustine demonstrates that the real gifts of the erotic are those that open us to change. More specifically, Augustine prompts teachers to discover places where their students' passions might be used to inspire new movements—to rewrite the structure, content, and leadership of the classroom. As Sharon Todd argues, this "flexible" approach to the erotic enables teachers to better address the increasing diversity of our campuses and fields of study:

> Given the multiple discourses currently informing transformative pedagogical discourse . . . it would seem that the shape, or morphology, of desire is something that must resist definite parameters and be open to constant amendment. A reconfiguration of desire for transformative pedagogy would need to be flexible in addressing itself to the particulars of a learning situation and would not be rendered a priori in terms.[59]

It is unlikely that any one-size-fits-all erotic arrangement will fit the bill. The conscientious development of these desires asks teachers to expect abundance—to anticipate, eagerly, that their students' passions will rearrange their courses and disciplines in surprising ways.

Finally, Augustine invites us to reflect upon the relationship between the erotic and gender. It was a gender-based question that led Augustine to reexamine the pedagogical effects of his own desires. It was Monica's willingness to give voice to her marginalization as a woman that pushed her son to alter his erotic practice. By extension, *De ordine* suggests that our amorous pursuits are at their most transformed when they also serve to disrupt the social/political status quo—when they direct us to reconsider why some individual's passions are deemed worthy while others are ignored. This critical endeavor does not presume that the classroom exists in some neutral world apart. Like Augustine, our approaches to desire are shaped by the "Ivory Tower" contours of our communities, including their ugly bits. However, as Rebecca Martusewicz argues, hope remains: "[T]here is also a kind of desire that motivates our struggles against domination and toward a shared truth. . . . Desire for a better world, for justice, and for truth generates questions and pushes us to challenge forms of social injustice by offering new ways of thinking and being."[60] When guided by our students' hunger for "a better world," the erotic gives birth to justice. It inspires us to push back against the current state of affairs, including the long lists of erotic abuses. To prompt such critique across our campuses—to nurture these longings—is to align the classroom with the efforts of the #MeToo movement. It is to allow education to become a form of social/political action.

NOTES

1. Plato, *Symposium*, trans. Seth Bernardete (Chicago: University Chicago Press, 1993).

2. Aristotle, *Metaphysics*, trans. W. D. Ross, in *The Complete Works of Aristotle*, ed. Jonathan Barnes. 2 vols. (Princeton: Princeton University Press, 1984), 980.b.22.

3. For an overview of the history of such abuse see, Carrie N. Baker, *The Women's Movement Against Sexual Harassment* (Cambridge: Cambridge University Press, 2008); Fred Strebergh, *Equal: Women Reshape American Law* (London: W. W. Norton and Company, 2009); Augustus B. Cochran III, *Landmark Law Cases & American Society: Sexual Harassment and the Law: The Mechelle Vinson Case* (Lawrence: University Press of Kansas, 2004).

4. See Anne Koedt, *Radical Feminism* (New York: Quadrangle, 1972); Susan Brownmiller, *Against Our Will: Men, Women and Rape* (London: Secker and Warburg, 1975); bell hooks, *Ain't I A Woman* (London: Pluto Press, 1982); Catherine MacKinnon, "Feminism, Marxism, and the State," *Signs* 7, no. 3 (1982): 515–44; Andrea Dworkin, *Intercourse* (New York: Basic Books, 1987/2006).

5. See Roberta M. Hall and Bernice R. Sandler, *Out of the Classroom: A Chilly Climate for Women* (Washington, D.C.: Association of American Colleges, Project on the Status and Education of Women, 1988); Billie Wright Dziech and Linda Weiner, *The Lecherous Professor: Sexual Harassment on Campus*, 2nd ed. (Urbana: University of Illinois Press, 1990); Alison Jones, "Desire, Sexual Harassment, and Pedagogy in the University Classroom," *Theory into Practice* 35, no. 2 (Spring 1996): 102–9.

6. One notable exception is Jane Gallop, *Feminist Accused of Sexual Harassment* (Durham and London: Duke University Press, 1997).

7. See Teresa Ebert, "For a Red Pedagogy: Feminism, Desire, and Need," *College English* 58, no. 7 (1996): 795–819; Miriam Wallace, "Beyond Love and Battle: Practicing Feminist Pedagogy," *Feminist Teacher* 12, no. 3 (1999): 184–97.

8. As Deirdre Golash explains: "The introduction of sex into the educational context has irredeemably poisoned the well; there is no going back." See, "Power, Sex, and Friendship in Academia," in *The Philosophy of Sex: Contemporary Readings*, ed. Alan Soble and Nicholas Power, 5th ed. (New York: Rowman and Littlefield Publishers, Inc, 2008), 450.

9. See Audre Lorde, "Uses of the Erotic," in *Sister Outsider* (Berkeley and Toronto: Crossing Press, 1984/2007), 53–65; bell hooks, *Teaching to Transgress* (New York and London: Routledge, 1994); Jyl Lynn Felman, *Never A Dull Moment* (New York and London: Routledge, 2001), 105–28; Angela Trethewey, "Sexuality, Eros, and Pedagogy: Desiring Laughter in the Classroom," *Women and Language* 27, no. 1 (Spring 2004): 34–39.

10. Lorde, "Uses of the Erotic," 54.

11. See Judith Chelius Stark, "Introduction," in *Feminist Interpretations of Augustine: Re-Reading the Canon*, ed. Judith Chelius Stark (University Park: Pennsylvania State University Press, 2007), 21.

12. See Rosemary Radford Ruether, "Augustine: Sexuality, Gender and Women," in *Feminist Interpretations of Augustine: Re-Reading the Canon*, ed. Judith Chelius Stark (University Park: Pennsylvania State University Press, 2007), 47–67; cf. John Cavadini, "Feeling Right: Augustine on the Passions and Sexual Desire," *Augustinian Studies* 36, no. 1 (2005): 195–217.

13. Augustine, *De ordine*, trans. Silvano Borruso (South Bend: St. Augustine's Press, 2007).
14. Augustine, *De ordine*, 1.1.2.5.
15. See Laura Holt, "Wisdom's Teacher: Augustine at Cassiciacum," *Augustinian Studies* 29, no. 2 (1998): 47–60.
16. See H.I. Marrou, *History of Education in Antiquity*, trans. George Lamb (Madison: University of Wisconsin Press, 1982).
17. For an overview of the research here, see Joanne McWilliam, "Cassiciacum Dialogues," in *Augustine Through the Ages: An Encyclopedia*, ed. Allan D. Fitzgerald (Grand Rapids: William B. Eerdmans, 1999), 135–43.
18. Certain textual components suggest that Augustine was more invested in exploring the technical form of the dialogue itself, especially those of Cicero. See Michael P. Foley, "Cicero, Augustine, and the Root of the Cassiciacum Dialogues," *Revue des Etudes Augustiniennes* 45, no 1 (1999): 51–77.
19. See Phillip Cary, "What Licentius Learned: A Narrative Reading of the Cassiciacum Dialogues," *Augustinian Studies* 29, no. 1 (1998): 142.
20. See Eugene Kevane, *Augustine the Educator: A Study in the Fundamentals of Christian Formation* (Eugene: Wipf and Stock, 1964/2009), 170–79; George Howie, *Educational Theory and Practice in St. Augustine* (London: Routledge and Kegan, 1969); William Harmless, *Augustine and the Catechumenate* (Collegeville: The Liturgical Press, 1995); Kim Paffenroth and Kevin Hughes, ed., *Augustine and Liberal Education* (Lanham: Lexington Books, 2000/2008); Karla Pollmann and Mark Vessey, ed., *Augustine and the Disciplines* (New York: Oxford University Press, 2005), 49–65.
21. Augustine, *De ordine*, 1.1.1.1.
22. Augustine, *De ordine*, 2.2.8.25.
23. Howie, *Educational Theory and Practice in St. Augustine*, 245.
24. See H. I. Marrou, *Saint Augustin et la Fin de la Culture Antique* (Paris, E. de Boccard, 1938–49).
25. For two differing accounts of Augustine's understanding of desire, see Anders Nygren, *Agape and Eros,* trans. Philip S. Watson (Chicago: University of Chicago Press, 1982) and John Burnaby, *Amor Dei: A Study of the Religion of St. Augustine* (Eugene: Wipf and Stock, 1938/2007).
26. Augustine, *De ordine*, 1.1.3.6.
27. Augustine, *De ordine*, 1.2.9.27.
28. Augustine, *De ordine*, 1.1.3.6.
29. Augustine, *De ordine*, 1.1.3.6.
30. Augustine, *De ordine*, 1.1.8.25.
31. Augustine, *De ordine*, 1.1.3.6.
32. Augustine, *De ordine*, 1.1.6.16.
33. Augustine, *De ordine*, 1.1.3.6.
34. Augustine, *De ordine*, 1.1.3.6.
35. Augustine, *De ordine*, 1.1.3.8.
36. Augustine, *De ordine*, 1.1.3.8.

37. See Ovid, *Metamorphoses*, trans. A.D. Melville (Oxford and New York: Oxford University Press, 2009).

38. Augustine, *De ordine*, 1.1.3.8.

39. Augustine, *De ordine*, 1.1.8.24.

40. For an account of the roots of this tension, see Raymond Barfield, *The Ancient Quarrel Between Philosophy and Poetry* (Cambridge: Cambridge University Press, 2011).

41. One might argue that such sentiments are what drive the ongoing analytic/continental divide within academic philosophy today.

42. For an overview, see Angelo Di Berardino, O.S.A., "Monnica," in *Augustine Through the Ages: An Encyclopedia*, ed. Allan D. Fitzgerald, O.S.A. (Grand Rapids: William B. Eerdmans, 1999), 570–71.

43. Rebecca Moore, "O Mother, Where Art Thou? In Search of Saint Monnica," in *Feminist Interpretations of Augustine: Re-Reading the Canon*, ed. Judith Chelius Stark (University Park: Pennsylvania State University Press, 2007), 147–66; Virginia Burrus and Catherine Keller, "Confessing Monica," in *Feminist Interpretations of Augustine: Re-Reading the Canon*, ed. Judith Chelius Stark (University Park: Pennsylvania State University Press, Pennsylvania, 2007), 119–45.

44. Augustine, *De ordine*, 1.2.11.31.

45. Augustine, *De ordine*, 1.2.11.31.

46. Augustine, *De ordine*, 1.2.11.31.

47. Early responses to this exclusion include Mary Wollstonecraft, *Vindication of the Rights of Women* (New York: Prometheus Books, 1989).

48. Augustine, *De ordine*, 1.2.11.31.

49. Augustine, *De ordine*, 1.2.11.32.

50. Augustine, *De ordine*, 2.1.1.1.

51. Augustine, *De ordine*, 1.2.11.31.

52. See Michael Foley, "The Other Happy Life: The Political Dimensions to St. Augustine's Cassiciacum Dialogues," *The Review of Politics* 65, no. 2 (Spring 2003): 165–83.

53. Augustine, *De ordine*, 1.2.11.32.

54. Augustine, *De ordine*, 1.2.11.32.

55. Augustine, *De ordine*, 1.2.11.32.

56. See Kari Elisabeth Børresen, "In Defense of Augustine: How *Femina* is *Homo*," in *Collectanea Augustiniana*, ed. B. Bruning, M. Lamberigts, and J. Van. Houtem (Leuven: Institut Historique Augustinien, 1990), 187–209; Judith Chelius Stark, "Augustine on Women: In God's Image But Less So," in *Feminist Interpretations of Augustine: Re-Reading the Canon*, ed. Judith Chelius Stark (University Park: Pennsylvania State University Press, 2007), 215–41.

57. Felman, *Never a Dull Moment*, 122.

58. Whatever education might entail, it need involve more than the mere reproduction of the teacher's longings. As education is irreducible to the epistemological transfer of content, it is also irreducible to the erotic transfer of desire. See Paulo Freire, *Pedagogy of the Oppressed*, trans. Myra Bergman Ramos (New York: Bloomsbury, 1968/1970/2000); Erica McWilliam, "Beyond the Missionary Position: Teacher

Desire and Radical Pedagogy," in *Learning Desire: Perspectives on Pedagogy, Culture, and the Unsaid*, ed. Sharon Todd (New York and London: Routledge, 1997), 217–35.

59. Sharon Todd, "Introduction," in *Learning Desire: Perspectives on Pedagogy, Culture, and the Unsaid*, ed. Sharon Todd (New York and London: Routledge, 1997), 6.

60. Rebecca Martusewicz, "Say Me to Me," in *Learning Desire: Perspectives on Pedagogy, Culture, and the Unsaid*, ed. Sharon Todd (New York and London: Routledge, 1997), 98.

Chapter 10

Augustine's *Confessions* and Monstrous Recognition

Daniel Jean Perrier

In her 1987 essay *The Empire Strikes Back: A Posttransexual Manifesto*, transgender theorist Sandy Stone responds to feminist criticisms of transsexuality. Admitting to the presence of strong binarism—and misogyny—in early trans autobiographies, Stone points out the demand on trans folks to produce a "plausible history"[1]—that is, to construct an autobiography that frames trans lives around the matrix of gender and sex, around suffering and discomfort, in which medical intervention is a tool not of transformation, but of correction.[2] Stone identifies a pattern in which the past self is supplanted by a new self, all behaviors categorized as masculine and feminine, and in the case of trans women, the masculine is wholesale denied and ignored, and femininity is privileged as ever present.[3] Under the scrutiny of political and medical authority, the eradication of a past self is deeply incentivized. The writers Stone examines dissociate themselves from the body "pre-" transition while asserting a persistent narrative of gender-stereotyped behavior that can serve for evidence of the truth of the writers' gender.

Transgender people must entrench themselves in a new set of gendered rules to "pass," first as authentically transgender to medical gatekeepers, and later to the world, to evade discrimination and violence. Passing is the requirement for security both in the body and the world. Stone's "plausible history" is a construction of self, a speaking of one's biography into the world for medical analysis. The history given to satisfy this need can be seen in the persistent quick and dirty definition of being transgender as being "born in the wrong body," a definition that requires of trans people a distinct alienation from their body. It must be proven through appropriately gendered artifacts, material and immaterial, thoughts and feelings and behaviors that all drive home the point that the body is *wrong* and is to be corrected.[4]

Life for trans people becomes, in this process, a before and after. Phrases like pre- and post-op, male-to-female, and female-to-male, among others, ensure this. Words like transgender and transsexual mark a change, and the status of the transgender person, if they do not want to be caught in between the two states, is one or the other. Often, it's whatever someone sees them as first. It becomes difficult to discuss the past without clothing it in the knowledge of the future, in clinging to parts of the past to submit as evidence. Old names and photos are hidden away, and hyperfemininity or hypermasculinity are taken on to smother any remainders. As Stone states in her analysis: "All these authors replicate the stereotypical male account of the constitution of woman. . . . No wonder feminist theorists have been suspicious. Hell, I'm suspicious."[5]

This process establishes a specific construction of outward identity that must conform to stereotypes of binary, cis gender to make up for the biological circumstances of birth. The possible self-directedness of transition is subsumed into complete control by the cisheteropatriarchy.[6] Asserting an internal consistency throughout life, one that preexists physical transition and justifies both medical intervention and social acceptance, itself creates the binary of pre- and post-transition. Transition becomes the fruit of a persistent identity that is gender-conforming, the body forced into sexual conformity.

In the *Confessions*, Augustine creates his own plausible history of self. This narrative is one driven by his own goals. He defines the moments in his life, even the ones he deeply despises, in terms of the person revealed in him through God. Augustine similarly splits his own life into a before and after, but he does not hide the past or shy away from it, even while hating it. Augustine states:

> They can go ahead and laugh at me, all those insolent people not yet flattened to the earth and smashed to pieces in wholesome fashion by you, my God, but for my part I want to plead to my humiliations because they glorify you. I beg you, let me, through today's memories, tour the detours of my bygone wrongheadedness and slaughter for you a victim, which is the gift of my rejoicing.[7]

Augustine recounts his past with strongly negative language, showing frequent disdain for his actions. However, the recounting itself is not a shameful experience. The past proves the present, and that makes the recounting joyful; it brings the present and the change Augustine experienced through God into sharp relief. Despite the distance in time, what Augustine becomes was always present, without denying the unsavory parts. Augustine says: "God, you saw me from far off, slipping on that slick surface. You saw, through thick smoke, my good faith sparking."[8] Augustine's faith is already present, simply hidden by the tarnish of his behaviors, misconceptions, and urges. He creates a before and after, but the transformation isn't a real change; it is the revelation of truth, within him, a recognition of truth that pre-exists in God. The two are not in battle, but a process toward the end, in which the endpoint brings to light what was missing or undesirable about the past.

The past, however, is not hidden or cleaved away, and the unsavory parts don't need to be hidden. In Augustine's self narrative, the intensity of the revealed truth only emphasizes its preexistence through emphasizing the perceived negative rather than hiding it to pretend Augustine only ever existed as he does at the end. For Augustine, the real endpoint is only found fully in God: "But still a mortal, a given portion of your creation, longs to extol you. In yourself you rouse us, giving us delight in glorifying you, because you made us with yourself as our goal, and our heart is restless until it rests in you."[9] An internal restlessness drives humanity toward its ultimate goal. Restlessness is a guide to search and to change. Joy confirms the path.

So too the transgender journey can be described; pushed by an internal, inexpressible knowledge, the transgender person who realizes sooner or later that they are transgender and begins to seek gender affirmation, finds themselves in joy and comfort. The transgender journey can be refigured as a path toward joy, rather than relying on a gender essentialist personal history that denies transness as an essential part of the validity of gender identity. If acknowledgment relies on erasure of the past, on eradicating the idea of change as thoroughly as possible through a stagnant internal identity that is gender confirming to the extreme, it is because the transness itself disqualifies a trans person from the gender category where they would place themselves. Nonbinary genders become entirely nonviable.

In the essay *My Words to Victor Frankenstein Above the Village of Chamounix: Performing Transgender Rage*, Susan Stryker figures the transsexual body as: "an unnatural body. It is the product of medical science. It is a technological construction. It is flesh torn apart and sewn together again in a shape other than that in which it was born."[10] This constructedness has consequences: human construction makes one less than human. As she describes:

> Like the monster, I am too often perceived as less than fully human due to the means of my embodiment; like the monsters as well, my exclusion from human community fuels a deep and abiding rage in me that I, like the monster, direct against the conditions in which I must struggle to exist.[11]

Existence becomes a struggle against not nature, but the conditions of the world, conditions that conflict with the transsexual body from the moment of creation. Trans people are confronted with a choice; be seen and risk violence or become invisible. For trans people, "passing" means being able to hide one's trans identity. The violence of this is the invisibility that Stryker describes permeating her existence as a trans woman:

> In the body I was born with, I had been invisible as the person I considered myself to be; I had been invisible as queer while the form of my body made my desires look straight. Now, as a dyke I am invisible among women; as a transsexual, I am invisible among dykes. As the partner of a new mother, I am often invisible as a transsexual, a woman, and a lesbian ... The high price of whatever visible, intelligible, self-representation I have achieved makes the continuing experience of invisibility maddeningly difficult to bear.[12]

Not rendering oneself invisible as trans has its own risks, from harassment to intense physical violence. Medical intervention is not available to all trans people, but for those who have access, their transition choices are always made under threat: the opposing threats of visibility and invisibility. But what is really at stake in visibility, and what is really lost in invisibility? Augustine provides an answer in the reason he displays his past:

> As to who I am right now, at this very period when I'm writing my confessions, many people are eager to know this, both those who're acquainted with me and those who aren't, as they've heard something from me or about me; but their ears aren't laid against my heart, where I *am* whoever I am. That's why they want to listen as I testify about what I myself, inside myself, am, where they can't direct their eyes or their ears or their minds. They want to hear, and they're ready to believe, but they're in no way able to *know*, are they? But the selfless love in them which makes them good people, tells them that I'm not lying in my testimony about myself. It is this love itself, in them, that believes me.[13]

It is selfless love that not only recognizes but seeks out recognition and understanding. There is a force in all of us that recognizes the other in the other's telling, in a process that is not just speaking, not just testifying, not just listening, but recognition, a recognition of sameness—and goodness—that can only be experienced between the recognizer and the recognized.

Augustine testifies not to others, but to God:

> But since selfless love believes all things, at least among those it binds to itself and thus unifies, I, too, Master, will join in, testifying to you in such a way that other people can hear me at the same time. I can't prove to them that what I confess is the truth, but those whose ears love opens to me believe me.[14]

For Augustine, recounting the past is a delight, because confessing the evils of the past means delighting in the change.[15] Writing about who he is allows others to extend selfless love to him and remain open to the truth of

Augustine's testimony. The rejection from humanity the monster faces in *Frankenstein* is created by the failure of the humans the monster encounters to extend the selfless love inside them—the uniting power of God throughout humanity—excluding the monster from humanity and goodness, dooming him to exile and isolation.

In recognition, one finds both rejection and love. In this way, there is a kind of true love possible between humanity and God that we can only find human-to-human, in the recognition of God in the other. And even as a cisnormative society rejects transgender people upon recognition as transgender, rejecting them specifically for the forms of their bodies, transgender people can find love in recognition. It has been done in traditions in transition houses run by house mothers, homes where trans women, largely trans women of color, would come together to provide mutual aid, and more experienced trans women would help others navigate their lives as trans women. This is a tradition that helped many trans women survive when socioeconomic conditions and social acceptance for trans people were even worse, and houses and organizations in that tradition continue to help trans people support each other today. The larger world might not provide recognition, but there is a more intimate recognition between trans folks, in part in the shared pain of not receiving it.

Ultimately, Frankenstein's monster accepts an outsider status, and it is with this status he returns to his human creator and asks for his match. Rather than continuing to seek community among humanity after his failure to pass as human causes rejection, he searches for something like himself, something that is also constructed. Though he found loving and intellectual community, the physical reality of his constructed-ness and unnatural passage from death to life makes him a horror when he is revealed.[16] Passing is not a simple choice. Like the monster, trans people accused of lying through passing are subject to transphobic and "gay panic" induced violence should they fail to measure up, thereby reaffirming the need to tell this "lie." Before medical intervention they too must pass, fulfilling a list of criteria that is, thankfully, less stringent than it once was. Those old autobiographies functioned in part as guides on how to construct the self for the medical institution that defines the transsexual and so, from our historical position, transgender, in such a way as to access body modifications that are classified as therapeutically beneficial to transgender people.

But, in being "clocked" (being recognized as transgender by someone who does not know that information prior), transgender people are opened to both violence, and to love. Passing eludes that love, the kind of love of recognition. Like the monster ultimately does, Stryker calls us to reject passing. She writes, "I am a transsexual, and therefore I am a monster."[17] Monster, she notes, "is derived from the Latin noun monstrum, 'divine portent,' itself formed on the root of the verb *monere*, or 'to warn.'"[18] Like angels, trans people bring a message and a misplaced fear; the binaries we've based our identities in are more malleable than we think.

Augustine opens up the shame of his past and refuses to shame it into silence; the confession of it is powerful proof of the strength of the internal light, and it cannot remain inside. Augustine is driven to speak a truth that requires the whole and does so unabashedly. It is this truth-telling that writers like Stone and Stryker encourage. Rather than hide away the evidence of a "disgraceful" past, Stone calls us not to deny it, and Stryker calls us to show it off, to become a physical announcement of existential truths, a holy portent. In Augustine, we can see that this narrative, for trans people written on the body, for the nonpassing proclaimed to all those who see, we find the same power driving his telling. Like Augustine, the temporal path taken by trans people, the narrative that strings their lives together, is one unit pointing to truth, and for trans people, the monstrous trans body holds that truth. It is only in embracing that monstrosity that trans people can experience real recognition, between each other, and between themselves and the world.

NOTES

1. Sandy Stone, "The *Empire* Strikes Back: A Posttransexual Manifesto," in *The Transgender Studies Reader,* ed. Susan Stryker and Stephen Whittle (New York: Routledge, 2006), 230.

2. Stone, "The *Empire* Strikes Back," 228.

3. Stone, "The *Empire* Strikes Back," 226.

4. Stone, "The *Empire* Strikes Back," 227.

5. Stone, "The *Empire* Strikes Back," 227.

6. Stone, "The *Empire* Strikes Back," 230.

7. Augustine, *Confessions,* trans. Sarah Ruden (New York: The Modern Library, 2017), 4.1.4.

8. Augustine, *Confessions,* 4.2.2

9. Augustine, *Confessions,* 1.1.2

10. Susan Stryker, "My Words to Victor Frankenstein above the Village of Chamounix," in *The Transgender Studies Reader*, ed. Susan Stryker and Stephen Whittle (New York: Routledge, 2006), 245.

11. Stryker, "My Words to Victor Frankenstein," 245

12. Stryker, "My Words to Victor Frankenstein," 251.

13. Augustine, *Confessions,* 10.4.3

14. Augustine, *Confessions,* 10.3.1

15. Augustine, *Confessions,* 10.4.1

16. Stryker, "My Words to Victor Frankenstein," 249.
17. Stryker, "My Words to Victor Frankenstein," 246.
18. Stryker, "My Words to Victor Frankenstein," 247.

Chapter 11

Finding an Ally in Augustine

Anne-Marie Schultz and Michael R. Whitenton

Throughout the late 1980s to the mid-2000s, many feminist scholars turned their attention to careful considerations of Augustine's extensive work. Some scholars regard him as a thinker deeply opposed to feminist concerns. For example, Margaret Maxey provocatively suggests, "The theological task of 'liberating' women would get underway primarily by rejecting and counteracting an Augustinian inheritance."[1] Indeed, given some of his remarks about women, it is not difficult to imagine why some feminists find little of value in his work.[2] However, other feminist scholars locate rich resources in his work that are helpful for rethinking the patriarchal structures of Western Christianity: its theology, institutions, individual and communal practices. For example, Anne-Marie Bowery argues that "Augustine presents Monica as a feminized image of Christ. Augustine's portrait of Monica allows us to reframe the masculine image of divinity that lies at the heart of the Christian doctrine."[3] Elizabeth Kari Børresen remarks, "Atypical use of female metaphors describing God or Christ in the Christian tradition can be used as a starting point for a new theology."[4] Jane Duran maintains, "Augustine shares with a thinker such as Kierkegaard a concern for inwardness and for the personal that may, after analysis and reflection, prove useful to feminist concerns."[5] More recently, Maggie Labinski explores the rich pedagogical resources of Augustine's thought. She considers "the moments of overlap between Augustine's pedagogical approach in *De magistro* and feminist theories of care." She argue[s] that "Augustine not only offers a useful model for those who wish to reclaim the centrality of students within education. He also encourages us to critique the narrative that women are more 'naturally' suited for caring relationships."[6] Elsewhere, she navigates the complex climate that pervades university campuses that make it difficult to explore pleasure in the classroom experience. She draws upon Augustine's discussion of pedagogical pleasure in Augustine's *De catechizandis rudibus*. She argues, "Despite his reputation as a pleasure-hater, Augustine spends the majority of his text defending the delights of teaching. In particular, Augustine argues that if teachers wish to find pleasure in teaching, they would do well to study the pleasures of mothers."[7]

In the past two decades, the academic conversations surrounding feminist discussions of gender have become increasingly complex. The rise of intersectional approaches that Black feminist and womanist scholars have advanced have led to much needed critiques of the privileged white focus of the American feminist movement from its inception in the mid 1800s to contemporary times. Intersectional approaches have also led to the increased recognition of women of color more broadly.[8] Feminist scholars from developing nations also offer critiques of capitalism and the rigid binary logic that maintains a politics of exclusion and dehumanization.[9] The increased recognitions of transgender, nonbinary, and gender-fluid persons also play an important role in developing broader implications of feminist critique.[10] Alongside these academic reconsiderations of gender, the social and political landscape with respect to gender and sexual identity has become more inclusive. Indeed, the Respect for Marriage Act was signed into law on December 13, 2022, a reflection of the fact that same sex and transgendered unions, adoptions, and diverse family structures have increasingly achieved mainstream acceptance.

However, alongside this increase in inclusivity in the secular world, many Christian communities have been much slower to reconsider gender and sexual orientation outside of traditional hetero-normative practices.[11] Furthermore, Augustine heavily influences conservative social/political religious value systems, such as the modern complementarian movement, an extension of the New Calvinism, led and maintained by Wayne Grudem, John Piper, and others. While this movement ostensibly focuses on upholding "traditional" gender roles, it is also heavily influenced by portions of Augustine's writing that fixate on sex and not having it.[12] More broadly, the influence of New Calvinism among conservative Christian student groups on college campuses ensures the proliferation of a particularly countercultural reading of the Bible and Christianity that is predicated on views regarding gender and sexuality that have come to be associated closely with Augustinian thought. Ironically, it is precisely these associations and dimensions of Augustine, if we can reread him skillfully, that expand his relevance beyond his typical allies. We seek to counterbalance certain aspects of his legacy by rediscovering him for new purposes. Our hope is that turning to certain aspects of Augustine's life and work might help LGBTQ+ Christians and allies navigate the sometimes difficult waters of balancing Christian commitment, identity, and inclusion. In what follows, we argue that a reconsideration of Augustine's writings provides a much needed resource to people with diverse perspectives on gender and sexuality.

More specifically, we turn to Augustine's writings as a way of showing how they offer us important resources to help students and faculty navigate what some perceive as a pernicious divide between increasing inclusivity and traditional Christian understandings of human sexuality, gender, and marriage. Augustine's struggles with his own sexuality and his treatment of Monica in the *Confessions* and his view of Biblical Interpretation are helpful not only with rethinking male/female dichotomies but also new issues that arise from greater LGBTQ+ representation. To this end, in section II, we discuss how Dr. Schultz teaches Augustine's *Confessions* in the philosophy classroom. In section III, we explore how Augustine is treated in a variety of contexts in the Baylor Interdisciplinary Core program, focusing particularly on Dr. Whitenton's use of *De Genese* and *De Doctrina* in Biblical Heritage and Contemporary Ethical Issues. We end by describing the difficulties an LGBTQ+ student group has faced while trying to get a charter at our historically conservative Christian university and some hopeful institutional responses that resonate with Augustine's understanding of the importance of Christian love and charity toward all people.

AUGUSTINE'S *CONFESSIONS* IN THE PHILOSOPHY CLASSROOM

Dr. Schultz often teaches Augustine's *Confessions* in her Introduction to Philosophy classes. She teaches him after several weeks on Plato and Aristotle and before a turn to Descartes, and Nietzsche. His prominent role in the history of philosophy is important for students to acknowledge. The autobiographical dimensions of Confessions is an excellent thread that the students can follow through the *Meditations* and *Ecce Homo*.[13] But larger historical considerations aside, the narrative is compelling on its own terms. Augustine's honesty with his own struggles with faith is helpful to evangelical Christian students who may well have doubts about their own faith and few venues in which to express it. Similarly, Augustine's struggles with sexual desire (properly framed) can become helpful resources for students constructing a sexual ethic, especially those who have grown up immersed in the purity culture of evangelical Christianity.[14] The examples of Augustine's influence on the New Calvinism mentioned above suggest that Augustine's self-loathing may be the archeological starting point for purity culture's shame-based system.[15] Indeed, those who have grown up within purity culture movements find consensual sexual experiences more traumatic (even within marriage),[16] are more likely to believe rape culture and domestic violence myths,[17] and thus experience greater trauma when faced with sexual assault. Such ideologies "splinter" its subjects both sexually and spiritually.[18]

Perhaps, amidst all this damage, there lies another reason Augustine can be a helpful ally. Augustine's hermeneutical approach, when placed in our modern world, promotes the consideration of viewpoints alternative to those espoused by Augustine himself.[19] Such an approach allows us to both uphold the importance of Augustine for Christian tradition and ethical reflection by teaching students to think Augustine-ly, while also suggesting that Augustine was reading the Bible through his own social and philosophical context of North African Christianity in Late Antiquity.[20]

Though his struggles with faith and sexuality are certainly entwined in Augustine's mind, for the purposes of this chapter, we will focus primarily on Augustine's struggles with sexual desire. His sexual drives, urges, and his willingness to indulge them pervade the early books of *Confessions*.[21] Here are just a few examples, "I was burning to find satisfaction in hellish pleasures. I ran wild in the shadowy jungle of erotic adventures."[22] He attests, "Sensual folly assumed domination over me, and I gave myself totally to it in acts allowed by shameful humanity but under your laws illicit."[23] He also laments that his parents did not push him to marriage for fear it would interfere with his rhetorical education. After his year break in his education, Augustine moves to Carthage to continue his studies, "and all around me hissed a cauldron of illicit loves."[24] Augustine falls in love and "in secret I attained the joy that enchains."[25] Augustine also mentions various other temptations like the theater, even as he emphasizes his dedication to his studies.

Students often find solace in the sincere expression of desire. And while Augustine's condemnation of it fits well with the purity culture ethic of abstaining until marriage, it is a helpful way to begin talking about sexual ethics with students regardless of sexual orientation. For example, in Book IV, Augustine describes aspects of his life from nineteen to twenty-eight. He recalls, "In those years I had a woman. She was not my partner in what is called lawful marriage. I had found her in my state of wandering desire and lack of prudence. Nevertheless, she was the only girl for me, and I was faithful to her."[26] He attests, "With her I learnt by direct experience how wide a difference there is between the partnership of marriage entered into for the sake of having a family and the mutual consent of those whose love is a matter of physical sex."[27] Augustine's frank discussion of different sexual relationships stimulates many conversations about student concerns over hook up culture, dating apps, and the additional challenges that COVID-19 has presented in developing deeper relational intimacy.

While Augustine ostensibly desires only women sexually, he also narrates a compelling story about the death of his close male friend with which LGBTQ+ people might identify. Their friendship starts when Augustine returns to Thagaste to teach, "I had come to have a friend who because of shared interests was very close. He was my age, and we shared the flowering of youth."[28] Augustine describes it as "a very sweet experience, welded by the fervour of our identical interests," even if the relationship does not deepen his faith.[29] While in no way suggesting Augustine had sexual desire for his friend, the relationship suggests that he would understand the depth of love that exists between same sex couples. He confesses, "My soul could not endure to be without him" and even though they were only close for a year before the friend died, "It had been sweet to me beyond all the sweetnesses of life that I had experienced."[30] Augustine then describes the depths of his despair after his friend's passing. He laments, "Everything on which I set my gaze was death. My home town became a torture to me."[31] He becomes a "vast problem" to himself[32] and reports that "I found myself heavily weighted down by a sense of being tired of living and scared of dying"[33] and "I was surprised that any other mortals were alive, since he whom I had loved as if he would never die was dead."[34] It is striking that Augustine spends more time talking about the depth of the love of his friend that he does describing his monogamous relationship. Though later in Book VI, Augustine conveys his despair when "the woman with whom I habitually slept was torn away from my side because she was a hindrance to my marriage. My heart which was deeply attached was cut and wounded, and left a trail of blood."[35] Despite what feelings he had for Adeodatus's mother, Augustine describes himself as "a slave for lust" and finds another woman for two years while he waits two years for his fiancé to turn thirteen. Making students aware of the fact that he had to wait two years to marry until the eleven-year-old turned thirteen calls attention to the social construction of what counts as acceptable desire. We would regard a union between a thirty-five-year-old man and a thirteen-year-old girl in quite different terms today. These details of Augustine's story often help students begin to think critically about the views they have inherited from their faith traditions. All of these aspects of the text can help students grapple with the complexities constructing their own sexual ethic regardless of their sexual orientation. The *Confessions* offers abundant resources for students to engage in ethical decision-making vis-à-vis their own sexual identity.

In *Augustine and the Dialogue*, Erik Kenyon draws attention to the ways in which Augustine inherits and develops a philosophical mode of inquiry from Plato and the Platonists. He writes, "The fact that we can inquire at all tells us various things about ourselves. By reflecting on our own act of inquiry, we are put in a position to improve how we go about inquiring."[36] Kenyon argues that this is the essential teaching that Augustine took from Plato, more than any doctrinal ascent. He explains, "If, while working through Augustine's works, we find that Augustine uses Platonic methods to draw conclusions that depart from orthodox Platonic doctrine, then why should we not engage in the same intellectual dance, engaging in Augustinian *aporia* and self-reflection as a way of reaching whatever conclusions strike us as most plausible today?"[37] Kenyon emphasizes the fact that "Augustine presents philosophical inquiry as a process that comes naturally to human beings, flowing from their rational desire to find unity in the world."[38]

In Kenyon's view, "The main task for a teacher of philosophy is not to impart new knowledge but merely to remove obstacles to this natural process."[39] Kenyon explains what these obstacles are: "Each individual has within himself everything needed to make this journey, yet the pursuit of sensual pleasures, the demands of everyday life and the opinions of human society present obstacles along the way. At the most basic level, a teacher's task is to remove these obstacles and support students as they embrace and develop their natural curiosity."[40] He notes that "Each of Augustine's dialogues ends by embracing some form of Christianity as the most plausible way forward."[41] Augustine's *Confessions* offers students a similar model of sustained self-reflective inquiry to engage with as they develop their own Christian understanding of identity.

AUGUSTINE IN THE BAYLOR INTERDISCIPLINARY CORE

The Baylor Interdisciplinary Core is an alternate pathway through the regular undergraduate core distribution requirements at Baylor. Approximately two hundred students enroll in the program each year. The courses are interdisciplinary and team taught. Students first encounter Augustine in their second semester World Cultures II where the students read Books I, II, IV, V, and VIII. They have one intro large group and two small group discussions on those books. It is the first text they read in the course. It offers an excellent transition from World Cultures I where the students study various cultures of the ancient world. It also represents one of the two main foundational strands of the medieval European world: 1) the Christian Classical/Mediterranean worldview and 2) Germanic warrior ethos. The students then read *Beowulf* right after Augustine to set up those two pillars of Western civilizations.

The following semester, the students read some of Augustine's letters, taken from his *Political Writings*, dealing with capital punishment and just war in Social World I,[42] a course which pairs social and political texts ranging from Plato, Aristotle, Augustine, and Machiavelli with contemporary thinkers in the social sciences like Jonathan Haidt. By the time BIC students take the junior-level Biblical Heritage and Contemporary Ethical Issues course, they have some familiarity with Augustine. Drawing upon that familiarity, Dr. Whitenton finds Augustine's *De Genese* and *De Doctrina* a useful resource to navigate a variety of contemporary ethical issues from a Christian perspective. This course is designed to be taught by two faculty members, from different disciplinary backgrounds, to represent and address better the interdisciplinarity of both the Bible and ethics. This team-taught course usually pairs a biblical scholar and either a historian, philosopher, or ethicist for the teaching pair. This pedagogical pairing multiplies the available paths of inquiry as professors and students explore the subject material together. It also checks professor bias and offers the opportunity to model the value of difference and disagreement.

The central goal of Biblical Heritage is to stimulate thinking about the role the Bible has played and might continue to play in contemporary ethics from a broadly Christian perspective. Dr. Whitenton relies heavily on case studies, which vary depending on the semester, but often include slavery and human trafficking, reproductive rights, gender, sexuality, disability, immigration, forced migration, physician-assisted death, interfaith cooperation, and food insecurity. Naturally, such a course runs the risk of begging the question of *how* one reads the Bible. In order to stimulate thinking about this topic, students read excerpts from Augustine's *De Genesi* and *De Doctrina*. While some of Augustine's ethical conclusions may trouble many twenty-first-century Bible readers, his manner of thinking with the Bible provides hermeneutical guides that bear extraordinary pedagogical fruit.

DE GENESI ON WHEN SCIENCE AND SCRIPTURE SEEM TO CONFLICT

In his *De Genesi ad litteram* (*On Genesis Literally Interpreted*), Augustine argues a Christian ought to read the Bible in a way that fits within what we know of the world through science. Using "Let there be light"[43] as an example, Augustine acknowledges an incongruity, which scholars of the Jewish scriptures have long pointed out: "light" (and "day" and "night") exists before the creation of celestial bodies, including the sun and moon.[44] For Augustine, in such instances where science conflicts with a particular reading of Scripture, Christians ought always to side with science. In so doing, Augustine upholds Scripture but dismisses Scriptural *readings* that run contrary to what we know through science. For example, he writes that "it is a disgraceful and dangerous thing for an infidel to hear a Christian, presumably giving the meaning of Holy Scripture, talking nonsense [about scientific] topics."[45] In order to protect the integrity of the Christian witness, Augustine maintains that the writers of Scripture must be presented as highly educated in all scientific matters (broadly conceived). His concern is worth quoting at length:

> If they find a Christian mistaken in a field which they themselves know well and hear him maintaining his foolish opinions about our books, how are they going to believe those books in matters concerning the resurrection of the dead, the hope of eternal life, and the kingdom of heaven, when they think their pages are full of falsehoods on facts which they themselves have learnt from experience and the light of reason?[46]

Notice that Augustine sets up a hierarchy of scriptural understanding, with matters pertaining to salvation at the top. His pragmatism leads him to reject as spurious any readings of Scripture that would jeopardize the opportunity for others to join the Faith—which he does not, at least in this context, attach to dogma outside of the heavenly things. What, we might wonder, would Augustine do with what many feel is a divide between the testimonies of Scripture on gender and sexuality and the growing literature on the complexities of these concepts, both of which, scientists and many philosophers maintain, are more of a culturally constructed spectrum?[47]

Augustine's concerns about the optics of Christians looking foolish to non-Christians and his prioritization of matters relating to salvation imply an instructive model for thinking with Scripture about ethics. Augustine's commitment to readings of Scripture that are compatible with science (reason and experience) emerges from his concern for the broader Christian witness. How will non-Christians take the Bible seriously regarding matters of salvation if they believe (erroneously for Augustine) that the Bible directly contradicts the accepted norms of science? Instead, Augustine insists that the writers of Scripture were educated men and would thus not espouse beliefs deemed false by those outside the Faith.

An Augustinian model of thinking with Scripture about ethics would suggest that all viable readings fit within contemporary sciences (broadly conceived), which have come a long way since Late Antiquity. From Einstein's Theory of Relativity to emerging sciences of happiness and communication to the (social) scientific study of different expressions of gender and sexuality, Augustine calls out from the grave that we ought to carefully consider research from the greatest minds, theoretical frameworks, and research laboratories, as we interpret the Scriptures for today. Further, if scriptural readings should not contradict contemporary science, they must also fit within the Love Command.

DE DOCTRINA ON THE LOVE COMMAND AS A GUIDE FOR SCRIPTURAL READING

In his *De Doctrina*, Augustine teaches that all skillful readings of Scripture must align with either the love of God and neighbor or the knowledge thereof. In *De Doctrina* 3.33–34, he writes,

> Anything in the [Scriptures] that cannot be related either to good morals or to the true faith should be taken as figurative. Good morals have to do with our love of God and our neighbor, the true faith with our understanding of God and neighbor.[48]

Beyond this, the Christian who "so far as he perceives that he has attained to the love and knowledge of God and his neighbor" may rely on conscience to decipher what ought to be interpreted as figuratively. In short, Scripture should be "interpreted according to the aim of love, whether it be love of God or love of one's neighbor, or both."[49] On the one hand, this is essentially the message of Jesus in the Gospel of Matthew, where Jesus thrice refers to the love command as the summation of all ethics before God and people.[50] Paul echoes this sentiment when he writes, "the one who loves another has fulfilled the law."[51] Indeed, the entire law is summed up in the commandment to "Love your neighbor as yourself. Love does no wrong to a neighbor; therefore, love is the fulfilling of the law."[52] However, Augustine's *ethos*, particularly among the New Calvinists, makes his directive more instructive, even though—or perhaps *because*—he is not found in Scripture. He is more accessible. And, perhaps most importantly, nobody questions Augustine's conservative *bona fides*. If the love command was enough for Jesus, Paul . . . and even Augustine, maybe it is good enough for us, as well.

Augustine's logic of reason, experience, and love may prompt some readers to scrutinize ancient views of gender reflected in Scripture. For example, the author of 1 Peter 3:7 refers to women as the "weaker vessel" (ἀσθενεστέρῳ σκεύει τῷ γυναικείῳ), a view that seems to draw upon ancient understandings of the female body as an incompletely formed male body, which was too cold, wet, and leaky.[53] Likewise, the author of 1 Tim 2:12 and an anonymous scribal addition we now call 1 Cor 14:33 maintain that women must not teach or have authority over men in church. An Augustinian hermeneutic might prompt us to reinterpret these passages in light of the love command, as well as any number of bodies of modern knowledge. In fact, scientific developments, contemporary psychology, and recent history all challenge straightforward interpretations of these texts. Crucially, Christian history is brimming with women preachers who have wrought change with skillful words and leadership. These developments should not be surprising considering the range of modern scientific, philosophical, and social advances. Read in this way, Augustine can prod us to consider interpretations of Scripture that yield a greater understanding of and love for one's (in this case, female) neighbors. Augustine's emphasis on science and love as guides for thinking ethically with the Scriptures invites us into a beautiful and difficult dance.

Such a love ethic is not without its critics. For example, preeminent New Testament scholar, Richard Hays, has argued against centering Christian ethical thinking on the love command because, in his estimation, love has "become debased in popular discourse; it has lost its power of discrimination, having become a cover for all manner of vapid self-indulgence."[54] However, in the Sermon on the Mount, the love Jesus describes is unique precisely for its *lack* of "discrimination." Jesus contrasts the typical discriminatory love, which excludes one's enemies, with a love that mimics God's love: "Love your enemies and pray for those who persecute you, so that you may be children of your Father in heaven" because God offers sun and rain to all people—evil and good.[55] Similarly, renowned Christian ethicist, Stanley Hauerwas, has described a love ethic as "often but a cover for what is fundamentally an assertion of ethical relativism."[56] Yet again, in the canonical gospels—and the Pauline corpus—Jesus's love is most clearly demonstrated in his embrace of the bloody ordeal of his death at the hands of powerful men in Rome. Even death could not stop such a love, which birthed God's paradoxical kingdom—where one finds strength in weakness, presence in absence, faith in doubt—when God raised him from the dead.[57] It is *this* love which Christians are called to embody as Christ embodies them.[58] Such caricatures of a love ethic bear no resemblance to love as prescribed by Jesus in the canonical gospels and Paul's writings—and by Augustine, who prescribes it as a dynamic hermeneutical tool.

Valarie Kaur uses birth metaphors to describe this kind of love—a "revolutionary love"—as "more than a feeling. Love is a form of sweet labor: fierce, bloody, imperfect, and life-giving—a choice we make over and over again."[59] Far from "vapid self-indulgence," such revolutionary love "is the choice to enter into wonder and labor for *others*, for our *opponents*, and for *ourselves* in order to transform the world around us."[60] Dismissing an ethic of love as a "cover for [. . .] ethical relativism" may provide an escape hatch for those unwilling to labor with a Christlike love, but it misses the beauty that waits on the other side of what may feel like insurmountable obstacles. An Augustinian love ethic provides essential flexibility that allows the Scriptures to permeate contemporary issues, and work synergistically with contemporary forms of knowledge, otherwise kept at arm's length.

By appealing to the tradition via Augustine's instructions for thinking with the Scriptures, Dr. Whitenton invites students into a dynamic process of Christian ethical inquiry in the Biblical Heritage course. While this journey backward may lead beyond vistas Augustine could not begin to imagine, we believe it is faithful to his instruction. Read in this way, Augustine prompts us to reevaluate our own views based on the twin guides of love and science.

STRUGGLES FOR INCLUSION AND BELONGING

We teach at a historically conservative Christian institution where these strands of the changing contemporary social political landscape with respect to gender and sexual identity are prevalent. There is also a growing awareness of the particular difficulties LGBTQ+ students face as they pursue their educational goals at Baylor. On the other hand, many faculty and students identify with a traditional conservative understanding of gender and sexual identity and often find these developments unsettling. Since the early 1990s, LGBTQ+ students have formed various unofficial student support groups and repeatedly asked for formal charter recognition from the Division of Student Life. In 2017, a new unofficial student group, ΓAY, formed. This group has repeatedly attempted to receive formal recognition as a student group. Reasons given for the rejection involve the belief that the group would be advocating for a position contrary to Baylor's official views on human sexuality.[61]

Though the student group charter requests continue to be denied, their ongoing attempts have pushed the conversation forward. For example, under the sponsorship of the School of Social Work, Christian gay activist and author Justin Lee spoke at Baylor in 2019. The Board of Regents has considered the student group issue at several recent meetings. In 2021, the Board approved the formation of an LGBTQ+ group that would work within the confines of the human sexuality policy.[62] This group, called "Prism," reflects "diversity, belonging, and opportunity in the LGBTQ+ community" at Baylor. In a public letter addressing these developments, Baylor president Linda Livingstone strikes an Augustinian note. She writes:

> A common theme emerging from all of the aforementioned conversations is the need for us to provide more robust and more specific training for students, faculty and staff in loving, caring for and supporting our LGBTQ+ students. It also became clear that we need to provide additional opportunities for our University community to listen to each other and discuss such matters in a civil, academic and supportive environment, as they are important to our faith and society. And, perhaps most importantly, we need to establish trust with our LGBTQ+ students so that, among other things, they might seek out the resources provided by Baylor—all of which must be done as a faithful expression of our Christian mission.[63]

Augustine stands uniquely poised to help navigate these contemporary waters. He can speak to both conservative elements of Christian communities that are resistant to full inclusion and to students struggling to find belonging. Augustine offers a powerful model of the quest to live authentically in relationship to God.

NOTES

1. Margaret Maxey, "Beyond Mary and Eve," *Religion for a New Generation*, ed. James Needleman et al., 2nd ed. (New York: Macmillan, 1977), 116–17.

2. See Anne-Marie Bowery for a brief overview: "Monica: The Feminine Face of Christ," in *Feminist Interpretations of Augustine: Re-Reading the Canon*, ed Judith Chelis Stark (University Park: Pennsylvania State University Press, 2007), 69–96, http://www.jstor.org/stable/10.5325/j.ctt7v22j.6. JSTOR.

3. Bowery, "Monica."

4. Kari Elizabeth Børresen, "In Defense of Augustine: How Femina Is Homo," *Augustiniana* 40 (1990): 425.

5. Jane Duran, "A Feminist Appraisal of Augustine," *New Blackfriars* 88, no. 1018 (2007): 666,
https://doi.org/10.1111/j.1741-2005.2007.00179.x.

6. Maggie A. Labinski, "Care and Critique: Augustine's *De Magistro*," *Epoché* 23, no. 1 (2018): 59, https://doi.org/10.5840/epoche2018720120.

7. Maggie A. Labinski, "Pedagogical Pleasures: Augustine in the Feminist Classroom," *Journal of Philosophy of Education* 51, no. 1 (2017): 281, https://doi.org/10.1111/1467-9752.12222.

8. See bell hooks, *Feminist Theory: From Margin to Center* (New York: Routledge, 1984); *Feminism Is for Everybody Feminism Is for Everybody: Passionate Politics* (Cambridge: South End Press, 1994); and Patricia Hill Collins, *Black Feminist Thought: Knowledge, Consciousness, and the Politics of Empowerment*, 2nd ed. (New York: Routledge, 1999). bell hooks passed on December 15, 2021. See this *New York Times* obituary about her life and work https://www.nytimes.com/2021/12/15/books/bell-hooks-dead.html.

9. See Ranjoo Seodu Herr, "Reclaiming Third World Feminism," *Meridians* 12, no. 1 (2014): 1–30, https://doi.org/10.2979/meridians.12.1.1; Asma Mansoor, "'Marginalization' in Third World Feminism: Its Problematics and Theoretical Reconfiguration," *Palgrave Communications* 2, no. 1 (2016): 1–9, https://doi.org/10.1057/palcomms.2016.26; María Lugones, "Toward a Decolonial Feminism," *Hypatia* 25, no. 4 (2010) 742–59.

10. See Kelly Oliver for a discussion of the 2017 Tuvel controversy: "If This Is Feminism . . . ," *The Philosophical Salon*, May 8, 2017, https://thephilosophicalsalon.com/if-this-is-feminism-its-been-hijacked-by-the-thought-police/.

11. See Justin Lee, *Torn: Rescuing the Gospel from the Gays-vs.-Christians Debate* (Nashville: Jericho Books, 2012).

12. See Wayne Grudem, *Evangelical Feminism and Biblical Truth: An Analysis of More Than 100 Disputed Questions* (Wheaton: Crossway, 2012) and John Piper and Wayne Grudem, *Recovering Biblical Manhood and Womanhood: A Response to Evangelical Feminism*, rev. ed. (Wheaton: Crossway, 2021). That the majority of the most influential popular literature on "biblical womanhood" comes from men should come as no surprise. However, women are also writing work heavily influenced by Augustine. See, e.g., Barbara Geer, *Confessions of a Godly Woman* (Grand Rapids: WestBow Press, 2014). On "biblical womanhood" as a construct of white patriarchal Christianity, see Beth Allison Barr, *The Making of Biblical Womanhood: How the Subjugation of Women Became Gospel Truth* (Grand Rapids: Baker, 2021). For a first person account of the harm these Augustinian systems can cause women, see Aimee Byrd, *Recovering from Biblical Manhood and Womanhood: How the Church Needs to Rediscover Her Purpose*. Illustrated edition (Grand Rapids: Zondervan, 2020); Brenda Marie Davies, *On Her Knees: Memoir of a Prayerful Jezebel* (Grand Rapids: Eerdmans, 2021).

13. J. Lenore Wright, *The Philosopher's "I": Autobiography and the Search for the Self* (Albany: SUNY Press, 2006).

14. The trauma from purity culture is well-documented. See, e.g., Amy DeRogatis, *Saving Sex: Sexuality and Salvation in American Evangelicalism* (Oxford: Oxford Univesity Press, 2014); Kelsy Burke, *Christians under Covers: Evangelicals and Sexual Pleasure on the Internet* (Oakland: University of California Press, 2016), http://www.ucpress.edu/book.php?isbn=9780520286337; Linda Kay Klein, *Pure: Inside the Evangelical Movement That Shamed a Generation of Young Women and How I Broke Free* (New York: Touchstone, 2018); Samuel L. Perry, *Addicted to Lust: Pornography in the Lives of Conservative Protestants* (Oxford: Oxford University Press, 2019); Aimee Byrd, *Recovering from Biblical Manhood and Womanhood*; Rachel Joy Watson and Scott Sauls, *Talking Back to Purity Culture: Rediscovering Faithful Christian Sexuality* (Downders Grove: InterVarsity, 2020).

15. Augustine has not borne this weight alone. Paul's sexual ethic in 1 Corinthians upholds celibay as the highest expression of sexual purity—even in marriage. This straightforward reading of 1 Corinthians 5–7 stands in stark contrast to the pro-family reading of Paul found in conservative circles today. On which, see David Wheeler-Reed, *Regulating Sex in the Roman Empire: Ideology, the Bible, and the Early Christians* (New Haven: Yale University Press, 2017).

16. See Katie Cross, "'I Have the Power in My Body to Make People Sin': The Trauma of Purity Culture and the Concept of 'Body Theodicy,'" in *Feminist Trauma Theologies: Body, Scripture & Church in Critical Perspective*, ed. Katie Cross and Karen O'Donnell (London: SCM Press, 2020): 21–42. Van Der Wyngaard's 2019 documentary, *I Survived I Kissed Dating Goodbye*, chronicles the sexual and religious trauma of a generation of American conservative Christians, who read and abided by Joshua Harris's 1997 book, *I Kissed Dating Goodbye*. See Jessica Van Der Wyngaard, *I Survived I Kissed Dating Goodbye*, 2019, https://www.youtube.com/watch?v=ybYTkkQJw_M. Harris recently announced that he had left Christianity, in large part over the immeasurable pain he had inflicted upon so many people. Harris opens up about his decision in Axios 2019. See Axios, *Former Evangelical Leader*

Josh Harris on Renouncing Christianity, 2019, https://www.youtube.com/watch?v=P8x-GEzCC78.

17. See Bretlyn Owens, *Purity Culture: Measurement and Relationship to Domestic Violence Myth Acceptance* (PhD diss., Biola University, 2021), https://www.proquest.com/docview/2533194829?pq-origsite=gscholar&fromopenview=true. Rape myths are conveyed to women in Christian dating books, as detailed in Kathryn R. Klement and Brad J. Sagarin, "Nobody Wants to Date a Whore: Rape-Supportive Messages in Women-Directed Christian Dating Books," *Sexuality & Culture* 21, no. 1 (2017): 205–23.

18. See Louisa Allen, "Denying the Sexual Subject: Schools' Regulation of Student Sexuality," *British Educational Research Journal* 33, no. 2 (2007): 231, https://doi.org/10.1080/01411920701208282; cf. Olivia Stanley, "A Personal Encounter with Purity Culture," *Bible & Critical Theory* 16 (2020): 202–3; Louisa Allen, *Young People and Sexuality Education: Rethinking Key Debates* (New York: Palgrave Macmillan, 2011), 139.

19. This is essentially Martin Luther's approach to Scripture, which Bultman called *Sachkritik* or a biblical criticism that "distinguishes between what is said and what is meant and measures what is said by what is meant." See Rudolph Bultmann, "The Problem of a Theological Exegesis of the New Testament," *The Beginnings of Dialectic Theology*, ed. James McConkey Robinson (Louisville: John Knox Press, 1968), 242. Robert Morgan would later describe this method as "a critical assessment of what a biblical text says in the light of the gospel that the author intended to communicate" (Morgan 175–90, quoting from 175). See further, Robert Morgan, "Sachkritik in Reception History," *Journal for the Study of the New Testament* 33, no. 2 (2010): 175, https://doi.org/10.1177/0142064X10385519.

20. On which, see Susanna Elm, *"Virgins of God": The Making of Asceticism in Late Antiquity* (Oxford: Clareon, 1994); cf. Virginia Burrus, *Begotten, Not Made: Conceiving Manhood in Late Antiquity* (Stanford: Stanford University Press, 2000); Matthew Kuefler, *The Manly Eunuch: Masculinity, Gender Ambiguity, and Christian Ideology in Late Antiquity* (Chicago: University of Chicago Press, 2001); esp. 13–36; Kyle Harper, *From Shame to Sin: The Christian Transformation of Sexual Morality in Late Antiquity* (Cambridge: Harvard University Press, 2016).

21. Before Augustine mentions sexual desire, it is worth noting that Book I is filled with references to the natural physical delights of receiving breastmilk. Here is just one of numerous examples: "For at that time, I knew nothing more than how to suck and to be quietened by bodily delights, and to weep when I was physically uncomfortable." See Augustine, *Confessions*, trans. Henry Chadwick (Oxford: Oxford University Press, 1991/98), I.vi.7. He also recounts fear of corporeal punishment (I.ix.14) and his discomfort with the models of imitation that his literary education was providing him with (I.xvii.28). We mention this just to emphasize that a concern with physicality of all sorts, not just sexuality, pervades the book as a whole.

22. Augustine, *Confessions*, II.i.i.

23. Augustine, *Confessions*, II.Ii.6.

24. Augustine, *Confessions*, III. i.i.

25. Augustine, *Confessions*, III.i.i.

26. Augustine, *Confessions*, IV.i.3.
27. Augustine, *Confessions*, IV.i.3.
28. Augustine, *Confessions*, IV.iv.7.
29. Augustine, *Confessions*, IV.iv.7.
30. Augustine, *Confessions*, IV.iv.7.
31. Augustine, *Confessions*, IV.iv.9.
32. Augustine, *Confessions*, IV.iv.9.
33. Augustine, *Confessions*, IV.vi.
34. Augustine, *Confessions*, IV.vi.

35. Augustine, *Confessions,* VI.xv.25; Margaret Miles, "Not Nameless but Unnamed: The Woman Torn from Augustine's Side," in *Feminist Interpretations of Augustine: Re-Reading the Canon*, ed. Judith Chelius Stark (University Park: Pennsylvania State University Press, 2007), 167–68.

36. Erik Kenyon, *Augustine and the Dialogue* (Cambridge: Cambridge University Press, 2018), 12.

37. Kenyon, *Augustine and the Dialogue*, 17.
38. Kenyon, *Augustine and the Dialogue*, 122.
39. Kenyon, *Augustine and the Dialogue*, 122.
40. Kenyon, *Augustine and the Dialogue*, 233.
41. Kenyon, *Augustine and the Dialogue*, 236.

42. See Augustine, *Political Writings*, ed. E. M. Atkins and R. J. Dodaro (Cambridge: Cambridge University Press, 2001).

43. Gen 1:3.
44. Gen 1:14–18.

45. Augustine, *The Literal Meaning of Genesis, Vol. 1 and 2*, trans. John Hammond Taylor S.J., vol. 41/42 *Ancient Christian Writers: The Works of the Fathers in Translation*, ed. Johannes Quasten, Walter J. Burghardt, and Thomas Comerford Lawler (New York: Paulist Press, 1982.), 1.19.39.

46. Augustine, *The Literal Meaning of Genesis*, 1.19.39.

47. See Lee, *Torn: Rescuing the Gospel from the Gays-vs.-Christians Debate*, 51–69, for an accessble overview of scientific views aimed at a Christian lay audience. Lee draws heavily on Simon LeVay, *Gay, Straight, and the Reason Why: The Science of Sexual Orientation* (Oxford: Oxford University Press, 2012). For a recent overview of the literature, see Anthony F. Bogaert and Malvina N. Skorska, "A Short Review of Biological Research on the Development of Sexual Orientation," *Hormones and Behavior* 119 (Mar. 2020): 1–5, https://doi.org/10.1016/j.yhbeh.2019.104659; Emmanuele A. Jannini et al., "Genetics of Human Sexual Behavior: Where We Are, Where We Are Going," *Sexual Medicine Reviews* 3, no. 2 (2015): 65–77, https://doi.org/10.1002/smrj.46.

48. Augustine, *De Doctrina Christiana*, trans. and ed. R. P. H. Green (New York: Clarendon Press, 1995), 3.33–34.

49. Augustine, *De Doctrina Christiana*, 3.48.
50. Matt 22:36–40.
51. Rom 13:8.
52. Rom 13:9–10.

53. Cf. Galen, *Hygiene,* in *Galen: Writings on Health: Thrasybulus and Health (De Sanitate Tuenda)*, trans. P. N. Singer (Cambridge: Cambridge University Press, 2023), 1.3; 5.2, https://doi.org/10.1017/9781009159524. See also, Hippocrates, *On Affections* and *Regimen in Acute Diseases*, vol. 6 *Hippocrates*, trans. Paul Potter, Loeb Classical Library 473 (Cambridge: Harvard University Press, 1988), 1.34; cf. Clement of Alexandria, *Christ the Educator*, trans. Simon P. Wood, C.P., vol. 23 *The Fathers of the Church* (Washington, D.C.: Catholic University of America Press, 2010), 3.3.

54. Richard B. Hays, *The Moral Vision of the New Testament*, 1st ed. (San Francisco: Harper San Francisco, 1996), 202. Cf. Richard B. Hays, "Response to Richard Burridge, Imitating Jesus," *Scottish Journal of Theology* 63, no. 3 (2010): 334, https://doi.org/10.1017/S0036930610000402.

55. Matt 5:43–44. Space does not permit a thorough treatment of Jesus's love ethic in the New Testament Gospels. For which, see Richard A. Burridge, *Imitating Jesus: An Inclusive Approach to New Testament Ethics* (Grand Rapids: William B. Eerdmans, 2007), 33–80; 155–346.

56. Stanley Hauerwas, *Vision and Virtue: Essays in Christian Ethical Reflection* (Notre Dame: University of Notre Dame Press, 1981), 124.

57. Cf. Phil 2:6–11; Rom 1:3–4; Mark 16:1–6.

58. Cf. Gal 2:19–20.

59. Valarie Kaur, *See No Stranger: A Memoir and Manifesto of Revolutionary Love*, illus. ed. (New York: One World, 2020), xv.

60. Kaur, *See No Stranger*, xvi (emphasis ours).

61. See Emily Cousins, *Baylor to Try to Charter LGBTQ Group This Semester*, 28 Sept. 2021, https://baylorlariat.com/2021/09/28/baylor-to-try-to-charter-lgbtq-group-this-semester/. Baylor's statement on human sexuality follows, "Baylor University welcomes all students into a safe and supportive environment in which to discuss and learn about a variety of issues, including those of human sexuality. Baylor affirms the biblical understanding of sexuality as a gift from God. Christian churches across the ages and around the world have affirmed purity in singleness and fidelity in marriage between a man and a woman as the biblical norm. Temptations to deviate from this norm include both heterosexual sex outside of marriage and homosexual behavior. It is thus expected that Baylor students will not participate in advocacy groups which promote understandings of sexuality that are contrary to biblical teaching." See https://news.web.baylor.edu/news/story/2004/baylor-statement-human-sexuality.

See further, "Human Sexuality at Baylor University" at https://diversity.web.baylor.edu/leadership-commitment/human-sexuality-baylor-university.

62. This group does not support or condone any sort of conversion therapy. Further, President Livingstone's statement explicitly rejects these practices. She emphasizes that "Baylor counselors do not practice or condone conversion or reparative therapy." See Linda A. Livingstone, "Human Sexuality at Baylor University," *Office of the President | Baylor University*, 2019, https://www.baylor.edu/president/news.php?action=story&story=212249.

63. Livingstone, *"Human Sexuality at Baylor University."*

Bibliography

Abelard and Heloise. *The Letters of Abelard and Heloise.* Translated by Betty Radici. New York: Penguin, 1974.

Allen, Louisa. "Denying the Sexual Subject: Schools' Regulation of Student Sexuality." *British Educational Research Journal* 33, no. 2 (2007): 221–34. https://doi.org/10.1080/01411920701208282.

———. *Young People and Sexuality Education: Rethinking Key Debates.* New York: Palgrave Macmillan, 2011.

Aristotle. *Metaphysics.* Translated by W.D. Ross. In *The Complete Works of Aristotle*, edited by Jonathan Barnes. 2 Vols. Princeton: Princeton University Press, 1984.

Ashbrook Susan Harvey. "Spoken Words, Voiced Silence: Biblical Women in Syriac Tradition." *Journal of Early Christian Studies* 9, no. 1 (2001): 105–31.

Augustine. *Against the Academics (Answer to the Skeptics).* In *The Happy Life; Answer to the Skeptics; Divine Providence and the Problem of Evil; Soliloquies.* Translated by Denis J. Kavanagh, O.S.A. Vol. 1 of *The Fathers of the Church.* New York: Cima Publishing Co., Inc, 1948.

———. *The Catholic Way of Life and the Manichean Way of Life.* In *The Manichean Debate.* Translated and notes by Roland Teske, S.J. Vol. I/19 of *The Works of Saint Augustine: A Translation for the 21st Century,* edited by Boniface Ramsey. Hyde Park: New City Press, 2006.

———. *On Christian Doctrine.* In *St. Augustine's City of God and Christian Doctrine.* Translated by James Shaw. Series 1, Vol. 2 of *Nicene and Post-Nicene Fathers*, edited by Philip Schaff. Buffalo: Christian Literature Publishing, 1886/87.

———. *City of God (books 1-10).* Series Latina 47 of *Corpus Christianorum*, edited by Bernhard Dombart and Alfons Kalb. Turnhout: Brepols, 1955.

———. *City of God (books 11-22).* Series Latina 48 of *Corpus Christianorum*, edited by Bernhard Dombart and Alfons Kalb. Turnhout: Brepols, 1955.

———. *The City of God.* Translated and introduction by William Babcock. Vol. I/6-7 of *The Works of Saint Augustine: A Translation for the 21st Century*, edited by Boniface Ramsey. Hyde Park: New City Press, 2012–13.

———. *Concerning the City of God against the Pagans.* Translated by Henry Bettenson. London: Penguin Books, 2003.

———. *Confessiones,* edited by J.J. O'Donnell. Oxford: Clarendon, 1992.

―――. *Confessions*. Translated and introduction by Maria Boulding, O.S.B. Vol. I/1 of *The Works of Saint Augustine: A Translation for the 21st Century*, edited by John E. Rotelle O.S.A. Hyde Park: New City Press, 1997/2002.

―――. *Confessions*. Translated by Henry Chadwick. Oxford: Oxford University Press, 1991/98.

―――. *Confessions*. Translated by Sarah Ruden. New York: The Modern Library, 2017.

―――. *On Continence*. In *Marriage and Virginity*. Translated by Ray Kearney. Vol. I/9 of *The Works of Saint Augustine: A Translation for the 21st Century*, edited by John E. Rotelle, O.S.A. Hyde Park: New City Press, 1999/2005.

―――. *Contra Academicos*. In *Opera Omnia: Patrologiae Latinae Elenchus*, edited by J.P. Migne. Paris: n.p., 1841–1845. http://www.augustinus.it/.

―――. *Divjak Letters*. Vol. 88 of *Corpus Scriptorum Ecclesiasticorum Latinorum*, edited by Johannes Divjak. Vienna: Tempsky, 1981/88.

―――. *De Doctrina Christiana*. Translated and edited by R. P. H. Green. New York: Clarendon Press, 1995.

―――. *Epistolae*. In *Opera Omnia: Patrologiae Latinae Elenchus*, edited by J.P. Migne. Paris: n.p., 1841-1845. http://www.augustinus.it/.

―――. *Essential Sermons, Part III: Homilies*. Translated by Edmund Hill. Vol. 25 of *The Works of Saint Augustine: A Translation for the 21st Century*, edited by Daniel Edward Doyle. Hyde Park: New City Press, 2007.

―――. *On the Excellence of Marriage*. In *Marriage and Virginity*. Translated by Ray Kearney. Vol. I/9 of *The Works of Saint Augustine: A Translation for the 21st Century*, edited by John E. Rotelle, O.S.A. Hyde Park: New City Press, 1999/2005.

―――. *Expositions of the Psalms, Vol. 1-6*. Translated and introduction by Maria Boulding, O.S.B. Vol III/15–20 of *The Works of Saint Augustine: A Translation for the 21st Century*, edited by John E. Rotelle, O.S.A. Hyde Park: New City Press, 2000–2004.

―――. *De Genesi ad litteram libri duodecim*. In *Opera Omnia: Patrologiae Latinae Elenchus*, edited by J. P. Migne. Paris: n.p., 1841–1845. http://www.augustinus.it/.

―――. *Genesis Against the Manichees*. In *St. Augustine on Genesis*. Translated by Roland Teske, S.J. Vol. 84 of *The Fathers of the Church*, edited by Ludwig Schopp et al. Washington, D.C.: Catholic University of America Press, 1991.

―――. *On Genesis: A Refutation of the Manichees*. In *On Genesis*. Translated by Edmund Hill, O.P. Vol. I/13 of *The Works of Saint Augustine: A Translation for the 21st Century*, edited by John E. Rotelle, O.S.A. Hyde Park: New City Press, 2002/04.

―――. *Good of Marriage*. Vol. 41 of *Corpus Scriptorum Ecclesiasticorum Latinorum*, edited by Joseph Zycha. Vienna: Tempsky, 1900.

―――. *Good of Widowhood*. Vol. 41 of *Corpus Scriptorum Ecclesiasticorum Latinorum*, edited by Joseph Zycha. Vienna: Tempsky, 1900.

―――. *On The Greatness of the Soul (The Magnitude of the Soul)*. In *The Immortality of the Soul; The Magnitude of the Soul; On Music; The Advantage of Believing; On Faith in Things Unseen*. Translated by John J. McMahon, S.J. Vol. 4 of *The Fathers of The Church*. Washington, D.C.: Catholic University of America Press, 1947.

———. *The Happy Life*. Translated by Ludwig Schoop. In *The Happy Life, Answer to Sceptics, Divine Providence and the Problem of Evil, Soliloquies*. Vol. 5/1 of *The Fathers of the Church*, edited by Ludwig Schoop et al. New York: Cima Publishing, 1948.

———. *The Happy Life*. In *Trilogy on Faith and Happiness*. Translated by Roland J. Teske, S. J., Michael Campbell, O.S.A., and Ray Kearney. Vol. I/3 of *The Works of Saint Augustine: A Translation for the 21st Century*, edited by Boniface Ramsey. Hyde Park: New City Press, 2010.

———. *On the Holy Trinity*. Translated by Arthur West Haddan. Series 1, Vol. 3 of *Nicene and Post-Nicene Fathers*, edited by Philip Schaff. Buffalo: Christian Literature Publishing, 1886.

———. *Holy Virginity*. Vol. 41 of *Corpus Scriptorum Ecclesiasticorum Latinorum*, edited by Joseph Zycha. Vienna: Tempsky, 1900.

———. *On Holy Virginity*. In *Marriage and Virginity*. Translated by Ray Kearney. Vol. I/9 of *The Works of Saint Augustine: A Translation for the 21st Century*, edited by John E. Rotelle, O.S.A. Hyde Park: New City Press, 1999/2005.

———. *Homilies (51-85)*. Vol. 30/1 of *Nuova Biblioteca Agostiniana* (Discorsi 2/1), edited and translated by Luigi Carrozzi. Rome: Città Nuova Editrice, 1982.

———. *Homilies (86-116)*. Vol. 30/2 of *Nuova Biblioteca Agostiniana* (Discorsi 2/2), edited and translated by Luigi Carrozzi. Rome: Città Nuova Editrice, 1983.

———. *Homilies (184-229)*. Vol. 32/1 of *Nuova Biblioteca Agostiniana* (Discorsi 4/1), edited and translated by P. Bellini, F. Cruciani, and V. Tarulli. Rome: Città Nuova Editrice, 1984.

———. *Homilies on the First Epistle of John*. Translated, introduction and notes by Boniface Ramsey. Vol. III/14 of *The Works of Saint Augustine: A Translation for the 21st Century*, edited by Daniel E. Doyle, O.S.A. and Thomas Martin O.S.A. Hyde Park: New City Press, 2008.

———. *Homilies on the Gospel of John*. Translated and notes by Edmund Hill, O.P. Vol. III/12 of *The Works of Saint Augustine: A Translation for the 21st Century*, edited, introduction, and notes by Allan Fitzgerald O.S.A. Hyde Park: New City Press, 2009.

———. *Instructing Beginners in Faith*. Translated, introduction, and notes by Raymond Canning. Vol. V of *The Works of Saint Augustine: A Translation for the 21st Century*, edited by Boniface Ramsey. Hyde Park: New City Press, 2009.

———. *Letters*. Vol. 31B of *Corpus Scriptorum Ecclesiasticorum Latinorum*, edited by K. D. Daur. Turnhout: Brepols, 2009.

———. *Letters (1-270)*. Translated, introduction, and notes by Roland J. Teske, S.J. Vol. II/1–4 of *The Works of Saint Augustine: A Translation for the 21st Century*, edited by Boniface Ramsey. Hyde Park: New City Press, 1997–2005.

———. *Letters (1-82), Vol. 1*. Translated by Sister Wilfrid Parsons, S.N.D. Vol. 12 of *The Fathers of the Church*, edited by Ludwig Schopp et al. Washington, D.C.: Catholic University of America Press, 1951.

———. *Letters*. In *Opera Omnia: Patrologiae Latinae Elenchus*, edited by J.P. Migne. Paris: n.p., 1865.

———. *The Letters of St. Augustine: Annotated Edition Including More Than 1500 Notes*. Translated and edited by John George Cunningham. Augsburg: Jazzybee Verlag, 2015.

———. *De Libero Arbitrio*. In *Opera Omnia: Patrologiae Latinae Elenchus*, edited by J.P. Migne. Paris: n.p., 1841–1845. http://www.augustinus.it/.

———. *On the Literal Interpretation of Genesis: An Unfinished Book*. In *St. Augustine on Genesis*. Translated by Roland Teske, S.J. Vol. 84 of *The Fathers of the Church*, edited by Ludwig Schopp et al. Washington, D.C.: Catholic University of America Press, 1991.

———. *The Literal Meaning of Genesis*. In *On Genesis*. Translated by Edmund Hill, O.P. In Vol. I/13 of *The Works of Saint Augustine: A Translation for the 21st Century*, edited by John E. Rotelle, O.S.A. Hyde Park: New City Press, 2002.

———. *The Literal Meaning of Genesis, Vol. 1 and 2*. Translated by John Hammond Taylor. New York: Newman Press, 1982.

———. *The Literal Meaning of Genesis, Vol. 1 and 2*. Translated by John Hammond Taylor, S.J. Vol. 41/42 of *Ancient Christian Writers: The Works of the Fathers in Translation*, edited by Johannes Quasten, Walter J. Burghardt, and Thomas Comerford Lawler. New York: Paulist Press, 1982.

———. *Lying*. Vol. 41 of *Corpus Scriptorum Ecclesiasticorum Latinorum*, edited by Joseph Zycha. Vienna: Tempsky, 1900

———. *On Marriage and Desire*. In *Answer to the Pelagians II*. Translated, introduction and notes by Roland J. Teske, S.J. Vol. I/24 of *The Works of Saint Augustine: A Translation for the 21st Century*, edited by John E. Rotelle, O.S.A. Hyde Park: New City Press, 1998.

———. "On Merit and the Forgiveness of Sins." Translated by Peter Holmes and Robert Ernest Wallace. Series 1, Vol. 5 of *Nicene and Post-Nicene Fathers*, edited by Philip Schaff, 113-297. Buffalo: Christian Literature Publishing, 1887.

———. *On Music*. In *The Immortality of the Soul; The Magnitude of the Soul; On Music; The Advantage of Believing; On Faith in Things Unseen*. Translated by Robert Catesby Taliaferro. Vol. 4 of *The Fathers of the Church*. Washington D.C.: Catholic University of America Press, 2002. https://ebookcentral.proquest.com/lib/bostoncollege.

———. *De ordine*. Translated by Silvano Borruso. South Bend: St. Augustine's Press, 2007.

———. *De Ordine*. In *Opera Omnia: Patrologiae Latinae Elenchus*, edited by J.P. Migne. Paris: n.p., 1841–1845. http://www.augustinus.it/.

———. *On Order (Divine Providence and the Problem of Evil)*. In *The Happy Life; Answer to the Skeptics; Divine Providence and the Problem of Evil; Soliloquies*. Translated by Robert. P. Russell, O.S.A. Vol. 1 of *The Fathers of the Church*. New York: Cima Publishing Co., Inc, 1948.

———. *Political Writings*, edited by E. M. Atkins and R. J. Dodaro. Cambridge: Cambridge University Press, 2001.

———. "On Rebuke and Grace." Translated by Peter Holmes and Robert Ernest Wallace. Series 1, Vol. 5 of *Nicene and Post-Nicene Fathers*, edited by Philip Schaff, 1276-1336. Buffalo: Christian Literature Publishing, 1887.

———. *Retractiones*. In *Opera Omnia: Patrologiae Latinae Elenchus*, edited by J.P. Migne. Paris: n.p., 1841–1845. http://www.augustinus.it/.

———. *The Rule of St. Augustine*. Translated by Robert Russell, O.S.A. Brothers of the Order of Hermits of Saint Augustine, Inc, 1976. Based on the critical text of Luc Verheijen, O.S.A. *La regle de saint Augustin*. In *Etudes Augustiniennes*. Paris: n.p., 1967.

———. *Sermones*. In *Opera Omnia: Patrologiae Latinae Elenchus*, edited by J.P. Migne. Paris: n.p., 1841–1845. http://www.augustinus.it/.

———. *Sermons (1-400)*. Translated and notes by Edmund Hill, O.P. Vol. III/1–10 of *The Works of Saint Augustine: A Translation for the 21st Century*, edited by John E. Rotelle O.S.A. Hyde Park: New City Press, 1990–1995.

———. *Soliloquia*. In *Opera Omnia: Patrologiae Latinae Elenchus*, edited by J.P. Migne. Paris: n.p., 1841-1845. http://www.augustinus.it/.

———. *The Teacher*. In *The Teacher; The Free Choice of the Will; Grace and Free Will*. Translated by Robert P. Russell, O.S.A. Vol. 59 of *The Fathers of the Church*. Washington D.C.: Catholic University of America Press, 1968

———. *Teaching Christianity*. Translated and notes by Edmund Hill, O.P. Vol. I/11 of *The Works of Saint Augustine: A Translation for the 21st Century*, edited by John E. Rotelle, O.S.A. Hyde Park: New City Press, 1995.

———. *Tractates on the Gospel of John*. Translated by John Gibb. Series 1, Vol. 7 of *Nicene and Post-Nicene Fathers*, edited by Philip Schaff. Buffalo: Christian Literature Publishing Co., 1888.

———. *De Trinitate*. In *Opera Omnia: Patrologiae Latinae Elenchus*, edited by J.P. Migne. Paris: n.p., 1841–1845. http://www.augustinus.it/.

———. *The Trinity*. Translated, introduction and notes by Edmund Hill, O.P. Vol I/5 of *The Works of Saint Augustine: A Translation for the 21st Century*, edited by John E. Rotelle O.S.A. Hyde Park: New City Press, 2012.

———. *Two Books on Genesis Against the Manichees*. In *Saint Augustine on Genesis*, edited and translated by Roland Teske, S.J. Washington, D.C.: Catholic University of America Press, 1991.

———. *On The Usefulness of Belief*. In *On Christian Belief*. Translated and notes by Edmund Hill, O.P., Ray Kearney, Michael G. Campbell, and Bruce Harbert. Vol. I/8 of *The Works of Saint Augustine: A Translation for the 21st Century*, edited by Boniface Ramsey. Hyde Park: New City Press, 2005.

———. *The Works of Saint Augustine: A Translation for the 21st Century*. Hyde Park: New City Press, 1990–.

———. *On the Work of Monks*. In *Saint Augustine: Treatises on Various Subjects*. Translated by Sister Mary Sarah Muldowney, R.S.M. et al. Vol. 16 of *The Fathers of the Church*, edited by Roy J. Deferrari. Washington, D.C.: Catholic University of America Press, 1952/2002.

Axios. *Former Evangelical Leader Josh Harris on Renouncing Christianity*. Accessed 2019. https://www.youtube.com/watch?v=P8x-GEzCC78.

Baker, Carrie N. *The Women's Movement against Sexual Harassment*. Cambridge: Cambridge University Press, 2008.

Barfield, Raymond. *The Ancient Quarrel Between Philosophy and Poetry.* Cambridge: Cambridge University Press, 2011.
Barker, Andrew. *Greek Musical Writings, Vol. 2 Harmonic and Acoustic Theory.* Cambridge: Cambridge University Press, 1989.
Barr, Beth Allison. *The Making of Biblical Womanhood: How the Subjugation of Women Became Gospel Truth.* Grand Rapids: Baker, 2021.
Barry, Jennifer. "So Easy to Forget: Augustine's Treatment of the Sexually Violated in the City of God." *Journal of the American Academy of Religion* 88, no. 1 (2020): 235–253.
Beard, Mary. "The Public Voice of Women." *Women's History Review* 24, no. 5 (2015): 809–818.
Bernau, Anke. *Virgins: A Cultural History.* London: Granta, 2007.
Blank, Hanne. *Virgin: The Untouched History.* New York: Bloomsbury, 2007.
Bogaert, Anthony F., and Malvina N. Skorska. "A Short Review of Biological Research on the Development of Sexual Orientation." *Hormones and Behavior* 119 (Mar. 2020): 1–5. https://doi.org/10.1016/j.yhbeh.2019.104659.
Børresen, Kari Elizabeth. "In Defense of Augustine: How Femina Is Homo." *Augustiniana* 40 (1990): 411–28.
———. "In Defense of Augustine: How *Femina* is *Homo*." In *Collectanea Augustiniana*, edited by B. Bruning, M. Lamberigts, and J. Van Houtem, 187–209. Leuven: Institut Historique Augustinien, 1990.
———. "God's Image, Man's Image? Patristic Interpretation of Gen. 1,27 and I Cor. 11,7." In *The Image of God: Gender Models in Judaeo-Christian Tradition*, edited by Kari Elizabeth Børresen, 187–209. Minneapolis: Fortress Press, 1995.
———. "Patristic 'Feminism': The Case of Augustine." *Augustinian Studies* 25 (1994): 139–52.
———. *Subordination and Equivalence: The Nature and Role of Woman in Augustine and Thomas Aquinas.* Kampen: Kok Pharos, 1995.
———. *Subordination and Equivalence: The Nature and Role of Woman in Augustine and Thomas Aquinas.* Translated by Charles H. Talbot. Washington, D.C.: University Press of America, 1981.
Bowery, Anne-Marie. "Monica: The Feminine Face of Christ." In *Feminist Interpretations of Augustine: Re-Reading the Canon*, edited by Judith Chelis Stark, 69–96. University Park: Pennsylvania State University Press, 2007. http://www.jstor.org/stable/10.5325/j.ctt7v22j.6.
Brachtendorf, Johannes. "Cicero and Augustine on the Passions." *Revue des Études Augustiniennes* 43 (1997): 289–308.
Bright, Pamela. *The Book of Rules of Tyconius: Its Purpose and Inner Logic.* Notre Dame: Notre Dame University Press, 1989.
Brooten, Bernadette. "Nature, Law, and Custom in Augustine's On the Good of Marriage." In *Walk in the Ways of Wisdom: Essays in Honor of E. Schüssler-Fiorenza*, edited by S. Matthews, C. Briggs Kittredge, and M. Johnson-Debaufre, 181–93. New York: Trinity Press International, 2003.
Brown, Peter. *Augustine of Hippo: A Biography, A New Edition with an Epilogue.* Berkeley and Los Angeles: University of California Press, 2000.

———. *The Body and Society: Men, Women and Sexual Renunciation in Early Christianity.* New York: Columbia University Press, 1988.

Brownmiller, Susan. *Against Our Will: Men, Women and Rape.* London: Secker and Warburg, 1975.

Bultman, Rudolph. "The Problem of a Theological Exegesis of the New Testament." In *The Beginnings of Dialectic Theology*, edited by James McConkey Robinson, 236–56. Louisville: John Knox Press, 1968.

Burke, Kelsy. *Christians under Covers: Evangelicals and Sexual Pleasure on the Internet.* Oakland: University of California Press, 2016. http://www.ucpress.edu/book.php?isbn=9780520286337.

Burnaby, John. *Amor Dei: A Study of the Religion of St. Augustine.* Eugene: Wipf and Stock, 1938/2007.

Burridge, Richard A. *Imitating Jesus: An Inclusive Approach to New Testament Ethics.* Grand Rapids: William B. Eerdmans, 2007.

Burrus, Virginia. *"Begotten, Not Made:" Conceiving Manhood in Late Antiquity.* Stanford: Stanford University Press, 2000.

———. "'Fleeing the Uxorious Kingdom': Augustine's Queer Theology of Marriage." *Journal of Early Christian Studies* 19, no. 1 (Spring 2011): 1–20.

———. "An Immoderate Feast: Augustine Reads John's Apocalypse." In *History, Apocalypse, and the Secular Imagination*, edited by Mark Vessey, Karla Pollmann, and Allan D. Fitzgerald, 183–94. Bowling Green: Philosophy Documentation Center, Bowling Green State University, 1999.

———. *Saving Shame: Martyrs, Saints, and Other Abject Subjects.* Philadelphia: University of Pennsylvania Press, 2008.

Burrus, Virginia, and Catherine Keller. "Confessing Monica." In *Feminist Interpretations of Augustine: Re-Reading the Canon*, edited by Judith Chelius Stark, 119–45. University Park: Pennsylvania State University Press, 2007.

Burrus, Virgina, and Karmen MacKendrick. "Bodies without Wholes: Apophatic Excess and Fragmentation." In *Augustine's City of God. Apophatic Bodies: Negative Theology, Incarnation, and Relationality*, edited by Chris Boesel and Catherine Keller, 79–93. New York: Fordham, 2010.

Byers, Sarah C. "Augustine and the Cognitive Cause of Stoic Preliminary Passions (Propatheiai)." *Journal of the History of Philosophy* 41, no. 4 (Oct. 2003): 433–48.

Bynum, Caroline Walker. *The Resurrection of the Body in Western Christianity, 200-1336.* New York: Columbia University Press, 1995.

Byrd, Aimee. *Recovering from Biblical Manhood and Womanhood: How the Church Needs to Rediscover Her Purpose.* Illustrated edition. Grand Rapids: Zondervan, 2020.

Cary, Phillip. "What Licentius Learned: A Narrative Reading of the Cassiciacum Dialogues." *Augustinian Studies* 29, no. 1 (1998): 141–63.

Cavadini, John C. "Feeling Right: Augustine on the Passions and Sexual Desire." *Augustinian Studies* 36, no. 1 (2005): 195–217.

Chrétien, Jean Louis. *Saint Augustin et les actes de parole.* Paris: Presses Universitaires de France, 2002.

Cicero. *"Orator."* In *Cicero: Brutus and Orator*. Translated by Robert A. Kaster, 184-188. Oxford: Oxford University Press, 2020.

Clark, Elizabeth A. "'Adam's Only Companion': Augustine and the Early Christian Debate on Marriage." In *The Olde Daunce: Love, Friendship, Sex and Marriage in the Medieval World*, edited by Robert R. Edwards and Stephen Spector, 15–31. New York: State University of New York Press, 1991.

———. "Adam's Only Companion: Augustine and the Early Christian Debate on Marriage." *Recherches augustiniennes* 22 (1986): 139–62.

———. ed. *St. Augustine on Marriage and Sexuality*. Washington, D.C.: Catholic University of America Press, 1996.

———. "Holy Women, Holy Words: Early Christian Women, Social History, and the 'Linguistic Turn.'" *Journal of Early Christian Studies* 6, no. 3 (1998): 413–29.

———. *Jerome, Chrysostom, and Friends*. New York and Toronto: Edwin Mellen Press, 1979.

———. *Reading Renunciation: Asceticism and Scripture in Early Christianity*. Princeton: Princeton University Press, 1998.

Clark, Gillian. "Adam's Engendering: Augustine on Gender and Creation." *Gender and Religion* 34 (1998): 13–22.

———. *Body and Gender, Soul and Reason in Late Antiquity*. Farnham: Ashgate, 2016.

———. *Women in the Early Church*. Collegeville: Liturgical Press, 1983.

———. *Women in Late Antiquity: Pagan and Christian Lifestyles*. Oxford: Oxford University Press, 1993.

Clement of Alexandria. *Christ the Educator*. Translated by Simon P. Wood, C.P. Vol. 23 of *The Fathers of the Church*. Washington, D.C.: Catholic University of America Press, 2010.

Coakley, Sarah. "The Eschatological Body: Gender, Transformation, and God." In *Powers and Submissions: Spirituality, Philosophy and Gender*, 153-67. Oxford: Blackwell, 2002.

Cochran III, Augustus B. *Landmark Law Cases & American Society: Sexual Harassment and the Law: The Mechelle Vinson Case*. Lawrence: University Press of Kansas, 2004.

Collins, Patricia Hill. *Black Feminist Thought: Knowledge, Consciousness, and the Politics of Empowerment*. 2nd ed. New York: Routledge, 1999.

Collins-Elliott, Jennifer. "'Bespattered with the Mud of Another's Lust': Rape and Physical Embodiment in Christian Literature of the 4th-6th Centuries C.E." PhD diss., Florida State University, Forthcoming.

Conybeare, Catherine. *The Irrational Augustine*. Oxford: Oxford University Press, 2006.

Couenhoven, Jesse. "St. Augustine's Doctrine of Original Sin." *Augustinian Studies* 36, no. 2 (2005): 359–96.

Cousins, Emily. *Baylor to Try to Charter LGBTQ Group This Semester*. Accessed September 28 2021. https://baylorlariat.com/2021/09/28/baylor-to-try-to-charter-lgbtq-group-this-semester/.

Cross, Katie. "'I Have the Power in My Body to Make People Sin': The Trauma of Purity Culture and the Concept of 'Body Theodicy.'" In *Feminist Trauma*

Theologies: Body, Scripture & Church in Critical Perspective, edited by Katie Cross and Karen O'Donnell, 21–42. London: SCM Press, 2020.

Daly, Mary. *Beyond God the Father: Toward a Philosophy of Women's Liberation.* Boston: Beacon Press, 1973/1985.

Davidson, James. "Dover, Foucault and Greek Homosexuality: Penetration and the Truth of Sex." *Past & Present* 170 (Feb. 2001): 3–51.

Davies, Brenda Marie. *On Her Knees: Memoir of a Prayerful Jezebel.* Grand Rapids: Eerdmans, 2021.

Denecker, Tim, and Gert Partoens. "*De uoce et uerbo*: Augustine's exegesis of John 1:1–3 and 23 in sermons 288 and 293A auct. (*Dolbeau* 3)." *Annali di Storia Dell'Esegesi* 31, no. 1 (2014): 95–118.

DeRogatis, Amy. *Saving Sex: Sexuality and Salvation in American Evangelicalism.* Oxford: Oxford University Press, 2014.

Derrida, Jacques. *Speech and Phenomena: And Other Essays on Husserl's Theory of Signs.* Evanston: Northwestern University Press, 1973.

Di Berardino, O.S.A., Angela. "Monnica." In *Augustine Through the Ages: An Encyclopedia*, edited by Allan D. Fitzgerald, O.S.A., 570–71. Grand Rapids: William B. Eerdmans, 1999.

Dover, Kenneth. *Greek Homosexuality.* Cambridge: Harvard University Press, 1978.

Drobner, Hubertus R. "The Chronology of St. Augustine's *Sermones ad populum*." *Augustinian Studies* 31, no. 2 (2000): 211–18.

Dunn, Geoffrey D. "The Functions of Mary in the Christmas Homilies of Augustine of Hippo." *Studia Patristica* 44 (2010): 433–46.

Duran, Jane. "A Feminist Appraisal of Augustine." *New Blackfriars* 88, no. 1018 (2007): 665–77. https://doi.org/10.1111/j.1741-2005.2007.00179.x.

Dworkin, Andrea. *Intercourse.* New York: Basic Books, 1987/2006.

———. *Intercourse.* New York: The Free Press, 1987.

Dziech, Billie Wright and Linda Weiner. *The Lecherous Professor: Sexual Harassment on Campus*, 2nd ed. Urbana: University of Illinois Press, 1990.

Ebert, Teresa. "For a Red Pedagogy: Feminism, Desire, and Need." *College English* 58, no. 7 (1996): 795–819.

Elm, Susanna. *"Virgins of God": The Making of Asceticism in Late Antiquity.* Oxford: Clarendon, 1994.

Felker Jones, Beth. *Marks of His Wounds: Gender Politics and Bodily Resurrection.* Oxford and New York: Oxford University Press, 2007.

Felman, Jyl Lynn. *Never A Dull Moment.* New York and London: Routledge, 2001.

Fitzgerald, Allan D., ed. *Augustine Through the Ages: An Encyclopedia.* Grand Rapids: William B. Eerdmans, 1999.

Foley, Michael P. "Cicero, Augustine, and the Root of the Cassiciacum Dialogues." *Revue des Etudes Augustiniennes* 45, no. 1 (1999): 51–77.

———. "The Other Happy Life: The Political Dimensions to St. Augustine's Cassiciacum Dialogues." *The Review of Politics* 65, no. 2 (Spring 2003): 165–83.

Foucault, Michel. *Confessions of the Flesh: The History of Sexuality, Vol. 4.* Translated by R. Hurley. New York: Pantheon Books, 2021.

———. *The Order of Things: An Archaelogy of the Human Sciences.* New York: Vintage Books, 1973.

Freire, Paulo. *Pedagogy of the Oppressed.* Translated by Myra Bergman Ramos. New York: Bloomsbury, 1968/1970/2000.

Gaarder, Jostein. *Vita Brevis: A Letter to St. Augustine.* Translated by Anne Born. London: Phoenix, 1997.

Gaca, Kathy L. "Martial Rape, Pulsating Fear, and the Sexual Maltreatment of Girls (παῖδες), Virgins (παρθένοι), and Women (γυναῖκες) in Antiquity." *American Journal of Philology* 135, no. 3 (2014): 303–57.

Galen. *Hygiene.* In *Galen: Writings on Health: Thrasybulus and Health (De Sanitate Tuenda).* Translated by P. N. Singer. Cambridge: Cambridge University Press, 2023. https://doi.org/10.1017/9781009159524.

Gallop, Jane. *Feminist Accused of Sexual Harassment.* Durham and London: Duke University Press, 1997.

Geer, Barbara. *Confessions of a Godly Woman.* Grand Rapids: WestBow Press, 2014.

Gleason, Maud. *Making Men: Sophists and Self-Presentation in Ancient Rome.* Princeton: Princeton University Press, 1995.

Golash, Deirdre. "Power, Sex, and Friendship in Academia." In *The Philosophy of Sex: Contemporary Readings*, edited by Alan Soble and Nicholas Power. 5th ed., 449–58. New York: Rowman and Littlefield Publishers, Inc, 2008.

Gregory of Nyssa. *The Life of Saint Macrina.* Translated by Kevin Corrigan. Eugene: Wipf and Stock, 2001.

Griffith, Susan Blackburn. "The Figure of Adam in the Sermons of Augustine." *Studia Patristica* 49 (2015): 161–68.

Grosse, Patricia. "Embodied Love and Extended Desire." PhD diss., Villanova University, 2017.

———. "Love and the Patriarch: Augustine and (Pregnant) Women." *Hypatia: A Journal of Feminist Philosophy.* Special Issue: Feminist Love Studies in the 21st Century 32, no. 1 (2017): 119–34.

Grudem, Wayne. *Evangelical Feminism and Biblical Truth: An Analysis of More Than 100 Disputed Questions.* Wheaton: Crossway, 2012.

Gunderson, E. *Staging Masculinity: The Rhetoric of Performance in the Roman World.* Ann Arbor: Michigan University Press, 2000.

Hall, Robert M., and Bernice R. Sandler. *Out of the Classroom: A Chilly Climate for Women.* Washington, D.C.: Association of American Colleges, Project on the Status and Education of Women, 1988

Hallisey, Charles. "The Surprise of Scripture's Advice." In *Religious Identity and the Problem of Historical Foundation: The Foundational Character of Authoritative Sources in the History of Christianity and Judaism*, edited by Judith Frishman, Willemien Otten, and Gerard Rouwhorst, 28–44. Leiden: Brill, 2004.

Harmless, William. *Augustine and the Catechumenate.* Collegeville: The Liturgical Press, 1995.

Harper, Kyle. *From Shame to Sin: The Christian Transformation of Sexual Morality in Late Antiquity.* Cambridge: Harvard University Press, 2016.

Harrison, Carol. "Confused Voices: Sound and Sense in the Later Augustine." In *The Intellectual World of Christian Late Antiquity*, edited by Lewis Ayres, Michael Champion, and Matthew R. Crawford. Cambridge and New York: Cambridge University Press, Forthcoming.

Hauerwas, Stanley. *Vision and Virtue: Essays in Christian Ethical Reflection*. Notre Dame: University of Notre Dame Press, 1981.

Hays, Richard B. *The Moral Vision of the New Testament*. 1st ed. San Francisco: Harper San Francisco, 1996.

———. "Response to Richard Burridge, Imitating Jesus." *Scottish Journal of Theology* 63, no. 3 (2010): 331–35. https://doi.org/10.1017/S0036930610000402.

Herr, Ranjoo Seodu. "Reclaiming Third World Feminism." *Meridians* 12, no. 1 (2014): 1–30. https://doi.org/10.2979/meridians.12.1.1.

Hill, Timothy D. *Ambitiosa Mors: Suicide and Self in Roman Thought and Literature*. New York and London: Routledge, 2004.

Hippocrates. *On Affections*. Vol. 6 of *Hippocrates*. Translated by Paul Potter. In Loeb Classical Library 473. Cambridge: Harvard University Press, 1988.

———. *Regimen in Acute Diseases*. Vol. 6 of *Hippocrates*. Translated by Paul Potter. In Loeb Classical Library 473. Cambridge: Harvard University Press, 1988.

Hockenbery, Jennifer. "The He, She and It of God: Translating Saint Augustine's Gendered Latin God-talk into English." *Augustinian Studies* 36, no. 2 (2005): 433–44.

———. *Wisdom's Friendly Heart: Augustinian Hope for Skeptics and Conspiracy Theorists.* Portland: Cascade, 2020.

Holt, Laura. "Wisdom's Teacher: Augustine at Cassiciacum." *Augustinian Studies* 29, no. 2 (1998): 47–60.

Hombert, Pierre-Marie. *Nouvelles Recherches de Chronologie Augustinienne*. Paris: Institut d'études augustiniennes, 2000.

hooks, bell. *Ain't I A Woman*. London: Pluto Press, 1982.

———. *Feminism Is for Everybody: Passionate Politics*. Cambridge: South End Press, 1994.

———. *Feminist Theory: From Margin to Center*. New York: Routledge, 1984.

———. *Teaching to Transgress*. New York and London: Routledge, 1994.

Howie, George. *Educational Theory and Practice in St. Augustine*. London: Routledge and Kegan, 1969.

Hunter, David G. "Augustine and the Making of Marriage in Roman North Africa." *Journal of Early Christian Studies* 11, no. 1 (2003): 63–85.

———. "Augustinian Pessimism? A New Look at Augustine's Teaching On Sex, Marriage and Celibacy." *Augustinian Studies* 25 (1994): 153–77.

———. "Augustine, Sermon 354A: Its Place in His Thought on Marriage and Sexuality." *Augustinian Studies* 33, no. 1 (2002) 39–60.

———. "Evil, Suffering, and Embodiment in Augustine." In *Suffering and Evil in Early Christian Thought*, edited by Nonna Verna Harrison and David G. Hunter, 143–60. Grand Rapids: Baker Academic, 2016.

———. "Introduction." *Marriage and Virginity*: The Excellence of Marriage; Holy Virginity; The Excellence of Widowhood; Adulterous Marriage; Continence.

Translated by Ray Kearney, edited by John E. Rotelle, O.S.A, 9-25. Hyde Park: New City Press, 1999/2005.

———. *Marriage, Celibacy and Heresy in Ancient Christianity: The Jovinianist Controversy.* Oxford and New York: Oxford University Press, 2007.

Ignatius. *Letter to the Magnesians.* In *The Apostolic Fathers: Greek Texts and English Translations.* Translated and edited by Michael W. Holmes. 2nd ed, 103–7. Grand Rapids: Baker Academic, 2007.

Irigaray, Luce. *Speculum de l'autre Femme.* Paris: Le Éditions de Minuit, n.d.

———. *Speculum of the Other Woman.* Translated by Gillian Gill, Ithaca: Cornell University Press, 1985.

Jannini, Emmanuele A., et al. "Genetics of Human Sexual Behavior: Where We Are, Where We Are Going." *Sexual Medicine Reviews* 3, no. 2 (2015): 65–77. https://doi.org/10.1002/smrj.46.

Jensen, Robin. *Living Water: Images, Symbols, and Settings of Early Christian Baptism.* Leiden: Brill, 2010.

Jones, Alison. "Desire, Sexual Harassment, and Pedagogy in the University Classroom." *Theory into Practice* 35, no. 2 (Spring 1996): 102–9.

Kannengiesser, Charles. "Athanasius and Traditional Christology." *Theological Studies* 34 (1973): 103–13. Reprinted in Kannengiesser, *Arius and Athanasius.* Hampshire: Variorum, 1991.

Kaur, Valarie. *See No Stranger: A Memoir and Manifesto of Revolutionary Love.* Illustrated ed. New York: One World, 2020.

Kenyon, Erik. *Augustine and the Dialogue.* Cambridge: Cambridge University Press, 2018.

Kevane, Eugene. *Augustine the Educator: A Study in the Fundamentals of Christian Formation.* Eugene: Wipf and Stock, 1964/2009.

Klein, Linda Kay. *Pure: Inside the Evangelical Movement That Shamed a Generation of Young Women and How I Broke Free.* New York: Touchstone, 2018.

Klement, Kathryn R., and Brad J. Sagarin. "Nobody Wants to Date a Whore: Rape-Supportive Messages in Women-Directed Christian Dating Books." *Sexuality & Culture* 21, no. 1 (2017): 205–23.

Koedt, Anne. *Radical Feminism.* New York: Quadrangle, 1972.

Kuefler, Mathew. *The Manly Eunuch: Masculinity, Gender Ambiguity, and Christian Ideology in Late Antiquity.* Chicago: University of Chicago Press, 2001.

Kugler, Robert A. "Tyconius' Mystic Rules and the Rules of Augustine." In *Augustine and the Bible*, edited and translated by Pamela Bright, 129–48. Notre Dame: Notre Dame University Press, 1986.

Labinski, Maggie A. "Care and Critique: Augustine's *De Magistro*." *Epoché* 23, no. 1 (2018): 59–84. https://doi.org/10.5840/epoche2018720120.

———. "Pedagogical Pleasures: Augustine in the Feminist Classroom." *Journal of Philosophy of Education* 51, no. 1 (2017): 281–97. https://doi.org/10.1111/1467-9752.12222.

Langlands, Rebecca. *Sexual Morality in Ancient Rome.* Cambridge: Cambridge University Press, 2006.

Lardinois, André, and Laura McClure, eds. *Making Silence Speak: Women's Voices in Greek Literature and Society.* Princeton: Princeton University Press, 2001.

Lee, Justin. *Torn: Rescuing the Gospel from the Gays-vs.-Christians Debate.* Nashville: Jericho Books, 2012.

LeVay, Simon. *Gay, Straight, and the Reason Why: The Science of Sexual Orientation.* Oxford: Oxford University Press, 2012.

Lienhard, Joseph T. "*Sacramentum* and the Eucharist in St. Augustine." *The Thomist* 77, no. 2 (2013): 173–92.

Lillis, Julia Kelto. "Paradox *in Partu*: Verifying Virginity in the *Protevangelium of James*." *Journal of Early Christian Studies* 24, no. 1 (2016): 1–28.

———. "Who Opens the Womb? Fertility and Virginity in Patristic Texts." *Studia Patristica* 81 (2017): 187–201.

———. *Virgin Territory: Configuring Female Virginity in Early Christianity.* Oakland: University of California Press, 2022.

Livingstone, Linda A. "Human Sexuality at Baylor University." *Office of the President | Baylor University.* Accessed 2023. https://president.web.baylor.edu/news/story/2019/human-sexuality-baylor-university.

Lorde, Audre. "Uses of the Erotic." In *Sister Outsider*, 53–65. Berkeley and Toronto: Crossing Press, 1984/2007.

Lugones, María. "Toward a Decolonial Feminism." *Hypatia* 25, no. 4 (2010): 742–59.

MacKendrick, Karmen. *Material Mystery: The Flesh of the World in Three Mythic Bodies*. New York: Fordham, 2021.

MacKinnon, Catherine. "Feminism, Marxism, and the State." *Signs* 7, no. 3 (1982): 515–44.

Mansfeld, Jaap. "'Illuminating What is Thought:' A Middle Platonist *Placitum* on 'Voice' in Context." *Mnemosyne* 58, no. 3 (2005): 358–407.

Mansoor, Asma. "'Marginalization' in Third World Feminism: Its Problematics and Theoretical Reconfiguration." *Palgrave Communications* 2, no. 1 (2016): 1–9. https://doi.org/10.1057/palcomms.2016.26.

Markus, Robert A. "Marius Victorinus and Augustine." In *The Cambridge History of Later Greek and Early Medieval Philosophy*, edited by Arthur Hilary Armstrong, 331–419. Cambridge: Cambridge University Press, 1967.

———. *The End of Ancient Christianity.* Cambridge: Cambridge University Press, 1990.

Marrou, H.I. *Saint Augustin et la Fin de la Culture Antique.* Paris: E. de Boccard, 1938–49.

———. *History of Education in Antiquity.* Translated by George Lamb. Madison: University of Wisconsin Press, 1982.

Martusewicz, Rebecca. "Say Me to Me." In *Learning Desire: Perspectives on Pedagogy, Culture, and the Unsaid,* edited by Sharon Todd, 97–113. New York and London: Routledge, 1997.

Matter, E. Ann. "Augustine and Women." In *Augustine Through the Ages: An Encyclopedia,* edited by Allan D. Fitzgerald, 887–92. Grand Rapids: William B. Eerdmans, 1999.

———. "Christ, God, and Woman in the Thought of St. Augustine." In *Augustine and his Critics*, edited by Robert Dodaro and George Lawless, 164–75. New York: Routledge, 2000.

———. "*De cura feminarum:* Augustine the Bishop, North African Women, and the Development of a Theology of Female Nature." *Augustinian Studies* 36, no. 1 (2005): 87–98.

———. "The Undebated Debate: Gender and the Image of God in Medieval Theology." In *Gender in Debate*, edited by Clare Lees and Thelma Fenster, 41–55. New York: Palgrave, 2002.

Maxey, Margaret. "Beyond Mary and Eve." In *Religion for a New Generation*, edited by James Needleman et al. 2nd ed. New York: Macmillan, 1977.

McInerney, Maud Burnett. *Eloquent Virgins from Thecla to Joan of Arc*. New York: Palgrave Press, 2003.

McLynn, Neil. *Ambrose of Milan: Church and Court in a Christian Capital*. Berkeley: University of California Press, 1994.

McWilliam, Erica. "Beyond the Missionary Position: Teacher Desire and Radical Pedagogy." In *Learning Desire: Perspectives on Pedagogy, Culture, and the Unsaid*, edited by Sharon Todd, 217–35. New York and London: Routledge, 1997.

McWilliam, Joanne. "Cassiciacum Dialogues." In *Augustine Through the Ages: An Encyclopedia*, edited by Allan D. Fitzgerald, 135–43. Grand Rapids: William B. Eerdmans, 1999.

Meltzer, Françoise. *For Fear of the Fire: Joan of Arc and the Limits of Subjectivity*. Chicago: University of Chicago Press, 2001.

Miles, Margaret R. *Augustine on the Body*. Missoula: Scholar's Press, 1979.

———. "From Rape to Resurrection: Sin, Sexual Difference, and Politics." In *Augustine's* City of God*: A Critical Guide*, edited by James Wetzel, 75-92. New York: Cambridge University Press, 2012.

———. "Not Nameless but Unnamed: The Woman Torn from Augustine's Side." In *Feminist Interpretations of Augustine, Re-Reading the Canon*, edited by Judith Chelius Stark, 167–88. University Park: Pennsylvania State University Press, 2007.

———. "Not Nameless but Unnamed: The Woman Torn from Augustine's Side." In *Rereading Historical Theology: Before, During, and After Augustine*, 127–48. Eugene: Cascade Books, 2008.

———. "Sex and the City (of God): Is Sex Forfeited or Fulfilled in Augustine's Resurrection of Body." *Journal of the American Academy of Religion* 73, no. 2 (June 2005): 307–27.

Moore, Rebecca. "O Mother, Where Art Thou? In Search of Saint Monnica." In *Feminist Interpretations of Augustine: Re-Reading the Canon*, edited by Judith Chelius Stark, 147–66. University Park: Pennsylvania State University Press, 2007.

Morales, Helen. "Rape, Violence, Complicity: Colluthus's Abduction of Helen." *Arethusa* 49, no. 1 (2016): 61–92.

Morgan, Robert. "Sachkritik in Reception History." *Journal for the Study of the New Testament* 33, no. 2 (2010): 175–90. https://doi.org/10.1177/0142064X10385519.

Nightingale, Andrea. *Once Out of Nature: Augustine on Time and the Body*. Chicago: University of Chicago Press, 2011.

Nisula, Timo. *Augustine and the Functions of Concupiscence*. Vol. 116 of *Supplements to Vigiliae Christianae*. Boston: Brill, 2012.
Nygren, Anders. *Agape and Eros*. Translated by Philip S. Watson. Chicago: University of Chicago Press, 1982.
O'Connell, Robert. *St. Augustine's* Confessions: *The Odyssey of the Soul*. Cambridge: The Belknap Press of Harvard University Press, 1969.
———. *Images of Conversion in St. Augustine's* Confessions. New York: Fordham University Press, 1996.
———. *Imagination and Metaphysics*. Milwaukee: Marquette University Press, 1986.
———. *Soundings in St Augustine's Imagination*. New York: Fordham University Press, 1994.
O'Donovan, Oliver. "*Usus* and *Fruito* in Augustine, *De Doctrina Christiana I*." *Journal of Theological Studies*, New Series 33 (1982): 361–97.
Oliver, Kelly. "If This Is Feminism . . ." *The Philosophical Salon*, May 8, 2017. https://thephilosophicalsalon.com/if-this-is-feminism-its-been-hijacked-by-the-thought-police/.
Otten, Willemien. "Augustine on Marriage, Monasticism and the Community of the Church." *Theological Studies* 59 (1998) 385–405.
———. "Between Praise and Appraisal: Medieval Guidelines for the Assessment of Augustine'sIntellectual Legacy." *Augustinian Studies* 43, no. 1 (2012): 201–18.
———. "Creation and Gender: A Theological Appraisal." In *The Cambridge Companion to Christianity and the Environment*, edited by Alexander Hampton, 303–18. Cambridge: Cambridge University Press, 2022.
———. "Creation and the Hexaemeron in Augustine." In *Thinking Nature and the Nature of Thinking: From Eriugena to Emerson*, 79-108. Stanford: Stanford University Press, 2020.
———. "Earthly Christianity between Divine Promise and Earthly Politics." In *Religious Identity and the Invention of Tradition*, edited by J.W. van Henten and A.W.J. Houtepen, 60-83. Assen: Royal van Gorcum, 2001.
———. "The Long Shadow of Human Sin: Augustine on Adam, Eve, and the Fall." In *Out of Paradise: Eve and Adam and Their Interpreters*, edited by B.E.J.H. Becking and S.A. Hennecke, 29–49. Sheffield: Sheffield Phoenix Press, 2010.
———. "Tertullian's Rhetoric of Redemption: Flesh and Embodiment in *De carne Christi* and *Deresurrectione mortuorum*." *Studia Patristica* 65 (2013): 331–48.
———. "Women in Early Christianity: Incarnational Hermeneutics in Tertullian and Augustine." In *Hermeneutics, Scriptural Politics, and Human Rights Between Text and Context*, edited by B. de Gaay Fortman, K. Martens, and M.A. Mohamed Salih, 219–35. New York: Palgrave Macmillan, 2010.
Ovid. *Metamorphoses*. Translated by A.D. Melville. Oxford and New York: Oxford University Press, 2009.
Owens, Bretlyn. *Purity Culture: Measurement and Relationship to Domestic Violence Myth Acceptance*. PhD diss., Biola University, 2021. https://www.proquest.com/docview/2533194829?pq-origsite=gscholar&fromopenview=true.
Paffenroth, Kim and Kevin Hughes, ed. *Augustine and Liberal Education*. Lanham: Lexington Books, 2000/2008.

Pagels, Elaine H. *Adam, Eve, and the Serpent*. New York: Random House, 1988.
Payne, Mark. *The Animal Part: Human and Other Animals in the Poetic Imagination.* Chicago: University of Chicago, 2010.
Perry, Samuel L. *Addicted to Lust: Pornography in the Lives of Conservative Protestants*. Oxford: Oxford University Press, 2019.
Piper, John, and Wayne Grudem. *Recovering Biblical Manhood and Womanhood: A Response to Evangelical Feminism*. Rev. ed. Wheaton: Crossway, 2021.
Plato. *Gorgias*. In *Plato: The Collected Dialogues*, edited by Edith Hamilton and Huntington Cairns, 229–307. Princeton: Princeton University Press, 1961.
———. *Symposium*. Translated by Seth Bernardete. Chicago: University Chicago Press, 1993.
Plutarch. "Advice to Bride and Groom/Praecepta Coniugalia." Vol. 2 of *Moralia*. Translated by Frank Cole Babbitt. Cambridge: Harvard University Press, 1928.
Pollmann, Karla and Mark Vessey, ed. *Augustine and the Disciplines*. New York: Oxford University Press, 2005.
Porter, James I. *The Origins of Aesthetic Thought in Ancient Greece: Matter, Sensation and Experience*. New York: Cambridge University Press, 2010.
Power, Kim. "Sed Unam Tamen: Augustine and His Concubine." *Augustinian Studies* 23 (1992): 49–76.
———. *Veiled Desire: Augustine on Women*. New York: Continuum, 1994/96.
Pranger, M. Burcht. *Eternity's Ennui: Temporality, Perseverance and Voice in Augustine and Western Literature*. Leiden: Brill, 2010.
Quintilian. *The Orator's Education 11.3*. Translated and edited by Donald A. Russell. In Loeb Classical Library 494. Cambridge: Harvard University Press, 2001.
Rackett, Michael R. "Anti-Pelagian Polemic in Augustine's *De Continentia*." *Augustinian Studies* 26 (1995): 25–50.
Ricoeur, Paul. *Time and Narrative, Vol. 1*. Translated by K. McLaughlin and D. Pellauer. Chicago: University of Chicago Press, 1984.
Rist, John. *Augustine Deformed: Love, Sin, and Freedom in The Western Moral Tradition*. Cambridge: Cambridge University Press, 2014.
Rosenberg, Michael. *Signs of Virginity: Testing Virgins and Making Men in Late Antiquity*. New York: Oxford University Press, 2018.
Ruether, Rosemary Radford. "Augustine: Sexuality, Gender and Women." In *Feminist Interpretations of Augustine: Re-Reading the Canon*, edited by Judith Chelius Stark, 47–67. University Park: Pennsylvania State University Press, 2007.
Schürmann, Reiner. *Broken Hegemonies*. Translated by Reginald Lilly. Bloomington: Indiana University Press, 2003.
———. *Des hégémonies brisées*. Mauvezin France: Trans-Europ-Repress, 1996.
Senellart, Michel. "Michel Foucault: une autre histoire du christianisme?" *Bulletin du centre d'études médiévales d'Auxerre*, 1–17. BUCEMA Hors-série n° 7 | 2013. Les nouveaux horizons de l'ecclésiologie: du discours clérical à la science du social.
Shanzer, Danuta. "Augustine's *Anonyma 1* and Cornelius's Concubines: How Philology and Literary Criticism Can Help in Understanding Augustine on Marital Fidelity." *Augustinian Studies* 48, no. 1-2 (2017): 201–24.

———. "*Avulsa a Latere Meo*: Augustine's Spare Rib: *Confessions* 6.15.25." *Journal of Roman Studies* 92 (2002): 157–76.

Smith, J. Warren. *Ambrose, Augustine, and the Pursuit of Greatness*. Cambridge and New York: Cambridge University Press, 2020.

———. *Passion and Paradise: Human and Divine Emotion in the Thought of Gregory of Nyssa*. New York: Crossroad, 2004.

Smith, Wilfred Cantwell. *What is Scripture? A Comparative Approach*. Minneapolis: Augsburg Fortress Press, 1993.

Soranus of Ephesus. *Gynecology*. In *Soranos d'Ephèse: Maladies des femmes*, edited by Paul Burguière, Danielle Gourevitch, and Yves Malinas. 4 Vols. Paris: Les Belles Lettres, 1988–2000.

Stanley, Olivia. "A Personal Encounter with Purity Culture." *Bible & Critical Theory* 16 (2020): 187–206.

Stark, Judith Chelius. "Augustine on Women: In God's Image, But Less So." In *Feminist Interpretations of Augustine: Re-reading the Canon*, edited by Judith Chelius Stark, 215–41. University Park: Pennsylvania State University Press, 2007.

———. "Introduction." In *Feminist Interpretations of Augustine: Re-Reading the Canon*, edited by Judith Chelius Stark, 1–45. University Park: The Pennsylvania State University Press, 2007.

Stock, Brian. *Augustine the Reader: Meditation, Self-Knowledge and the Ethics of Interpretation*. Cambridge: The Belknap Press of Harvard University, 1996.

———. *The Integrated Self: Augustine, the Bible, and Ancient Thought*. Philadelphia: University of Pennsylvania Press, 2017.

Stone, Geoffrey R. *Sex and the Constitution: Sex, Religion, and Law from America's Origins to the Twenty-First Century*. London and New York: W. W. Norton & Company, 2017.

Stone, Sandy. "The Empire Strikes Back: A Posttransexual Manifesto." In *The Transgender Studies Reader*, edited by Susan Stryker and Stephen Whittle, 221–235. Routledge: New York, 2006.

Stowe, Harriet Beecher. "Sojourner Truth, the Libyan Sibyl." *Atlantic*, April 1863.

Strebergh, Fred. *Equal: Women Reshape American Law*. London: W. W. Norton and Company, 2009.

Stryker, Susan. "My Words to Victor Frankenstein above the Village of Chamounix." In *The Transgender Studies Reader*, edited by Susan Stryker and Stephen Whittle, 244–56. Routledge: New York, 2006.

Teske, Roland. "Augustine's Philosophy of Memory." In *The Cambridge Companion to Augustine*, edited by Eleonore Stump and Norman Kretzmann, 148–58. Cambridge: Cambridge University Press, 2005.

———. "Introduction." In *St. Augustine on Genesis*. Translated by Roland Teske, S.J. Vol. 84 of *The Fathers of the Church*, edited by Ludwig Schopp et al., 1–39. Washington, D.C.: Catholic University of America Press, 1991.

Thompson, Jennifer J. "'Accept This Twofold Consolation, You Faint-Hearted Creatures': St. Augustine and Contemporary Definitions of Rape." *Simile* 4, no. 3 (2004) 1–17.

Todd, Sharon. "Introduction." In *Learning Desire: Perspectives on Pedagogy, Culture, and the Unsaid*, edited by Sharon Todd, 1–13. New York, London: Routledge, 1997.

Trethewey, Angela. "Sexuality, Eros, and Pedagogy: Desiring Laughter in the Classroom." *Women and Language* 27, no. 1 (Spring 2004): 34–39.

Undheim, Sissel. *Borderline Virginities: Sacred and Secular Virgins in Late Antiquity*. New York: Routledge, 2017.

Van Der Wyngaard, Jessica. *I Survived I Kissed Dating Goodbye*, 2019. https://www.youtube.com/watch?v=ybYTkkQJw_M.

Vessey, Mark. "Response to Catherine Conybeare: 'Women of Letters.'" In *Voices in Dialogue: Reading Women in the Middle Ages,* edited by Linda Olson and Kathryn Kerby-Fulton, 86–87. Indiana: Notre Dame University Press, 2005.

Walker, Abbe Lind. *Bride of Hades to Bride of Christ: The Virgin and the Otherworldly Bridegroom in Ancient Greece and Early Christian Rome*. London and New York: Routledge, 2020.

Wallace, Miriam. "Beyond Love and Battle: Practicing Feminist Pedagogy." *Feminist Teacher* 12, no. 3 (1999): 184–97.

Walsh, P. G., ed. *Augustine: De Civitate Dei (books I & II)*. Translated by P. G. Walsh. Oxford: Oxbow Books, 2005.

Walters, Jonathan. "Invading the Roman Body: Manliness and Impenetrability in Roman Thought." In *Roman Sexualities*, edited by Judith P. Hallett and Marilyn B. Skinner, 29–43. Princeton: Princeton University Press, 1997.

Watson, Rachel Joy, and Scott Sauls. *Talking Back to Purity Culture: Rediscovering Faithful Christian Sexuality*. Downers Grove: InterVarsity, 2020.

Watts, William. *St. Augustine's Confessions with an English Translation by William Watts*. London: William Heinemann, 1631.

Webb, Melanie Gibson. "Rape and Its Aftermath in Augustine's *City of God*." PhD diss, Princeton Theological Seminary, 2016.

Wessel, Susan. *Passion and Compassion in Early Christianity*. Cambridge: Cambridge University Press, 2016.

Wetzel, James. "Agony in the Garden: Augustine's Myth of Will." In *Parting Knowledge: Essays after Augustine*, 9–27. Eugene: Cascade Books, 2013.

Wheeler-Reed, David. *Regulating Sex in the Roman Empire: Ideology, the Bible, and the Early Christians*. New Haven: Yale University Press, 2017.

Wollstonecraft, Mary. *Vindication of the Rights of Women*. New York: Prometheus Books, 1989.

Wright, J. Lenore. *The Philosopher's "I": Autobiography and the Search for the Self*. Albany: SUNY Press, 2006.

Xenophon. *Symposium*. In *Memorabilia Oeconomicus; Symposium; Apology*. Translated by Jeffrey Henderson, E. C. Marchant, and O. J. Todd. In Loeb Classical Library 168. Cambridge: Harvard University Press, 2014.

Yarnold, Edward. *Cyril of Jerusalem*. New York: Routledge, 2000.

Index

1 Corinthians, 16, 46, 50, 83, 136, 146, 198, 201
1 Peter, 197–98
1 Timothy, 197

Abelard, 116, 121, 207
Adam and Eve, ix, x, 3–4, 6, 8–15, 48, 51–53, 83–84, 86–95, 99, 146–51, 153–55
Adeodatus, 32, 34–35
Alaric, 6
Allen, Louisa, 202, 207
Alypius, 152
Ambrose, 70, 90, 93, 143, 145
amor, 8
Antony, 92, 100
apatheia, 47
Aristotle, 26, 42, 163, 164, 176, 191, 195, 207
Artemidoros, 85–86
Ashbrook, Susan Harvey, 207
Athanasius of Alexandria, 89, 99
Augustine:
    on creation, 79–101;
    on desire, 21, 28;
    on emotions, 44–45, 52–53;
    on gender, 79–101;
    on happiness, 22–24, 27–28;
    interpretation of Genesis, ix, 3–6, 8–10, 13–15, 47, 49, 81, 85, 91, 93–95, 114, 143–59, 195–97;
    interpretation of Gospel of John, 44, 62, 125, 127, 132;
    interpretation of Gospel of Luke, 126, 131;
    interpretation of Gospel of Matthew, 44, 197;
    on language, 30–31;
    on love, 43, 197–99;
    on marriage, 39, 46, 50–51, 81–87;
    misogyny of, vii–viii, 7, 20;
    on power, 117–18;
    on sex/sexuality, 33, 39, 45–46, 50–52, 54, 64, 85, 87;
    on virginity, x, 59–77;
    women and, ix, 11–12, 14, 20, 24, 29, 31–34
Aumiller, Rachel, 16
Axios, 211

Baker, Carrie N., 176, 211
Barfield, Raymond, 178, 212
Barker, Andrew, 136, 212
Barr, Beth Alison, 201
Barry, Jennifer, 72, 76, 212

Basil of Caesarea, 90, 99, 100
Baylor University, 191, 194–99, 203
Beard, Mary, 136, 212
Beowulf, 195
Bernard of Clairvaux, 115
Bernau, Anke, 75, 212
Blank, Hanne, 75, 212
Bogaert, Anthony F., 204, 212
Borresen, Kari Elisabeth, viii, xiii, 56, 76, 96, 178, 189, 200, 212
Bowery, Anne-Marie, 189, 200, 212
Brachtendorf, Johannes, 55, 212
Bright, Pamela, 100, 212
Brooten, Bernadette, 80, 81, 85–86, 96, 98, 212
Brown, Peter, 80, 85, 90, 96, 98, 99, 101, 136, 213
Brownmiller, Susan, 176, 213
Bultmann, Rudolph, 202, 213
Burke, Kelsy, 201, 213
Burnaby, John, 177, 213
Burridge, Richard A., 204, 213
Burrus, Virginia, 13, 18, 75, 76, 93, 95, 100, 153, 158, 159, 178, 202, 213
Butler, Judith, 99–100
Byers, Sarah C., 55, 213
Bynum, Caroline Walker, 213
Byrd, Aimee, 201, 213

Cain, 17
caritas, ix, 4, 8, 9
Carthage, 60, 72, 192
Cary, Phillip, 177, 213
Cassiciacum, 165–68, 170–73
De catechizandis rudibus (*On Instructing the Unlearned*), 190
Cavadini, John C., 6–7, 16, 17, 56, 176, 213
Chadwick, Henry, 11
Chrétien, Jean Louis, 214
Christ, xi, 39, 44–45, 62, 75, 85–86, 88–91, 94, 98, 99, 107, 109–11, 113, 115, 118, 120, 126–131, 134–36, 137, 140, 145–46, 149–50, 153–54; as female, 154, 189

Chrysostom, 96
Cicero, 43, 140, 177, 214
City of God, x, 4, 6, 14, 16, 18, 36, 43, 45, 53, 54, 59–70, 72, 74, 75, 76, 77, 80, 84, 91, 95, 144, 157, 158, 207
Clark, Elizabeth, viii, xiii, 10, 17, 81–87, 89, 94, 95, 96, 97, 98, 99, 100, 137, 157, 214
Clark, Gillian, 137, 157, 214
Clement of Alexandria, 204, 214
Clifford, Anne, 112
Coakley, Sarah, 99–100, 214
Cochran, Augustus B., III, 176, 214
Collins, Patricia Hill, 200, 214
Collins-Elliot, Jennifer, 72, 75, 214
Confessions, ix, xi, xii,4–5, 11, 14, 17–18, 19–38, 83, 95, 96, 107–8, 110–11, 119, 120, 134, 135, 139, 140, 141, 143–44, 147, 151, 152–55, 157–59, 182–84, 186, 191–94, 203, 207–208
concupiscentia, ix, 4, 6, 8–11, 15
Conybeare, Catherine, 214
Couenhoven, Jessie, 3, 16, 214
Cousins, Emily, 205, 214
Cross, Katie, 202, 214
Cyprian, 60, 86
Cyril of Jerusalem, 138

Daly, Mary, viii, xiii, 105, 110, 118, 119, 214
Davidson, James, 41, 53, 215
Davies, Brenda Marie, 201, 215
Denecker, Tim, 137, 215
DeRogatis, Amy, 201, 215
Derrida, Jacques, 36, 215
Descartes, Rene, 191
desire, 20–21, 29–30, 33, 45, 115–16, 149–51, 152, 154; erotic, 163–79
De Doctrina Christiana (On Christian Doctrine or *Teaching Christianity)*, xi, 22–23, 25, 28, 36, 135, 141, 144, 150, 155, 191, 195, 197, 204
Di Berardino, Angelo, 178

Donatism/Donatist/Donatists, 5, 81, 92
Dover, Kenneth, 40–41, 53, 215
Drobner, Hubertus R., 73, 215
Dunn, Geoffrey D., 73, 215
Duran, Jane, 189, 200, 215
Dworkin, Andrea, 6, 17, 176, 215
Dziech, Billie Wright, 176, 215

Ebert, Teresa, 176, 215
Eden. *See* Adam and Eve
Elm, Susanna, 202, 215
emotions, 39–56
education, 163–79
Einstein, Albert, 196
Ephrem the Syrian, 139
Epistles. *See* letters
Eriugena, 97
Eve, xi, 8, 17, 48–49, 52, 143–59
Expositions of the Psalms, 138–40

the Fall. *See* sin, original
Felker Jones, Beth, 76, 215
Felman, Jyl Lynn, 174, 176, 178, 215
Fitzgerald, Allan D., xiii, 215
Foley, Michael P., 177, 178, 215
Foucault, Michel, 27, 37, 95, 96, 98, 101, 216
Frankenstein, 185
Freire, Paolo, 178, 216

Gaarder, Jostein, 121, 216
Gaca, Kathy L., 72, 216
Galen, 204, 216
Gallop, Jane, 176, 216
Geer, Barbara, 201, 216
gender:
    and creation, 79–101;
    and desire, ix, xi–xii, 40;
    and emotion(s), ix–x, 39–56;
    and God, xi;
    and voice, x–xi, 123–41
De Genesi ad litteram (*On Genesis Literally Interpreted* or *The Literal Meaning of Genesis*), 4, 6, 9, 10, 14, 16–18, 56, 82, 96–99, 121, 156, 195, 204, 208, 210
Gleason, Maud, 136, 216
God, xi, 28–29;
    as feminine, 105–21;
    as mother, 107–10;
    as object of desire, 21, 45, 115–16, 149–51, 152, 154
Golash, Deirdre, 176, 216
Gregory of Nyssa, x, 80, 88–91, 93, 96, 99, 100, 216
Griffith, Susan Blackburn, 16, 216
Grosse Brewer, Patricia, ix, 17, 216
Grudem, Wayne, 190, 201, 216
Gunderson, E., 136, 216

Haidt, Jonathan, 195
Hall, Roberta M., 176, 216
Hallisey, Charles, 100, 216
Harmless, William, 177, 216
Harper, Kyle, 202, 217
Harris, Joshua, 202
Harrison, Carol, x–xi, 139, 217
Harvey, Susan Ashbrook, 139
Hauerwas, Stanley, 198, 204, 217
Hays, Richard B., 204, 217
Heloise, 116, 121, 207
Herr, Ranjoo Seodu, 201, 217
Hildegard of Bingen, 112, 117, 118
Hill, Timothy D., 217
Hippocrates, 204, 217
Hockenberry, Jennifer, xi, 119, 120, 137, 217
Holt, Laura, 177, 217
Hombert, Pierre-Marie, 73, 217
hooks, bell, 176, 200, 217
Howie, George, 166, 177, 217
Hughes, Kevin, 177, 222
Hunter, David G., 9–10, 17, 54, 73, 77, 86, 99, 217

Ignatius, 140, 218
Irigaray, Luce, 26, 37, 218
Isham, Elizabeth, 112

Jacob of Sarug, 139
Jannini, Emmanuele A., 204, 218
Jensen, Robin, 141, 218
Jerome, 16, 79, 82
John the Baptist, 128, 132, 133, 135
Jones, Alison, 176, 218
Jovinian, 73, 77, 82
Julian, x, 39, 47, 50–53
Julian of Norwich, 109

Kannengeiser, Charles, 101, 218
Kant/Kantian, 22, 24
Kaur, Valerie, 198, 204, 205, 218
Keller, Catherine, 13, 18, 178
Kelto Lillis, Julia, x
Kenyon, Erik, 194, 203, 218
Kevane, Eugene, 177, 218
Kierkegaard, Soren, 116, 189
Klein, Linda Kay, 201, 218
Klement, Kathryn R., 202, 218
Koedt, Anne, 176, 218
Kuefler, Matthew, 202, 218
Kugler, Robert, 92, 100, 218

Labinski, Maggie Ann, xi–xii, 189, 200, 218
Langlands, Rebecca, 219
Lardinois, André, 219
Lee, Justin, 201, 204, 219
Lee, Richard A., Jr., ix
Letters (of Augustine), 74;
    Letter 11, 65, 75;
    Letter 18, 25, 27, 37;
    Letter 130, 111–12;
    Letter 147, 112;
    Letter 264, 111;
    Letter 266, 111
LeVay, Simon, 204, 219
Licentius, xii, 168–70
Lienhard, Joseph T., 77, 219
Lillis, Julia Kelto, 71, 72, 77, 219
Livingstone, Linda A., 205, 219
Lorde, Audre, 164, 176, 219
love, 43, 166, 197–99
Lucretia, 72

Lugones, María, 201, 219
Luther, Martin, 202

Machiavelli, Nicolo, 195
MacKendrick, Karmen, xi, 158
MacKinnon, Catherine, 176, 219
Macrina, 90, 100
De magistro (*On the Teacher*), 189
Mani/Manichaeans/Manichaeism/Manichees, x, 5, 25, 39, 47–48, 50, 52–53, 54, 73, 81, 106, 108, 114, 143, 145
Mansfeld, Jaap, 137, 219
Mansoor, Asma, 201, 219
Markus, Robert, 82, 89, 93, 97, 99, 100, 101, 219
marriage, 10, 17, 39, 46, 50–51
Marrou, H. I., 177, 219
Martusewicz, Rebecca, 175, 179, 219
Mary (mother of Jesus), xi, 62–63, 65–66, 69–70, 73, 126, 128, 130–36, 140, 148–49, 151
Mary Magdalene, 149, 151
Matter, E. Ann, 18, 144, 155, 220
Maxey, Margaret, 189, 200, 220
McClure, Laura, 219
McInerney, Maud Burnett, 75, 220
McLynn, Neil, 220
McWilliam, Erica, 178, 220
McWilliam, Joanne, 177, 220
Meltzer, Francoise, 75, 220
Miles, Margaret, viii, xiii, 16, 38, 76, 77, 98, 157, 203, 220
Milton, John, 12
Monica, xii, 34, 37, 38, 110–11, 113, 135, 170–73, 189, 191, 200
Moore, Rebecca, 178, 220
Morales, Helen, 72, 220
Morgan, Robert, 202, 221
Moses, 144

Naas, Michael, 36
Nebridius, 152
New Calvinism/Calvinists, 190, 192, 197

Nietzsche, Friedrich, 191
Nightingale, Andrea, 80, 81, 88–89, 93–94, 96, 97, 99, 221
Nisula, Timo, 10, 17, 47, 55, 221
Nygren, Anders, 177, 221

O'Connell, Robert, 106–7, 115, 119, 121, 221
O'Donovan, Oliver, 22, 24, 36, 221
Oliver, Kelly, 201, 221
Optatus, 16
De Ordine (On Order or *On Providence)*, 110, 120, 164–66, 170–71, 174–75, 177, 178, 210
Origen, 45, 79, 89–90, 97, 101
Otten, Willimien, x, 97, 98, 100, 101, 221
Ovid, 178, 221
Owens, Bretlyn, 202, 222

Paffenroth, Kim, 177, 222
Pagels, Elaine, vii–viii, xiii, 4, 16, 81, 97, 100, 222
Paradise. *See* Adam and Eve
Partoens, Gert, 137, 215
passions. *See* emotions
Paul, 46, 83, 99, 146–47, 150–52, 197–98, 201
Payne, Mark, 139, 222
Pelagian/Pelagianism/Pelagius, 47, 54, 55, 86, 87, 91, 94, 99
Perrier, Daniel Jean, xii
Perry, Samuel L., 201, 222
Philo, 90
Piper, John, 190, 201, 222
Plato/Platonism/Platonists, 5, 11, 25–27, 37, 40–42, 45, 53, 80, 90, 107–8, 143, 163, 164, 175, 191, 194, 195, 222
Plutarch, 85, 86, 98, 99, 222
poetry, 168–70
Pollmann, Karla, 177, 222
Porter, James I., 140, 222
Power, Kim, viii, xiii, 38, 96, 101, 222
Pyramus and Thisbe, 169

Quintilian, 140, 222

Rackett, Michael R., 222
rape, 6, 16, 59–60, 65–71, 72
reason, 39, 115
Respect for Marriage Act, 190
Retractions, 116
Ricoeur, Paul, 96, 222
Rist, John, 40, 43–45, 53, 54, 222
Romanianus, 152
Rosenberg, Michael, 75, 222
Rousseau, Philip, 100
Ruden, Sarah, 107
Ruether, Rosemary Radford, 176, 222
Rule of St. Augustine, 112–13, 120

Sagarin, Brad J., 202
Sandler, Bernice R., 176
Sauls, Scott, 201
Scholz, Sally, 16
Schultz, Ann-Marie, xii, 191
Schürmann, Reiner, 37, 222
Seneca, 41, 44, 53, 72
Senellart, Michel, 101, 223
Sermons (of Augustine), 69, 73, 74, 127, 138, 139, 140, 141, 209
Sermon 51, 159
Sermon 117, 159
Sermon 291, 131
Sermon 293, 133
sex/sexuality, 33, 39–42, 45, 50–52, 54, 64, 83, 87, 92
Shanzer, Danuta, 12–13, 18, 153–54, 158, 159, 223
Sin, original, 3–4, 31–32, 45, 47–49, 64, 92, 95
Skorska, Malvina N., 204
Smith, J. Warren, 72, 223
Smith, W. C., 100, 223
Socrates, 32, 41–42, 48
Soliloquies, 115, 121
Soranus of Ephesus, 71–72, 223
Stanley, Olivia, 202, 223
Stark, Judith Chelius, viii, xiii, 17, 76, 176, 178, 223

Stebergh, Fred, 176
Stock, Brian, 77, 92, 100, 101, 223
Stoics/stoicism, x, 39, 42–45, 47, 52–53, 114
Stone, Geoffrey, 87, 89, 99, 223
Stone, Sandy, 181, 182, 186, 223
Stowe, Harriet Beecher, 112, 120, 223
Strebergh, Fred, 223
Stryker, Susan, 183–87, 223
suicide, 61, 66, 72
Sweeney, Elaine C., ix–x

The Teacher, 128, 129, 138
Tertullian, 60, 83–84, 86, 98
Teske, Roland, 37, 38, 156, 223
Thagaste, 193
Theiner, Georg, 16
Thomas Aquinas, 36, 79, 96
Thompson, Jennifer J., 72, 224
Todd, Sharon, 174–75, 179, 224
Toppo, Greg, 224
transgenderism, 181–87
Trethewey, Angela, 176, 224
De Trinitate (On the Trinity), 120, 124, 126, 137, 144–47, 156, 157
Truth, Sojourner, 112
Tyconius, 92, 100

Undheim, Sissel, 75, 224

Van Der Wyngaard, Jessica, 202, 224
Vessey, Mark, 138, 177, 224
virginity, x, 59–77
Visigoths, 61
Vitale, Sarah, 16

Walker, Abbe Lind, 75, 224
Wallace, Miriam, 176, 224
Walsh, P. G., 75, 224
Walters, Jonathan, 41–42, 53, 224
Watson, Rachel Joy, 201, 224
Watts, William, 120, 224
Webb, Melanie Gibson, 72, 75, 76, 224
Weiner, Linda, 176
Wessel, Susan, 224
Wetzel, James, 8, 11–12, 16, 17, 224
Wheeler-Reed, David, 201–202, 224
Whitenton, Michael R., xii, 191, 195
Wollstonecraft, Mary, 178, 224
Wright, J. Lenore, 201

Xenophon, 40, 53, 225

Yarnold, Edward, 138, 255

About the Contributors

Patricia Grosse Brewer (née Patricia L. Grosse) is a professional philosopher and writer living in the Upper Peninsula of Michigan. She received her PhD in Philosophy from Villanova University. Her research interests include the thought of St. Augustine of Hippo, the philosophy of love and sex, and bioethics. She is currently an Adjunct Assistant Professor at Michigan Technological University, teaching ethics, logic, and general philosophy. She has five cats.

Carol Harrison is Lady Margaret Professor of Divinity and a Canon of Christ Church Cathedral, Oxford University. She was previously Professor of the History and Theology of the Latin West at the University of Durham, where she has worked for twenty-five years. Her publications include four works on Augustine: *Beauty and Revelation in the Thought of Saint Augustine* (OUP, 1992); *Augustine in Context: Christian Truth and Fractured Humanity* (OUP, 2000); *Rethinking Augustine's Early Theology: An Argument for Continuity* (OUP, 2006) and *Reading Augustine: On Music, Sense, Affect and Voice* (Bloomsbury, 2019). She is currently working on a theology of the voice, which developed from her work on *The Art of Listening in the Early Church* (OUP, 2013). She was elected a Fellow of the British Academy in 2018.

Jennifer Hockenbery is Dean of Humanities and Professor of Philosophy at St. Norbert College. Her books *Wisdom's Friendly Heart: Augustinian Hope for Conspiracy Theorists and Skeptics* (Cascade, 2020) and *Thinking Woman: A Philosophical Approach to the Quandary of Gender* (Cascade, 2015) both address the importance of Augustine's theology for thinking philosophically about the quest for truth and the search for understanding one's self.

Maggie Ann Labinski is Associate Professor of Philosophy at Fairfield University. She is also a member of the Women, Gender, and Sexuality Studies Program and Peace and Justice Studies Program. Her research focuses on the intersection of feminist and medieval philosophies. She has published several articles and chapters on questions concerning sex, sexuality, and education.

Richard A. Lee, Jr., is Professor of Philosophy at DePaul University. He works on Medieval and Early Modern Philosophy, the Frankfurt School (particularly Adorno), and Marx and Marxism. He is the author, most recently, of *The Thought of Matter: Materiality, Conceptuality, and the Transcendence of Immanence* (Roman and Littlefield, 2016).

Julia Kelto Lillis is Assistant Professor of Early Church History at Union Theological Seminary in the City of New York. She was previously Visiting Assistant Professor of Religion at Luther College in Decorah, Iowa and Postdoctoral Fellow and Lecturer in New Testament and Early Christianity at the University of Virginia. Her primary research interests concern ancient constructions of social difference, especially gender and sexuality, and their significance in early Christian literature. She has written several publications focused on virginity; among them are a monograph titled *Virgin Territory: Configuring Female Virginity in Early Christianity* (University of California Press, 2022) and an article about the *Protevangelium* of James (*Journal of Early Christian Studies*, 2016), which was awarded the American Society of Church History's Jane Dempsey Douglass Prize as an outstanding contribution on women in the history of Christianity. Her current research examines the possibility of human genderless-ness in early Christian thought.

Karmen MacKendrick is Professor of Philosophy at Le Moyne College in Syracuse, New York. She works primarily in philosophical theology, with elements of literary, cultural, feminist, and queer theories in engagement with late ancient and medieval texts. MacKendrick is the author of several books including *Material Mystery: The Flesh of the World in Three Mythic Bodies* (Fordham, 2021), *Divine Enticement: Theological Seductions* (Fordham, 2012), and *Failing Desire* (SUNY, 2017). With Virginia Burrus and Mark Jordan, she is the coauthor of *Seducing Augustine: Bodies, Desires, Confessions* (Fordham, 2010). She is currently engaged in a consideration of exile and loss in terms of proximity and distance.

Willemien Otten is Dorothy Grant Maclear Professor of Theology and the History of Christianity at the University of Chicago Divinity School, where she specializes in medieval and early Christian thought. She has a longstanding and ongoing interest in Augustine. With Karla Pollman she edited the three-volume *Oxford Guide to the Historical Reception of Augustine* (Oxford, 2013) and with Susan Schreiner a volume of essays for theologian David Tracy, *Augustine Our Contemporary: Examining the Self in Past and Present*

(Notre Dame, 2018). Her latest book, which includes a chapter on Augustine, is *Thinking Nature and the Nature of Thinking: From Eriugena to Emerson* (Stanford, 2020).

Kim Paffenroth graduated from St. John's College (Annapolis), Harvard Divinity School, and the University of Notre Dame. He directed the Honors Program at Iona University for nine years. Besides editing the "Augustine in Conversation," series he has published extensively on Augustine, including most recently, *On King Lear, The Confessions, and Human Experience and Nature* (Bloomsbury, 2021). He lives in upstate New York with his cat, Cordelia.

Daniel Jean Perrier received their bachelor's degree in religious studies and English from Iona University and their master's degree in Theological Studies from Harvard Divinity School. He is continuing independent writing and research in religious studies. Their interests include the history of American religious movements, the development of nonbinary religions, queer theology, and leftist religious movements. He currently works in a public library and as an independent author. He is privileged to work in Connecticut, named with a European corruption of the Algonkian Quinnetukut, on unceded tribal land historically cared for by Indigenous peoples.

Anne-Marie Schultz is Professor of Philosophy at Baylor University. She also serves as Undergraduate Program Director and recently received the designation of Master Teacher. She has published numerous articles on Plato, Augustine, and the Scholarship of Teaching and Learning. She is also the author of *Plato's Socrates as Narrator* (Lexington, 2013) and *Plato's Socrates on Socrates* (Lexington, 2020). She is currently at work on the third volume of the trilogy: *Socratic Epics and Platonic Legacies: Pedagogy in the Midst of Political Strife*. In her outside of academia life, she enjoys spending time with her husband, Jeff, and their Rhodesian Ridgebacks, Dante and Guthrie.

Eileen C. Sweeney is Professor of Philosophy at Boston College and the author of *Logic, Theology and Poetry in Boethius, Abelard, and Alan of Lille: Words in the Absence of Things* (Palgrave, 2006) and *Anselm of Canterbury and the Desire for the Word* (Catholic University of America Press, 2012). She served as president of the Society for Medieval and Renaissance Philosophy and is the author of many articles on topics in the early and high Middle Ages on language, science, and the liberal arts, the literary forms of Medieval philosophy, natural law, and the passions. She is working on two projects, one on a history of theories of the passions from Augustine to Modern Philosophy with the support of a Humboldt Fellowship, and the second, on the transition from the organization of knowledge around the seven liberal arts to Aristotelian science from the twelfth century to the thirteenth century.

Michael R. Whitenton is Lecturer in the Baylor Interdisciplinary Core at Baylor University. His primary research interests focus on ancient & cognitive rhetorics, emotions, and early Christian narrative, drawing especially upon linguistics, cognitive psychology, social psychology, and narratology. He has written several publications related to ancient rhetoric, cognitive sciences, and early Christian narrative. Most recently, he has written a monograph, *Configuring Nicodemus: An Interdisciplinary Approach to Complex Characterization* (Bloomsbury, 2019), an article pioneering an adaptation of cognitive blending for understanding ancient characters (*Biblical Interpretation*, 2021), and a book chapter on humor in the Infancy Gospel of Thomas (Wipf & Stock, 2023). His current research expands applications of cognitive blending in ancient narrative.

Milton Keynes UK
Ingram Content Group UK Ltd.
UKHW011825290224
438701UK00004B/87

9 781666 954852